Civil Disobedience

A Wadsworth
Casebook in Argument

Sharon K. Walsh

Loyola University Chicago

Evelyn D. Asch

Northwestern University

THOMSON
WADSWORTH

Australia • Canada • Mexico • Singapore • Spain
United Kingdom • United States

THOMSON

WADSWORTH

Civil Disobedience
A Wadsworth Casebook in Argument
Sharon Walsh/Evelyn Asch

Publisher: *Michael Rosenberg*
Acquisitions Editor: *Dickson Musslewhite*
Associate Production Project Manager: *Karen Stocz*
Marketing Manager: *Carrie Brandon*
Print Buyer: *Marcia Locke*

Cover Image: © *Franklin McMahon/CORBIS*
Compositor/Project Manager: *Shepherd, Inc.*
Photography Manager: *Sheri Blaney*
Permissions Manager: *Bob Kauser*
Cover Designer: *Joseph Sherman*
Printer: *Malloy Lithographing, Inc.*

For permission to use material from this text or product, submit a request online at http://www.thomsonrights.com

Any additional questions about permissions can be submitted by email to thomsonrights@thomson.com

For more information contact Thomson Wadsworth, 25 Thomson Place, Boston, Massachusetts 02210 USA, or you can visit our Internet site at http://www.thomson.com

ISBN 1-4130-0665-5

Credits appear on pages 339–340, which constitute a continuation of the copyright page.

Contents

Preface

We have focused this book, both the section on argument and the Casebook on Civil Disobedience, on the relationship between reading and writing and readers and writers. Our philosophy of teaching and our classroom practice have convinced us that good writing is stimulated by the challenges that meaty texts present. The readings you will find here come from the fields of religion, politics, and history and from the genres of the essay, personal narrative, drama, and speech. They center on the crucial issue of citizens' responsibility to the state and to their conscience. The writers of these texts are thinkers and doers who confront injustice perpetuated by law. The philosophers like Socrates, Thoreau, and King articulated the theory underlying civil disobedience but also practiced it. Such activists as Frederick Douglass, John Lewis, and Dorothy Day framed their actions with their ideas and beliefs. Because these writers and actors are so aware of the tradition out of which they come, their words and actions create a conversation that they invite us to join. Some of us will be convinced by their arguments; others will want to debate the claims and conclusions. All of us must acknowledge that injustice must be remedied by some means.

The two parts of the book move from reading to writing. In Part I, Chapters 1 and 2 focus on understanding argument and its failures, with emphasis on analyzing exemplary texts. Chapter 3 presents a method for writing argumentative essays that are based on reading and research. Part II, the Casebook on Civil Disobedience, also moves from reading to writing. Each chapter supplies background for each writer, includes questions about the texts and their argument, raises issues worth exploring, and provides ideas for writing as both conversation and argument. We have designed these features of the text to make challenging readings accessible to students. Chapter 4 explores early examples of civil disobedience. Chapter 5 presents the seminal texts for modern civil disobedience. Chapter 6 focuses on abolitionism, Chapter 7 chronicles the unfinished struggle for civil rights, and Chapter 8 traces American peace movements.

There is also another relationship between readers and writers that we would like to explore: between you the readers of this book and us the authors. We imagine that you instructors are like us, enjoying the give and take of the classroom, sometimes snowed under by the papers we assign, but convinced that our students can learn to write well. We want our students to learn to write well by observing good writers in action, engaging in worthwhile discussion, and experiencing the urge to have their say. We imagine that you students are like our students: lively; bright; often engaged with the class, but sometimes not; sometimes unsure of what you think; sometimes unwilling to say what you think; and often lacking confidence in your writing skills.

We write this book for all of you, hoping that you will discover, as we did, that it is satisfying to chew on the ideas, engaging to enter a conversation with the writers and each other, and—even—fun to make one's own voice heard through argument.

Acknowledgments

This casebook on civil disobedience, like our previous one on just war, owes much to the Loyola University Chicago English Department Shared-Text Project. Many colleagues shared their ideas with us, and we have enjoyed the give and take of collegial discussion with them. Research colleagues at Northwestern University have been understanding and supportive of the joys and pains of writing.

Loyola writing students continue to make teaching challenging and rewarding. English 106 students in particular have contributed to this casebook by their stimulating discussions of the casebook readings and by their unexpected and insightful responses. Special thanks to John Anneken, Caitlin Cunningham, Andrew Packman, and Saudur Rahman, whose work appears in Chapter 3 and in Appendix B.

We also very much appreciate Kathy Kelly, peace activist, educator, and civil disobedient, for giving her time, ideas, and memories to us in her August 2003 interview. Talking with her helped us see the practice of civil disobedience more clearly and, we hope, made us better thinkers about the issues.

Once again, we are grateful to Jain Simmons, of Thomson Learning, for her ongoing support. We thank our editor, Dickson Musslewhite, and Karen Judd and Karen Stocz at Wadsworth, who have trusted our choices and judgment.

And, finally, our families continue to put up with our many hours away from them. We thank Richard Hartenstein and John, Rachel, and Nathaniel Tingley for their unfailing love, support, and encouragement.

Why Should We Care
about Civil Disobedience?

Most of us will never participate in civil disobedience, though many of us will witness others practicing it. Demonstrators may block a street we wish to go down or a door we wish to enter. The nightly news may cover an illegal demonstration, photojournalists record it with powerful images, and editorial cartoonists highlight it. Why should we care about it? Civil disobedience has a long intellectual history, and it has changed—and continues to change—our country in notable ways. Most important, it challenges us to raise fundamental ethical and political questions about our government and about ourselves. What is an unjust law? Will normal democratic processes work to change an unjust law? If not, what other actions are morally correct? Are we willing to take those actions? Are we willing to accept the consequences of those actions? Can nonviolent resistance work? Is complete nonviolence even possible?

Civil disobedience began long ago when the Hebrew midwives refused the royal command to kill baby boys, and continues today with protesters interrupting meetings of the World Trade Organization or preventing loggers from clear-cutting forests. To do justice to the idea of civil disobedience, though, we must look beyond what those practicing civil disobedience do to why they do it. Over time, many writers have considered this question. Sophocles spells out why Antigone openly refuses to follow King Creon's command, and Socrates lays out his reasons for accepting the penalty of death rather than abandon his search for truth. Thoreau coins the term "civil disobedience" and meditates on its meaning when he becomes a tax refuser rather than contribute to a government that permits slavery and wages an unjust war. Tolstoy, Gandhi, and King each add a new dimension to the idea when they concur that true civil disobedience must be more than a negative refusal to

1

obey and a willingness to accept consequences; rather, it must include an active commitment to nonviolence. Thus, the readings we include in Chapters 4 and 5 create a debate over time about the motives for refusing to obey the state and the necessary conditions for civil disobedience.

In the United States, civil disobedience has played an important role in our history. Acts of civil disobedience like the Boston Tea Party predated our revolution. Conductors on the Underground Railroad defied the Fugitive Slave Act to lead slaves out of bondage. Numerous activists challenged laws upholding segregation and restricting voting rights with illegal sit-ins and marches. Draft resisters targeted the Vietnam War because they considered it unjust. More recently, peace activists have spoken out against the nuclear arms race by trespassing at nuclear missile sites and have resisted the sanctions against Iraq by deliberately violating them. Chapters 6, 7, and 8 chronicle the attempts, which are sometimes very successful, to challenge unjust laws.

Ideas do matter, and they have consequences. We have only to read the interview with Kathy Kelly, the memoir of John Lewis, or the diary entries of Merrill Proudfoot to encounter serious people who think before they act, act on what they value, and may even effect necessary change. At the very least, to enter this conversation on civil disobedience pushes us to examine our principles and responsibilities as ethical citizens.

PART ONE

Analyzing and Writing Arguments

1

Analyzing Arguments

Recognizing Arguments

Imagine this scene: Two adults are screaming at each other, hurling insults and accusations back and forth. Or this: Children trying to decide on which game to play engage in a shouting match. Because we describe these activities by the term "argument," we often think of argument as a negative activity. We might ask our children or our friends not to argue, as if arguing were only the equivalent of fighting or disagreeing. For our purpose though, argument refers to a very common and widespread process by which we draw conclusions from evidence that has been laid out or make decisions based on reasons provided. Argument is not so much about winning or losing, though we do talk about debate in those terms; it is more about concluding, deciding, solving or resolving, persuading, all very positive and practical human activities.

Where Is Argument Found?

Argument pervades our private and public discourse. We make arguments, whether in speech or in writing, when we raise questions and answer them; demonstrate problems and solve them; or outline issues or alternatives and delineate the ways to address or decide them. Through argument we weigh evidence, alternatives, and competing claims. Through argument we may come to theoretical answers and solutions, but we also make decisions or choices that will lead to action in the real world.

The Private Sphere

Argument is a large component of our private thoughts, our stream-of-consciousness. A writer debates internally how she should organize her text; she sketches out possibilities, evaluates them, and then chooses. A student lays out problem-solving strategies and selects the one most likely to succeed. We argue with ourselves: I should major in business because I'll be able to get a job. We engage imaginary opponents: Dad, you should help me with grad school because I received a scholarship for college tuition.

Important also to family life, argument ranges from the trivial to the serious as a way to negotiate differences: Who will sit in the front seat? What movie shall we see? Where shall we go on our vacation? How shall we budget our money? What values shall we teach our children?

The Professional and Business Domain

Argument is central to contemporary medical practice as doctors can no longer rely on their patients' unquestioning acceptance of the doctors' dictates. Rather, canny doctors list the pro and con reasons for a medical procedure or treatment, weigh them, and offer a medical opinion.

Underpinning business and commercial life, argument appears in business plans, proposals, loan applications, marketing strategies, ad campaigns, and stock recommendations. From team decision making to the deliberations of the board, both employees and managers use argumentative strategies to arrive at decisions.

The Public Forum

Intrinsic to making a case in our law courts, argument structures a trial as the prosecutor opens with what is to be proved, provides the requisite evidence to support this claim, and makes a closing statement demonstrating what has been proved. The defense's role is to undermine or rebut the prosecutor's argument. Demonstrating that the prosecutor's evidence is flawed, countering it with other evidence, or constructing an alternative theory of the case are all ways defense attorneys strive to attack the prosecutor's case.

Argument is crucial to our democratic deliberations, particularly in the debate format where the reasons for or against an issue or proposition are weighed. We see it in speeches given in Congress to argue for the passage of a bill or by the president to the American people to lay out the reasons for going to war.

The Academic Classroom and Symposium

Finally, argument is fundamental to our academic discourse. Every time we formulate a thesis and prove it, or establish criteria and weigh the value of a work of art against them, or provide statistics or other evidence to support an assertion, we engage in argument. Students write essays, professors write articles, and scholars give papers. Faculties debate curricula and policy, departments argue for appointments and tenure, and students debate issues. These argumentative strategies have a long history, begun by Aristotle in his *Rhetoric*. More recent discussions of argument include the Toulmin and Rogerian methods. **Toulmin** argument is rooted in Aristotelian logic, but replaces the syllogism with a **claim** and **warrants** for that claim. The **Rogerian** method (explained fully in Robert Miller and Robert Yagelski's *The Informed Argument* [Wadsworth]) focuses on locating a common ground between arguers or arriving at consensus.

What Are the Components of Aristotelian or Classical Argumentative Strategy?

Argument is closely allied to **rhetoric**, the study of how language may be used to achieve a desired effect. Those who follow Aristotle's guidance utilize or respond to three elements of argument: **ethos**, the persona that speakers or writers project to their audience; **logos**, the type of reasoning on which the argument is based as well as the content of the argument; and **pathos**, the emotional appeals that speakers and writers make to their audience. Each of these strategies may be used legitimately or validly, or they may be used fallaciously.

Notice that both speakers and **audience**, the listeners to or readers of the argument, have reciprocal roles in each element of this triad. Speakers and writers must always keep the audience in mind when trying out an argumentative strategy. Unless the audience responds as expected to this strategy, the argument cannot be called truly successful.

Ethos: Evaluating the Writer's Assumptions, Credentials, Reputation, and Use of Authority

Discussions of argument based on the Aristotelian model generally begin with ethos because we intuitively give much weight to the trustworthiness of the speaker or writer. If we do not trust the speaker or believe the writer to be qualified, we are likely to dismiss the argument no matter how good the logic. We can determine the persona that writers project to their audience by asking questions like the following: What kind of person is the speaker or writer? What does he or she believe? How do those beliefs underlie the argument? Is this someone with appropriate credentials? How do we know from evidence within the text? Are there sources outside the text that will help us find out? How do other experts and the writer's peers esteem this writer? What sources or authorities does the writer rely on? Given the answers to the preceding questions, how can we judge the writer's credibility?

Assumptions

What are the speaker's assumptions, premises, beliefs, and values that underlie or stand behind the argument? Does the speaker or writer make them explicit, presume the readers share them, or hide them?

Thomas Jefferson's *Declaration of Independence* (see p. 178) makes explicit a set of beliefs or convictions from which his premises follow. His thinking is grounded in eighteenth-century political philosophy. He spells out his assumptions, so all his readers can make the connections between his assumptions and premises. Probably few of Jefferson's readers could have enunciated the basis for the claim that "whenever any Form of Government becomes destructive of these ends, it is the right of the People to alter and abolish it," so Jefferson does it for them, making an interlocking chain of assumptions: Men are created equal and are also given inalienable rights by their creator to "Life, Liberty, and the pursuit of Happiness"—the divine rights of humans rather than the Divine Right of Kings! And wonder of wonders: "to secure these rights, Governments are instituted among Men"! Governments are not put in place merely to perpetuate power or to ensure the prosperity of the rulers, nor should they be imposed upon the governed through might; rather, they derive their power from the consent of the governed. When all these preconditions are in place, then and only then can Jefferson state his first premise with some possibility that it will be accepted.

One might think that the Reverend Martin Luther King, Jr., has set himself the fairly simple task in "Letter from Birmingham Jail" (see p. 156) of answering the criticisms of his fellow clergy. He can assume a shared set of beliefs in God, in justice as a cardinal virtue, in the Judeo-Christian tradition, and in the importance of obeying the law. Instead, because it is clear that these clergy repudiate some of his strategies, he has to reiterate—or make explicit—these assumptions to show how a given value or belief underpins his actions. For example, to answer the objection against "outsiders coming in," King recalls how the eighth-century prophets and the Apostle Paul were called to go "beyond the boundaries of their home towns" to carry the message of God (p. 156). So too are King and his followers called to Birmingham not only because they were invited and had organizational ties there but also because "injustice is here" (p. 156).

Credentials

What education, training, experience, knowledge, and expertise does the speaker or writer have? What evidence of the speaker's credentials is there within the text? What outside sources can help us determine these credentials? We suggest consulting such biographical and bibliographical sources as the *Encyclopedia Britannica, Who's Who, Contemporary Authors,* university or department Web sites, and library listings.

Even if we did not know that Jefferson had a wide-ranging intelligence and would serve his country as ambassador to France and as president, we can discern from *The Declaration of Independence* his skills as a logician and rhetorician.

Frederick Douglass, like Jefferson, lacks credentials that we might expect of twentieth- and twenty-first-century writers represented in a text like this: a college degree as well as postgraduate education. He certainly more than compensates for this lack of formal education by his determination to educate himself as he movingly portrays in his autobiography. His own experience of slavery and his work on the Underground Railroad, where he helped many other slaves escape to freedom; his editing of *The North Star,* a journal that won many Americans to the cause of emancipation; and his many official positions in post–Civil War America—all confirm his expertise and contributions to the cause of freeing the slaves.

Reputation

How do peers and colleagues review the work? Do they value its contributions to the field? What is the quality of the forum in which the writer is published? Is it a major newspaper or a respected press? How has the response to a writer or speaker changed over time? Has the reputation increased or diminished? To find book reviews, good sources are the London *Times Literary Supplement* (TLS), *New York Times, New York Review of Books, Book Review Digest, Chicago Tribune,* journals of opinion, and professional and scholarly journals. *Contemporary Authors* and the *Dictionary of Literary Biography* provide assessments of authors' reputations.

To illustrate the importance of evaluating both the credentials and reputation of a writer, let us examine the credentials of Abe Fortas, a Supreme Court justice in the 1960s. Fortas became a kind of spokesperson for the importance of civil disobedience in a democracy. A member of the court that ruled on the legality of the injunction against Martin Luther King's march in Birmingham, Fortas knew both the circumstances and the constitutional issues well. His book, *Concerning Dissent and Civil Disobedience,* was taken very seriously due to his position and his knowledgeable argument. The book generated at least two collections of essays that either critiqued his views or developed them further.

Use of Authority

We use the word *authority* in various ways. For example, a CEO has the authority (from the board or the stockholders) to make a decision; here, the CEO derives his power from those who employ him. As another example, I have the authority to sign checks for my aunt who signed a legal power of attorney permitting me to act in her name. The writer, however, speaks with the authority earned by credentials and position. The words writers choose and the rhetorical and argumentative strategies they employ most certainly help create ethos. But authors can also add weight to their words by appealing to the authority of someone higher, more expert, more experienced, or more credible. Important questions to ask about credentials include the following: How does the writer use other authorities? Whom does the writer enlist or cite as an authority? Are they people with better credentials than the writer's, ones pertinent to the topic, ones that readers will understand and appreciate?

Thomas Jefferson has authority to speak for the colonists, having been designated by the Continental Congress to draft *The Declaration.* He also uses God as his ultimate authority. In the introduction, he claims that "Nature's God" entitles a people, having found it necessary to dissolve its "political bands," to have a "separate and equal station." He assumes that "all men are created equal" and "that they are endowed by their Creator with certain unalienable rights." In his conclusion he also calls upon God as "Supreme Judge of the world" to witness their right intentions and expresses their "firm reliance on the protection of divine Providence." Calling on God as Creator, Providence, and Judge reminds his readers of their commonly held beliefs that God is all-encompassing and all-powerful, and reassures them that the colonists' cause is just, binding them together in a series of morally necessary actions. For those among the British or the colonists who are frightened by the revolutionary nature of *The Declaration*, calling upon God strengthens the case for revolution.

Like many abolitionists who used religion as their authority, Martin Luther King, Jr., draws extensively on scripture and theology as his source of authority. In his "Letter," King makes numerous references to figures like Shadrach, Meshach, and Abednego and to the Christian martyrs as civil disobedients. He names such "extremists for justice" as Jesus, Amos, St. Paul, Martin Luther, and John Bunyan. He turns to theologians like St. Augustine for his dismissal of unjust laws as "no law at all" and to St. Thomas Aquinas for his definition of unjust law (p. 161). These are all figures that are certainly familiar to his clerical audience. For a wider audience, King also refers to secular history, naming Lincoln and Jefferson among the extremists for justice and noting that the Hungarian freedom fighters acted illegally under Hitler's occupation. These multiple allusions have a two-pronged effect, strengthening his argument by supporting his assertions and strengthening his own authority, a significant part of his ethos.

Audience: Considering the Reader's Needs

The writer usually has a specific initial audience in mind, and the greater the writer's knowledge of those who comprise this audience, their values and assumptions, their desires, their knowledge, and their mental capacity, the more likely the argument is to succeed. Crucial questions for the writer are: Who is the intended audience? Does this differ from the actual audience? Is the audience likely to be receptive to or agree with the writer's assumptions? Is the audience either uninformed or neutral about the writer's argument? Is the audience likely to be hostile to the argument? Given that a writer may be addressing all these audiences at once, what strategies might be used to find some common ground to get the audience on the writer's side? Is the audience likely to agree with the writer's assumptions? What are the tone and language appropriate for the intended audience? In addition to the intended audience, we can think of the actual audience as a series of concentric circles radiating from the original audience. For a speech, the actual audience is people in the room, people who see it on television or the

Web, people who hear it on the radio, people who read it the next day, and so on. Writers like Jefferson or King who see their works as possibly extending to a wide-ranging audience must hope to keep in mind the needs of all their readers.

The audience must also assess the choices the writer has made. Has the writer kept the needs and desires of the various audiences in mind? Has the writer given them the information they need to understand the argument and done so without talking down to them or talking over their heads?

Jefferson, for example, must have had the colonists first and foremost in mind because he wishes to convince them that action to overturn the government is justified. The lengthy list of grievances must be intended to persuade them as well to pay "decent respect" to the views of the world. King George III and Parliament are unlikely to be convinced by this argument, so Jefferson can expect only to declare that the American colonies are independent, not that Britain will accept this action. As for their British brethren, Jefferson hopes for some sympathy; from other countries like France that are sympathetic to the desire to overturn a tyrannous king, he hopes for more concrete forms of support like money and troops. Of course, Jefferson, well aware of the momentous nature of *The Declaration*, must also have been writing for the ages.

The first audience that King has in mind must be the clergymen who signed the now famous letter calling him to task for his "unwise" and "untimely" actions, for being "an outsider coming in," and for his willingness to break laws. King's task is a difficult one: to win them over to his view. He must take their criticisms very seriously, and he does, answering them specifically and in order. He must demonstrate that he shares their values and concerns, and, as we noted in the previous section, his allusions are well selected to establish common ground with his fellow clergy. Rather than hastening to make countercharges or counterarguments, he must take the time to make thoughtful responses and provide careful explanations. All this he does. But after making multiple attempts to win them over, he turns on this audience more in sadness than in anger to express his disappointment with the white Church. Perhaps like the preacher he is, he hopes these other clergy will measure themselves against the extremists for justice, find themselves wanting, and now be willing to admit their own failures.

As must be obvious to any reader of this book, King's audience is a very wide one. "Letter from Birmingham Jail" speaks not only to the signers of the clergymen's letter, to King's followers in 1963, and to the

Americans who read it at the time. It also reaches down to us several decades later to remind us of the principled and well-reasoned strategies to attain equal rights for African Americans and to demonstrate the power of rhetoric and argument to change people's minds and hearts.

Rogerian Argument: Finding Common Ground with Readers

Anyone who has worked on committees, boards, or councils understands the importance of finding common ground on which to base a decision; otherwise, decisions may be delayed or, if reached, so displease some members of the group that the group cannot function effectively. Here is where listening techniques derived from the field of psychology, especially from the work of Carl Rogers, are very valuable. If listeners can restate the positions of the other group members clearly and fairly, acknowledge the strengths of a position they disagree with, recognize the weaknesses of their own position, and remind themselves of their common goals, the group will have a much better chance of reaching the consensus needed to make a decision. The outcome is less likely to be a narrowly won victory and more likely to be a satisfactory determination.

While it is certainly possible to construct a written Rogerian argument using the process indicated above, argumentative essays are less likely to follow the Rogerian pathway, especially with hotly debated issues. Effective arguers do, however, borrow elements from this approach, particularly in introductions intended to draw readers into a discussion.

Raising objections to their own arguments is another way writers acknowledge the importance of their readers' positions. The latter strategy fails, however, if writers see readers' objections only as impediments to be removed from the argumentative ground. Rather, writers must sincerely explore the strengths of a position contradictory to their own. Dorothy Day, for example, answers the questions of *Catholic Worker* readers with respect, not with defensiveness. In "On Pilgrimage," she notes that some readers think there is "too much stuff about war and preparation for war." She admits, "We still need to build up the vision of a new social order . . . and to work for it here and now. We still need to perform the works of mercy because . . . there is still sin, sickness, and death, and the hunger and homelessness and destitution that go with so much sickness." Only after having granted the legitimacy of her readers' concerns does she make her claim that "the work of non-violent resistance to our militarist state must go on" (p. 259).

Another peace activist, Presbyterian minister Maurice McCrackin, rather than answering objections, implicitly acknowledges his audience's right to an explanation. Suspended indefinitely from his pastoral position after being jailed for nonpayment of taxes, McCrackin writes his "Pilgrimage of a Conscience" as a kind of apologia, or justification of his evolution of conscience, directed to both his congregation and the Presbyterian church as a whole. He stakes out common ground with them when he says, "For us as Christians to know Jesus personally has reality only as we try earnestly to grow more like him" (p. 255). He also affirms that "I agree wholeheartedly with the affirmation of Presbytery made in February of 1958, that, 'A Christian citizen is obligated to God to obey the law but when in conscience he finds the requirements of law to be in direct conflict with his obedience to God, he must obey God rather than man'" (p. 256). His tone is never defensive, nor does he bring up the criticism he no doubt received. He assumes his readers are people of conscience who will understand the necessity of an act of conscience.

Logos: Understanding the Writer's Reasoning

Although logos suggests the English word "logic," it goes beyond logic to consider the ways we think or proceed rationally. We think of logos as the heart of argument, for here we provide both the necessary information and the logical structure to convince our readers.

Induction

Inductive reasoning is the process by which we draw conclusions or generalizations based on a series of experiences or examples. It is the way much of our learning takes place. For example, if a child gets sick every time she drinks milk, we conclude that the milk has caused the illness. If a toddler burns himself by touching the lit burner of a stove and a lighted candle, he very quickly concludes that flames burn.

How Does Inductive Reasoning Translate to Argumentative Writing?

Induction can lead to very sophisticated and successful arguments. *The Declaration of Independence* relies heavily on a series of examples to prove its case. The body of the document is a lengthy list of the outrages perpetrated by the government of Great Britain against the American colonists. Jefferson lists eighteen categories of outrages that King George III has perpetrated against the colonies, what Jefferson calls "a history of repeated injuries and usurpations, all having in direct object the establishment of absolute Tyranny over these States." A short list of grievances would not have the same impact. He also builds his case by saving the most heinous offenses, assaults on life, for the last five positions in his list. At the end of these "Facts . . . submitted to a candid world," few could argue that his generalization is unfounded.

Induction also plays a significant role in Frederick Douglass' speech given at Canandaigua, New York, on August 3, 1857 (see p. 193). In this speech, Douglass argues that "the whole history of the progress of human liberty shows that all concessions yet made to her august claims have been born of earnest struggle." Like Jefferson, he draws this claim from the enumeration of multiple examples. Jefferson lists the abuses of King George's government to support the assertion that the government of Great Britain must be overturned; Douglass names those who have gone to great lengths to avoid re-enslavement, thus supporting his assertion that "the progress of human liberty" has come as a result of such "earnest struggle." The struggles of his more recent exemplars have interfered with the ability of the manhunters to function in the North. The more distant exemplars like Margaret Garner and Joseph Cinque have embraced death willingly rather than submit to slavery. Garner killed her baby rather than risk the child's enslavement; Cinque led the uprising on the *Amistad* slave ship.

Argument by Analogy

Argument by analogy is a legitimate form of inductive reasoning that uses similarities between examples to draw conclusions. When we draw on our experiences, we may reason by analogy. For example, a teacher might reason that students in class A are like those in class B and that the same lesson would therefore work as well in B as it did in A.

Many writers also seek out historical analogies to bolster a point. Martin Luther King, Jr., draws an analogy between the civil disobedients of 1963 and the early Christians who went to the lions rather than obey Roman laws prohibiting their practice of religion. The analogy rests on the conviction that it is moral to resist an unjust law (p. 164). Mohandas Gandhi, in arguing for a *satyagraha* (civil disobedience) campaign against Hitler, sees an "exact parallel" between the Indians in South Africa and the Jews in Germany:

"Indians occupied precisely the same place that the Jews occupy in Germany. The persecutions had also a religious tinge. . . . [T]he white

Christians were the chosen of God and Indians were inferior beings created to serve the whites. . . . There too the Indians were consigned to ghettos described as locations" (p. 148).

Both of the analogies in the preceding paragraph raise the question of how many points of similarity are necessary to make the analogy valid. In the following example, there appear to be important points of comparison:

Jewish immigrants to the United States have thrived economically due to their strong belief in education and solid family structure. Korean immigrants also value education highly and have tight family networks. Therefore, Korean immigrants will succeed the way the Jews did.

These apparent similarities may not hold up under scrutiny, however. Perhaps the two groups may have different views of the role of education. Other differences may also be significant: Jews came earlier to the United States in large numbers, they have a different religion from the American majority, and they are not racially identifiable. Koreans, on the other hand, have arrived more recently, almost all are Protestants, and are racially distinct in appearance. Such differences outweigh the similarities given above.

Deduction

Deductive reasoning starts with a generalization (either drawn from induction or stated as an unproven assumption), applies it to a particular case, and draws a conclusion.

Syllogisms

These are the classic format for deductive reasoning. A syllogism has two premises, or propositions, from which a conclusion may be drawn. The following is Aristotle's famous syllogism, illustrating the deductive process:

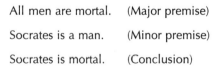

All men are mortal.   (Major premise)

Socrates is a man.   (Minor premise)

Socrates is mortal.   (Conclusion)

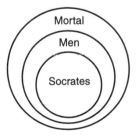

Figure 1-1

Note that here the **major premise** results from an inductive premise (though this is not always the case): All the people who lived in the past eventually died; we know people who have died; we do not know of any exceptions. It thus makes sense to state as a proposition that all men are mortal. The **minor premise** places Socrates in the category of men, that is, he shares the characteristics of men. Given that the entire category of men belongs within the category of mortal being, it makes sense that Socrates, who belongs to the category of men, must also be included within the category of mortal beings. Thus, we can conclude that Socrates is mortal.

To test whether a syllogism is valid, we can both apply rules and diagram the syllogism. Note that validity is not the same as truth. A syllogism may follow all the rules and still not be true because one or both of the premises are not true.

Rule 1. There must be three and only three terms (men, mortal, Socrates), each of which must refer to a discrete entity.
We can draw no secure conclusion from the following premises because the meaning of the middle term shifts. Being a Marxist and teaching Marxism are not the same. Belonging to one group does not mean automatically belonging to the other group:

All Marxists are communists.

Professor Jones teaches Marxism.

Professor Jones is a communist.

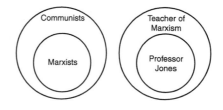

Figure 1-2

Rule 2. The middle term must be distributed at least once.
The **middle term** appears in both premises (in our first example, the middle term is "men") but not in the conclusion. To understand **distribution**, think of the meaning of the statement "All men are mortal." In a positive proposition or statement, the subject term "men" is distributed because "all" refers to every member of the group. Had "men" been modified by "some" or "most," it would not be distributed. The predicate term "mortal" is undistributed. We are essentially saying that men are only some of the mortal beings—others would

be dogs, cats, carrots, roses, and so on. Note the illustration of this statement:

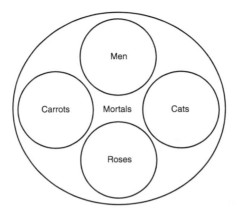

Figure 1-3

In a negative proposition or statement, the subject term is distributed if it is modified by "no." The predicate term is also distributed. In the statement "No cat is a human," we are saying that no member of the class of cats is any part of the class of humans. A diagram illustrates this proposition with two nonintersecting circles:

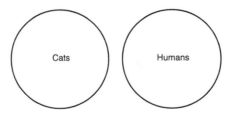

Figure 1-4

Rule 3. If a term is distributed in the conclusion, it must be distributed in the premise.

No local students are dormitory residents.

Some seniors are local students.

Some seniors are not dormitory residents.

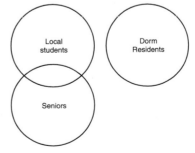

Figure 1-5

The conclusion is valid. Here the term "dormitory residents" is distributed both in the conclusion and in the premise. Look at what happens, though, in the following syllogism:

> All local students are dormitory residents.
> Some seniors are local students.
> All seniors are dormitory residents.

The above conclusion is not valid. We cannot conclude "All seniors are dormitory residents" because the term "seniors" is now distributed in the conclusion although it is undistributed in the premise. We cannot make the extension from "some seniors" to "all." Try to draw your own diagram to illustrate this syllogism.

Rule 4. If a premise is negative, the conclusion must also be negative.

> No British are Germans.
>
> Carla is British.
>
> Carla is not German.

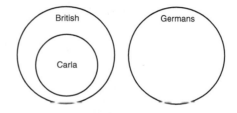

Figure 1-6

In this example, if Carla belongs to one group, she cannot belong to the other. Thus, we cannot logically conclude that "Carla is German."

Rule 5. No conclusion may be drawn from two particular premises.

> Some cats are mean animals.
>
> Some mean animals are rabid.

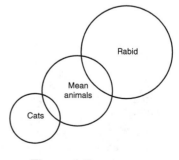

Figure 1-7

Here we cannot conclude "some cats are rabid." Because there are, in addition to cats, other types of mean animals, and because some of these other mean animals are rabid, we cannot know for certain whether cats are rabid. We could draw a valid conclusion that "some cats are rabid," if we were to say that "all mean animals are rabid" and "some cats are mean animals" because then the middle term would be distributed.

Rule 6. No conclusion may be drawn from two negative premises.

> All bimsy are not fimsy.
> All fimsy are not mimsy.

We cannot conclude either that "all bimsy *are* mimsy" or "all bimsy *are not* mimsy." They may or may not be:

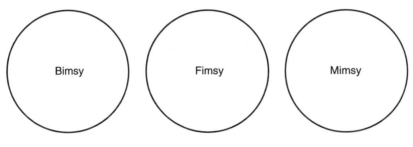

Figure 1-8

Exercises

Test the validity of the following syllogisms both by diagramming them and applying the rules. If no conclusion is supplied, supply the conclusion that will follow logically from the premises.

All humans are rational animals.
Mary is a human.

All humans are rational animals.
Mary is not a rational animal.
Mary is a human.

All good students study for finals
Marge did not study for finals.

Some people are robots.
All robots are intelligent.
Some people are intelligent.

Some A are B.
All B are C.

Some robots are intelligent machines.
Some intelligent machines are
expensive.

Some A are C.

Some robots are expensive.

No A are B.
No B are C.
No A are C.

All A are B.
All B are C.

Hypothetical Syllogisms

These syllogisms start with a first premise consisting of an **antecedent** from which a **consequent** follows: If students get 70 percent or above (antecedent), they will pass the course (consequent). The second premise may either **affirm** or **deny** the antecedent or affirm or deny the consequent. The syllogism is **valid** if the second premise affirms the antecedent or denies the consequent.

If students receive 70 percent or above, they will pass the course.

This student received 70 percent or above. She will pass the course.	(Affirms the antecedent, so it is VALID.)
This student did not receive 70 percent or above. He will not pass the course.	(Denies the antecedent, so it is INVALID. There are other possibilities. Perhaps the teacher decided to curve the grade, so the student passed.)
This student will not pass the course. She did not receive 70% or above.	(Denies the consequent, so it is VALID.)
This student will pass the course. Therefore, she received 70% or above.	(Affirms the consequent, so it is INVALID.) (That same kind teacher!)

Enthymemes

Enthymemes are shortened syllogisms that we use frequently in speech and sometimes in writing. We might say, "John is mortal because he's human." Or "John is human, so he's mortal." In such structures, it is usually the major premise we omit, perhaps because it is obvious. Sometimes, though, we may not want to call attention to the major premise because it does not fully meet the test of distribution. For example, in the enthymeme "Professor White is a good writer because she teaches English," we may not be able to preface the major term with *all* but only *nearly all* or *most*. We certainly cannot say that *all* professors of English are good writers, but we probably can say that *many* or *most* are. The following examples show strategies for expanding the enthymeme. Note that such linguistic clues as "because" and "so" may signal a premise or conclusion:

Because Mary was elected class president, we know she is popular. Because the word "because" points to a premise—usually the minor premise—the main clause must be the conclusion. So far, the syllogism is taking shape like this:

Major premise:	[What belongs here?]
Minor premise:	Mary was elected class president.
Conclusion:	Mary is popular.

"Elected class president" must be the middle term because it appears in a premise, but not in the conclusion, and it also must be distributed at least once. So the major premise must be "All those elected class president are popular." The syllogism is valid, but is it true? Must a student be popular to be class president? Certainly this is often the case, but is it always the case? Might someone be elected because she is competent or a good leader though not popular? Probably the best we can do is say that *most* or *almost all* of those elected class presidents are popular.

When linguistic clues are missing, it can be harder to expand the enthymeme. If we are told, "John must be frugal. He was elected class treasurer," we assume there must be some connection between the two statements, but we cannot assume that the first statement is the premise and the second the conclusion. We can try each statement as the conclusion and work back from there to see if we can derive a major premise that will make a valid syllogism.

If "John is elected class treasurer" is placed as the conclusion, the syllogism would look like one of the following:

Major premise: Those elected class treasurer are frugal.
Minor premise: John is frugal.
Conclusion: John is elected class treasurer.

Or

Major premise: Frugal people are elected class treasurer.
Minor premise: John is frugal.
Conclusion: John is elected class treasurer.

But in the first case the middle term, "frugal," is not distributed at least once. In the second case, there is also a problem because we certainly cannot claim that all frugal people are elected class treasurer. If we make "John is frugal" the conclusion, we can get closer to validity, especially if we qualify the statement: Those elected class treasurers are likely to be frugal; John is elected class treasurer; therefore, John is likely to be frugal.

Exercises

Try your hand at analyzing the following hypothetical syllogisms, rephrasing the statements as necessary to determine their validity. Do not merely apply the rules, but try to think through why the conclusion does not follow from the premises:

1. If you file your taxes late, you will receive a penalty. You received a penalty. Therefore, you must have filed your taxes late.

2. I know you cannot graduate if you don't complete 168 units. Because you will graduate, you must have completed all 168 units.
3. If you don't have your passport, you won't be allowed on the plane for France. You have your passport. So you must have been allowed on the plane.

Expand the following enthymemes to make a valid syllogism. Is the syllogism also true?

4. Martha wears glasses, so she must be studious.
5. George is sick because he ate green apples.
6. Heather is gorgeous. She gets lots of dates.

How Do Deductive Reasoning and Syllogisms Transfer to Longer Arguments?

Essentially, deduction not only logically structures the reasoning process but also provides a framework for the argumentative essay or speech.

In *The Declaration of Independence,* for example, Thomas Jefferson sets up his first or major premise that a "government which becomes destructive of these ends" (ensuring the right to life, liberty, and pursuit of happiness of its citizens) may rightfully be altered or abolished. The body of the argument provides plentiful support for the second or minor premise: The government of Great Britain is destructive of these ends ("The history of the present King of Great Britain is a history of repeated injuries and usurpations, all having in direct object the establishment of an absolute Tyranny over these States").

The conclusion of the argument also provides the ineluctable conclusion of the syllogism: The government of Great Britain may rightfully be and is abolished ("We, therefore, the Representatives of the united States of America . . . are, and of Right ought to be Free and Independent States; that they are Absolved from all Allegiance to the British Crown, and that all political connection between them and the State of Great Britain, is and ought to be totally dissolved").

Though "Letter from Birmingham Jail" may at first sight appear primarily as a refutation, Martin Luther King, Jr., derives his own argument that it is justified to break an unjust law from two categorical syllogisms:

Major Premise:	A just law is a manmade code that squares with the law of God.
Minor Premise:	Segregation laws are not manmade codes that square with the law of God.
Conclusion:	Therefore, segregation laws are not just laws.

And

Major premise:	Unjust laws may be broken.
Minor premise:	Segregation laws are unjust laws.
Conclusion:	Therefore, segregation laws may be broken.

For other examples of deductive reasoning structuring an argument, see William Lloyd Garrison's "Declaration of the National Anti-Slavery Convention (p. 183) and student John Anneken's "Brief for Argument" (p. 46).

In Maurice McCrackin's "Pilgrimage of a Conscience" (p. 254), we see a different way of using deduction in an argument. Although he writes in the form of a chronological narrative, each stage of his pilgrimage rests upon deduction. His third paragraph contains several interlocking hypothetical syllogisms. He ends with:

"But if, as a committed follower, I believe that Jesus would do none of these things [support conscription, throw a hand grenade, or release the bomb over Hiroshima], I have no choice but to refuse at whatever personal cost, to support war."

I am a committed follower of Jesus.

Therefore, I must refuse to support war.

Toulmin Argument: Moving from Certainty to Probability

The contemporary philosopher Stephen Toulmin has contributed another way of understanding deductive reasoning in his book, *The Uses of Argument* (Cambridge UP), by allowing for a lesser degree of certitude. The Aristotelian syllogism sets up a system that leads ineluctably from a universal statement or major premise to a conclusion. As our discussion of the enthymeme has suggested, though, there are many cases where we cannot argue with complete certainty. How often can we say something that applies to every member of a group? Instead of saying *all*, we may hedge our bets and say *almost all*, *most*, or *many*. We often use adverbs to qualify our statements: *usually, frequently, often*. The terms Toulmin uses for the elements of argument reflect this lesser degree of certainty: The **claim** is what is to be proved; **qualifiers** indicate exceptions to or limitations of the claim; the **data** are the evidence or support for the claim; and the **warrants** are the assumptions, principles, and beliefs—stated or, often, unstated—that both underpin the claims we make and allow us to link the data with the claim. Toulmin includes two other terms, the **backing**, additional support for the warrant, and the **rebuttal**, either critiques of an argument or counterarguments.

The Toulmin method, though quite complex, can be simplified and adapted for the composition classroom; we call this a claim/reasons/

specific evidence method, which many students agree is a useful process for analyzing and constructing arguments.

Claim: What is the proposition to be argued or defended? What, if any, qualifications or exceptions does it have?

> Motorcyclists and bikers who do not wear helmets should not be covered by insurance because this risky behavior often contributes to the severity of accidents and to raising their cost.

The qualifier here is the word *often*. Is the fact that risky behavior does not always lead to severe accidents or high cost enough to undermine the claim?

> **Reason I** (or subclaim) for supporting the claim: *Not wearing helmets contributes to the severity of accidents.*
>
> **Specific evidence** (data) supporting this reason or subclaim: *Frequency and types of severe motorcycle and bike accidents.* **Warrants:** *These injuries must clearly relate to having the head unprotected.*
>
> **Reason II:** *Not wearing helmets helps to raise the cost of accidents.*
>
> **Specific evidence:** *Head injuries can lead to various types of mental and physical impairment, necessitating costly treatments.* **Warrants:** *Must show both how the injuries lead to impairments and provide data on the cost of such treatments.*
>
> **Reason III:** Does not apply here, though many arguments have multiple reasons.
>
> **Specific evidence**
>
> **Reason IV and so on:** Does not apply.
>
> **Specific evidence**

Warrants   How can one justify connecting each reason with the claim as well as each piece of evidence with the reason it supports? The main warrant for the argument is *"Risky behavior that often contributes to the cost and severity of accidents should not be covered by insurance."* Whether one accepts this reasoning or not probably depends on how much store one places on taking responsibility for one's own acts.

Refutation

Dealing with objections raised about an argument or countering evidence supplied to support an alternative position is an essential strategy to win a hearing from readers who may be leaning to the other side or have already made up their minds. Many readers will raise objections that you fail to raise and may then decide your argument is not worth following because you have not shown yourself to be fair-minded.

Martin Luther King, Jr., devotes a significant portion of "Letter from Birmingham Jail" to refuting the objections to his Birmingham March made in the "Clergymen's Letter." To counter their objections to "outsiders coming in," King details his organizational ties with affiliates of the Southern Christian Leadership Conference (paragraph 2) and claims a biblical precedent in the eighth-century prophets and St. Paul (paragraph 3). In paragraph 14, he answers the clergymen's charge that his actions are "untimely" with an impassioned defense of his actions, stating, "We have waited more than 340 years for our God-given rights." To address the anxiety over "our willingness to break laws," King employs logos in his closely reasoned advocacy of breaking unjust laws: clearly defining unjust laws, repudiating tactics of "evading or defying the law," and placing his movement within the historical development of civil disobedience (paragraphs 15–22). To rebut the objection that King's actions "precipitate violence," King uses an analogy to Socrates, asking whether he should be blamed because his refusal to abandon his teaching of the truth led to his death sentence (paragraph 25). King defends the actions in Birmingham against being labeled as "extreme," for he stands between the complacent and the "force of bitterness and hatred" (paragraphs 27–30). Such a lengthy refutation (thirty out of fifty paragraphs) demonstrates how seriously King takes the clergymen's objections and how much he wishes to win over such an audience of "moderates" to his side. King then turns his sights on his interlocutors, in essence challenging them to take greater responsibility for changing unjust laws. It would be interesting to know how the clergymen would have responded to King.

Pathos: Weighing Appeals to Emotion

Appeals to emotion can be a very powerful part of argument. Such legitimate appeals often speak to the best parts of our humanity, our sympathy for the sufferings of others, our altruistic desires to improve our world, and our outrage against those twisted individuals who inflict harm on the innocent, the unprotected, and those who cannot protect themselves.

Through pathos, we also recognize that we are subject to multiple fears that may paralyze us or move us to action. Even when used judiciously, such appeals to emotion may, however, raise the hackles of some readers, so they must be used carefully.

Some useful questions to ask of appeals to emotion are: Does the argument lend itself to emotional support? Most likely, a medical discussion of the advisability of taking one drug therapy or another does not lend itself to the use of emotion. Is the audience one that will respond positively or negatively to emotion? An academic audience may be turned off by emotional appeals, for example. Does the use of emotion strengthen or weaken the argument? Does the emotional appeal substitute for a strong logical structure?

Appeals to emotion can function legitimately in arguments as an adjunct to the logic they employ. *The Declaration*, for example, appeals for solidarity with the colonists' British brethren: "We have appealed to their native justice and magnanimity, and we have conjured them by the ties of our common kindred to disavow these usurpations." The list of causes, though generally couched in measured terms, does in fact name heinous deeds: "He has plundered our seas, ravaged our Coasts, burnt our towns, and destroyed the lives of our people." The powerful verbs Jefferson uses must heighten the sense of outrage the colonists feel.

Jefferson makes emotional appeals that, while effective, are subordinate to the logical structure. Martin Luther King's use of pathos in paragraph 14 of "Letter from Birmingham Jail" is much briefer than his use of logos, but it is truly a stunning example of the appeal to emotion. Most of the paragraph consists of a periodic sentence: a long sentence that withholds its main point until the end or period. This sentence is constructed of a series of subordinate clauses beginning with "when." Each depicting a moving situation, the clauses are designed to enable readers to participate imaginatively in the black experience: lynch mobs attacking one's parents; policemen beating black brothers and sisters; 20 million Negro brothers "smothering in an airtight cage"; a six-year-old daughter who cannot go to a public amusement park; a son who asks, "Why do white people treat colored people so mean?"; a family on a cross-country trip who cannot find a motel that will accept them. These experiences, even stripped of King's moving descriptors, evoke powerful images of discrimination by the surrounding society. The next set of "when" clauses turn inward to trace the psychological alienation inflicted by signs addressed "white" and "colored"; the depersonalization caused by the loss of one's name and title; the constant discomfort of "living constantly at tiptoe stance"; and the ultimate sense of the loss of self or "nobodiness" that results. Of course, many of King's readers would not have experienced these things firsthand, but the cumulative impact of piling up example after example is great. King intensifies this impact by repeating "when" again and again, like nails pounded into a wall. He also uses the repetition of alliteration to underscore his point: "lynch . . . at will" and "drown . . . at whim"; policemen who "curse, kick, and even kill"; "harried by day and haunted by night." Only after one has experienced all of the above, King says, "only then you will understand why we find it difficult to wait." It is difficult to imagine that any reader could fail to grasp the power of this writing. To be sure, such high-voltage writing should be used sparingly if it is to be effective. King knows this.

This discussion of pathos should make us remember our obligations to our readers if we have forgotten them as we become preoccupied with the mechanics of arguments. Readers are flesh-and-blood people who occupy a moral universe and care what ethos we present. They want to see our character as well as our credentials, reputation, and skill in finding authorities to support us. Readers are intelligent people who dislike being talked down to and recognize when we play fast and loose with logic or evidence. They respect order and clarity and truthfulness. Readers have hearts that make them respond to the predicaments of others, to the poor, the victims, the unfortunate. At the same time, readers resent being manipulated by writers who overdo appeals to emotions by relying on sentimentality or exaggeration. In the next two chapters, we will explore both how we can lose the trust of our readers by fallacious reasoning and how we can gain it by careful, respectful reading, research, and writing.

2

Avoiding Fallacies

Fallacies, whether deliberate or inadvertent, are failures in logical reasoning and argument. They can be categorized as failures in ethos, in logos, and in pathos. These fallacies may be found at every level of argumentative discourse. The child arguing that she should be allowed to go to bed late because her mother does and the teenager claiming that he should be able to have a beer because his father does are both making fallacious claims. Newspaper letters to the editor are gold mines of fallacies with some writers oversimplifying issues, creating false dilemmas, and attacking leaders and candidates based on spurious reasons. Political ads may attack the character of a candidate rather than her positions or may misstate the position of a candidate. To sell a product, television commercials, whether selling beer, lingerie, or cars, often appeal to multiple human desires, relying little on the intrinsic worth of the product and more on the product's purported ability to make the buyer happy or desirable.

Recognizing fallacies is important to you as a reader or viewer so that you can evaluate the claims that others make. It is crucial to you as a writer so that you can avoid distorting facts, overstating a claim, or drawing invalid conclusions.

Attacks on Ethos

Usually, attacks on ethos are unjustified or irrelevant assaults on the character or credentials of the speaker. Not every attack on credentials or character is unjustified, however, so it is necessary to make clear distinctions. Making a claim without the credentials to back it up can make the speaker a legitimate target. For example, Linus Pauling, who advocated large doses of vitamin C without the nutritional background or studies to support his claim, was excoriated by the scientific community despite being a Nobel laureate. A failure in ethics can also undercut a speaker's credibility. People charged with enforcing laws cannot break them without losing credibility. Both Presidents Nixon and Clinton discovered that the American people take covering up wrongdoing and lying under oath very seriously.

Ad Hominem or Attack on the Person

An ad hominem attack is on the speaker rather than the argument, focusing on something that has nothing to do with the argument:

- He's divorced. How can he have anything to say about funding for childcare?

Tu Quoque or You Too

A favorite of children addressing their parents, this fallacy suggests that people cannot advise against or prohibit a behavior that they themselves practice.

- You smoke. How can you tell me not to do it?
- You're telling me to save my money? Look how much money you spent last year!

False Authority

We know that legitimate authority is vital to the writer's ethos. In the false authority fallacy, the argument relies on someone without the knowledge, position, or credentials to be an authority on the issue discussed. This fallacy is often seen in ads.

Michael Jordan may be granted authority to promote a brand of athletic shoes. However, this authority most likely does not extend to promoting a particular restaurant or car. There is no reason to think he has those credentials.

Failures in Logos

Errors in Reasoning

Many logical fallacies are related directly to failing to derive valid conclusions or construct valid syllogisms. The following might be called errors in reasoning:

Hasty or Illicit Generalization

Induction requires sufficient relevant examples on which to base a conclusion. A hasty generalization occurs when too small a sample leads to a suspect conclusion:

- I know two redheads who have bad tempers. It's clear that redheads have bad tempers.
- Terrorists who were Muslim were responsible for September 11. Muslims are a threat to the United States.

Stereotyping

Related to hasty generalization, a stereotype begins with a conclusion drawn about a group of people from a too-limited sample and then applies that conclusion to a member of the group, implying that every member of the group shares that characteristic:

- Joan must be a gossip. You know what women are like.
- Men are sports freaks. Mark must spend his weekend glued to the TV watching football games.
- The Irish (or the Polish, French, Russians, Jews, Catholics, or Protestants . . .) are all _____ (fill in the blank). What can I say? She's Irish.
- I saw a picture of an Arab terrorist the other day. I'll avoid anyone who looks like him.

Stacked Evidence

Here the evidence supporting an assertion may be valid, but the writer or arguer omits other evidence that may weigh against it. In a criminal trial, for example, if the prosecutor were to omit a relevant fact that might lead to exoneration—perhaps an alibi—that would be stacked evidence.

Invalid Syllogisms

In deductive reasoning, failure to follow the rules of the syllogism, whether categorical or hypothetical, leads to an invalid conclusion, often called a non sequitur. You will recall that hypothetical, categorical, and invalid syllogisms are discussed in Chapter 1.

Faulty Analogy

Analogies can become faulty when similarities are stretched too far or are outweighed by the differences between the examples being compared:

- A teacher reasons that two students, both named Meghan and both having blond hair, should receive the same grade.

Obviously, the unimportant similarities between the two students are inadequate for reasoning by analogy.

Fuzzy Thinking

These next fallacies may be attempts to sound as if one is arguing logically. Instead, they are fuzzy thinking or replacements for logic.

Begging the Question

Begging the question means restating a claim, in one form or another, without supplying any proof:

- The theory of evolution is just that; a theory. Charles Darwin has not made his case for evolution. Evolution has not been proven.

Circular Reasoning

This is an attempt at argument that goes nowhere, landing us back at the beginning:

- I have to have a car in order to get to work. And I need to work in order to buy the car.

False Cause

Assigning the wrong cause for an outcome or an incident is a kind of oversimplification, assuming that there is only one cause for an effect:

- Our sales shot up by 25 percent after we started using an Internet pop-up.

This alone *might* have produced the result, but other factors might apply: The product might have been improved or the proximity of Christmas might have stimulated sales.

Post Hoc Ergo Propter Hoc or "After This, Because of This"

Another type of false cause involves saying that because something happened first in time, it caused what followed. Eating spicy food may indeed produce heartburn, but many superstitions ascribe causality to an incident merely because it preceded the effect in time:

- You walked under a ladder today. That's why you had bad luck.
- Your horoscope warned you not to engage in financial transactions today. No wonder you lost money on the stock market.

"What's One More or Less?"

The question implies that numbers do not really matter, but they do. Too many people in a boat **will** make it capsize. Other examples include:

- I know the registration system says the class is full. Please let me in anyway. One person won't make a difference. (Not true: The teacher will have more work to do and the students will have fewer chances to participate.)
- Why should it matter if we have less than the required number for the tour group? What difference can one person make? (The missing person's fare would have helped cover the expenses of the chaperone.)

Attempts to Deceive

The following fallacies are usually deliberate attempts to deceive, sometimes by oversimplifying, sometimes by misdirection, sometimes by narrowing options:

Straw Man

This fallacy consists of constructing a weak or exaggerated argument in order to tear it down, claiming that it is the argument your opponent is making. However, your opponent has not made this argument. For example:

- Consider this argument against pacifism: Pacifists always oppose violence. They think that the world can be changed by not responding to violence. They clearly do not understand the real world because they are blinded by their idealism. If pacifists were elected, we would be invaded the next day.

Here the arguer, by distorting the pacifist position, makes the argument seem poorly reasoned, even dangerous.

Red Herring

The red herring is named after a strategy used to train hunting dogs to follow the original scent. Dogs learn to ignore a strongly scented object like a herring that has been drawn across a trail. Thus, irrelevant or misleading statements that pull the audience away from the real argument are called red herrings.

- You've argued that our candidate has not been fiscally responsible. She has, however, beautified the city, constructing planters along every major street.

False Dilemma

Sometimes called **black or white reasoning** or the **either/or fallacy,** this fallacy is usually improperly couched as an either/or proposition. As long as there might be another possibility, the statement is fallacious:

- To have peace in the Middle East, either Ariel Sharon or Yasser Arafat must resign. (Note that another possibility is that both must resign.)
- Either we go to war with Iraq, or Iraq will sell nuclear weapons to terrorists who want to attack us. (Certainly there are other possibilities, including pursuing arms inspection and elimination through the United Nations.)

Inappropriate Appeals to Pathos

Though appeals to emotion may be a legitimate adjunct to logic (see Martin Luther King Jr.'s powerful use of the harm that discrimination does to children in "Letter from Birmingham Jail"), they can also be used to *replace* logic.

Ad Populum or Pandering

These are appeals to emotions or desires that many people feel. Commercials and ads might appeal to sexual instincts, selling cars by implying that the gorgeous model will come with them.

At Christmas, children's toys are much more than toys, and Christmas cards more than a seasonal greeting: Ads for these products are targeted to adults as well as children and bring with them happy memories of home and a promise of warmth and good times.

The ad populum fallacy may also involve an appeal to fear. It was used during World War II to justify interning Americans of Japanese descent with the claim that they might aid the Japanese in attacking the U.S. mainland. In the current war on terror, it might take this form:

- Look at Ground Zero and the grieving survivors. Terrorists are plotting another massive attack on the United States. We must suspend civil liberties in order to prevent this attack.

Bandwagon

This fallacy invites us to join the parade or jump on the bandwagon. Because everyone is doing something, we should too. A favorite ploy of political consultants, the bandwagon appeal often involves showing a large group of people rallying around a candidate. A commercial example is the well-known Coke ad showing a huge group of diverse people while the jingle "I'd like to teach the world to sing" is playing.

Slippery Slope

This is a kind of fearmongering that argues that any step down a path will lead to the worst possible outcome:

- Any restriction of abortion means that *Roe vs. Wade* will be overturned.
- Experiments with gene therapy for diseases will lead to designer or made-to-order babies.

Exercises

1. Work in groups to review the letters to the editor of several newspapers. Read a week's worth of these letters, selecting those letters with weak arguments. In your group, decide which fallacies are represented.
2. Also in groups, review the ads in several magazines that you read regularly. What needs, instincts, or feelings do these ads appeal to? Which do you think are legitimate appeals; which are not?
3. Identify the fallacious thinking in the following examples:

   - Susan Sarandon, a famous actress, and other entertainment figures used the Academy Awards ceremony to protest the war in Iraq. You should listen to what they have to say.
   - I don't get good grades because my teachers don't like me.
   - 98 percent of my high school class are attending college, many because "it's what everyone does."
   - Adopting the Equal Rights Amendment will mean that women will be drafted.
   - In his zeal to make his argument a strong one, Joshua presented all the evidence that supported his position, omitting any data that seemed to weaken it.

- After the plane crash, investigators discovered that the airline's ticket agents had allowed several passengers to bring on excess baggage even though they knew the plane was carrying a full cargo load.
- My dad told me that if I do not finish college, I will end up as a waitress or a sales clerk.
- When a ship disappeared after entering the Bermuda Triangle, investigators of paranormal phenomena reasoned that the Bermuda Triangle had triggered the disappearance.

3

Writing the Source-Based Argumentative Paper

Becoming the Arguer: Creating a Conversation among Writer, Readers, and Authorities

The first two chapters of Part One have focused on understanding how argument works and reading arguments written by others to determine how they make their argument and whether they avoid fallacious reasoning. The kind of repeated careful analysis that we undertake together in class has undoubtedly honed our analytic skills. As we study how masters of the form make their case, we no longer read passively. We question; we disagree; we put forward our own arguments; we demand additional evidence; we contradict the support that is provided. No longer do we think of reading argument as a private activity, but we enter a conversation with the writer, other readers, and the authorities cited in the text. We say to the writer, "Who are you to tell me what I should think? Prove to me that you are competent to make this case." "My, you really did make a powerful *Declaration*, Mr. Jefferson." Or, "You didn't think I'd let you get away with that, did you, Mr. Thoreau?" With other readers, we dispute their interpretations and evaluations and sometimes reach an agreement: "You are just plain wrong that civil disobedience can involve violence." Or, "You convinced me that Martin Luther King does more than refute his critics." The sources and authorities cited within the text are thus no longer merely providers of dry data but people whose ideas and arguments are so familiar that we feel as if we know Socrates, Tolstoy, Gandhi, or Kelly.

No matter how actively we have engaged in the conversation described above, at some point we decide to initiate our own conversation. Sometimes it is our own need to clarify or defend our ideas that urges us to write; often it is an assignment that requires us to do so. Whatever the motive, we need to take charge of the conversation, acquiring and demonstrating expertise, respecting our readers, and taking heed of their needs. Most of all, we need to lay claim to our position with conviction, passion, and authority, to be as willing to engage with our readers as we were to be critical readers.

The following steps work for any source-based argumentative writing, though some may be eliminated for a shorter essay based on a few primary sources. For the longer argumentative research paper, following the process in detail will assure a carefully researched, thoughtful, well-written paper that creates the kind of conversation we have been discussing.

Choosing a Topic

Select a topic that interests you and lends itself to research. For a successful paper, you will need to find multiple relevant and academic sources (that is, from significant journals and magazines, respected national newspapers, and books by scholars and experts). Your topic should raise important questions about serious issues.

You will be spending a great deal of time doing research and writing your essay, so you need a project that you will find worthwhile. Even if your topic has been somewhat limited by the topic of this casebook or by your assignment, you can find a way to tailor it to your interests. You might connect your topic with what you have been learning in another class or with a subject in which you are already interested. For example, one student decided to examine the argument in *Antigone* and used what she had been learning in a communications class to find a framework for analyzing the speeches. Another connected his peace studies class with his topic from the casebook, finding good sources for his support of the pacifist position. Others took historical periods that fascinated them and focused on the nineteenth century or the Vietnam War.

A quick survey of the topic will help you decide whether your topic is doable within the time frame and manageable within the parameters of the assignment. Read about the subject in a good encyclopedia like *Britannica.* Look at the bibliography provided after the article, as well as the bibliography provided in the casebook. Does your library have a good selection of these sources, or are public and other university libraries easily accessible? Do a quick subject search of your library's catalog and databases and of InfoTrac® College Edition to determine whether there is ample and varied material available on your topic.

Narrowing a Topic and Developing a Working Thesis or Claim

Try to narrow your topic as soon as possible. Do not research poverty in general, but research and explore the causes of poverty, the governmental or private remedies for poverty, or the impact of poverty on children. Narrow down the topic of capital punishment to the morality of the death penalty, or its deterrent effect, or the question of retribution, or the question of whether capital punishment is fairly administered. Focus on one war, not several; on a few speeches, not ten. Narrowing allows you to focus on more specific sources and to avoid getting lost in reading sources that will not be relevant to your project. Narrowing will also ensure that you can develop adequate support in the time and space you have. Always keep in mind that you need to be able to make a claim and that you will be writing an argument, not merely a report.

As soon as you can, write a working thesis (or claim). It is often helpful to start with a question. Given the information you have already, which questions are most appropriate; for which do you have the most supportive information? For example: Is capital punishment moral? Does it deter murderers? Does it provide retribution? Is it unfair in its application? In a short paper you might want to try to answer only one of these questions; in a longer paper you might want to tackle them all. Next, provide a tentative answer to your question. This answer is your thesis or claim. Be sure that it is arguable, that not everyone is in agreement: "Capital punishment is moral because _____." Or, "Capital punishment is unfair in its application because _____."

Your subsequent research will help you determine whether your claim is defensible, whether it will hold up to scrutiny. It is helpful to think of your claim as a hypothesis, one that you will test. Should the evidence not support the claim, you as a responsible and honest arguer will need to reformulate your thesis. Student Caitlin Cunningham, for example, began with a thesis claiming that those who worked on the Underground Railroad were not practicing civil disobedience. In the course of doing her research, however, she modified her claim to argue that despite the secrecy (to avoid capture and penalty) of their actions, those helping slaves to escape were civil disobedients.

Selecting and Evaluating Sources

Make effective use of library resources to find good sources. Check your library's online catalog of books and articles, and locate articles through databases such as InfoTrac College Edition. Books provide a more comprehensive look at a topic and often include extensive data or thorough development of important ideas; articles are, of course, shorter and more focused on a portion of the topic. Your bibliography should usually include both types of material.

Depending on your topic, your most up-to-date sources will be from journals, magazines, newspapers, and Web sites. Be wary of Web sites because they differ widely in source, reliability, and usable content. Look for those set up by universities, reputable institutions, and authorities. The following are useful questions to ask in order to evaluate sources:

1. Examine the cover of a magazine or journal, the front page of a newspaper, or the opening pages of Web sites. Determine how its images and words affect you. What feelings do you think it is intended to stimulate? What would motivate someone to buy it if it is a magazine, or continue reading or subscribe to it if it is a newspaper, Web site, or other electronic publication?
2. What is the publication's social and political viewpoint? Who owns or publishes it?
3. Study the table of contents, look at the range of subjects offered, and skim some articles. What can you infer about the political orientation, purpose, and assumptions of this publication?
4. Look at ads and generalize about which sponsors sell their products in this publication. What social class would they appeal to? What kinds of advertisements are missing? How might the advertisers influence the publication's policies and attitudes?
5. Analyze the language in the articles. How does the language indicate the targeted readers and their level of education?

Taking Notes

As you read, you will need to keep track of material helpful to your argument. It is a good idea to print out or copy any sources not in your text because transcribing material directly into your text can lead to many types of errors and, in some cases, to charges of plagiarism. In addition, your instructor may wish that you submit this material with your completed essay in order to check that you have cited material correctly, either by direct and accurate quotation, paraphrase, or summary. Many researchers start by highlighting relevant material in a source. Some researchers are then reluctant to allocate the time to take notes, but omitting this step can make it difficult to locate a quotation or piece of information and arrange material in the best order. When downloading sources, try to find sources that indicate original page numbers, such as PDFs.

We recommend using note cards or fairly small slips of paper for your notes. This way, you avoid having too much information on one card and do not lose the flexibility of shuffling cards to determine the correct ordering of the information you have amassed. Usually it is a good idea to have three types of note cards: a card with complete bibliographic information for each source; cards containing the background information, quotations, or evidence you think will be helpful for your argument; and cards on which you jot down ideas, questions, examples, etc., as they occur to you. Bibliography cards can then be alphabetized to serve as the source for your Works Cited or References page. The notes you take on each source should have at least the author and an abbreviated title at the top left and a topic on the right (these topics will help you sort your cards). Be sure to indicate page number (or paragraph number for an Internet source). Use quotation marks to indicate quoted material. For summarized or paraphrased material, be sure to rewrite the material in your own words. Do not merely change a word or two. These three types of cards are invaluable when you write your draft. Many students have told us that after they have arranged their notes in a logical order, the paper almost writes itself. Andrew Packman's note cards on pages 41–42 will give you an idea of how to proceed. Some students find it convenient to take notes on the computer and then print them out for easy reference.

Construct your Works Cited or References page (for example, a minimum of 8–10 sources for an 8–10-page essay) from your bibliography cards. As you add sources, add them to a computer file you have created to list your sources. You can directly copy or download the bibliographic information from your library catalog. Include a wide range of sources: books, articles, and Web sites covering a time frame appropriate for your topic. For each source, do you have complete bibliographic information, including pages or paragraph numbers? Have you used correct MLA or APA bibliographic format?

Ashe, Geoffrey. <u>Gandhi.</u> New York: Stein and Day, 1968.

Ashe provides explanation of the Rowlatt Bill, showing people accused of sedition were tried w/out jury and interned w/out trial.

Nanda, <u>Mahatma Gandhi</u>   Violence

Context: G writing to Nehru about Chauri Chaura

" 'I assure you . . . if this thing [mass demonstration] had
not been suspended we would be leading not a non-violent
struggle, but essentially a violent struggle'" (236).

My Ideas

What contributes to outbreak of violence in nonviolent
mass movements?

—Lack of control at the fringe
—Geographical separation from leader
—Lack of commitment to leader's program
—Impatience, disappointment with failure?

Annotating a Bibliography

Many instructors require more than an initial list of your sources as a
way to help decide if you have the sources you need. The annotated bibliography includes the following steps: Skim each source you have
selected. Write your own brief, but specific, summary of the source.
Using the abstract in the database is not acceptable because it may often
not include the specific information that makes the source valuable to
you. Include a paragraph indicating your evaluation of the source: What
is its relevance to your project? How pertinent and accurate is the information it contains? Does it make an argument that supports yours, or
does it provide important counterarguments to your position? Keep
looking for additional sources as you find holes in your research.

Student Caitlin Cunningham prepared the following entries for her
annotated bibliography on the topic of whether conductors on the Underground Railroad can truly be considered civil disobedients. Note that
Caitlin has succinctly stated the main point of her sources and reflected
on their utility for her paper. She has included materials representing
diverse viewpoints and drawn from recent and more contemporary
sources. She has also been careful to use correct MLA citation form:

Annotated Bibliography

Breyfogle, William. <u>Make Free: The Story of the Underground Railroad.</u> Philadelphia and New York: J. B. Lippincott, 1958.

This book emphasizes the secrecy of the Underground Railroad and its goal to put itself out of business. Without such a system, Breyfogle argues, Negroes' discontent would have turned into violence. In "Some Leaders of the Underground" appear outlines of the lives and achievements of exemplary figures such as Isaac Hopper and Harriet Tubman. Conductors' general characteristics are presented as well. The Fugitive Slave Law of 1850 is discussed in detail in "1850," and "The Last Days" explains the Proclamation of Emancipation and informal ending of the Underground Railroad.

Breyfogle's writing will be useful in describing methods, examples, and reasons for running the Underground Railroad in secret. Concealment, proven essential to the system's survival, relates directly to the question of whether or not the Underground Railroad is, nonetheless, a true act of civil disobedience. Specific leaders' stories provide concrete support for a need for silence, and Breyfogle presents the Underground Railroad as an alternative far superior to uprisings and violence. Reflections on the railroad's character and ultimate success justify it as a proper, even if unlawful, response by an oppressed group.

Hudson, J. Blaine. <u>Fugitive Slaves and the Underground Railroad in the Kentucky Borderland.</u> Jefferson, NC: McFarland, 2002.

Hudson refers to Frederick Douglass's statement that freedom from bondage is but a small step in a long journey to equal treatment for African Americans. "It is perfectly fitting," Hudson adds, "that the biological and ideological children, grandchildren, and great-grandchildren of fugitive slaves and those who assisted them would become the leaders of black America." Because of slaves' worth as property and in labor (and, in the case of women, the value of her children), advertisements for fugitive slaves were prevalent. This danger, in addition to the threat of slave-catchers seeking profit, proves yet one more reason for concealment of illegal action. "Armed, not with guns," Hudson writes, "but with tenacity, courage, patience and above all, incisive intelligence, slaves waged a continual war against slavery [by means of the Underground Railroad]." He repeatedly refers to the Underground Railroad as a "conspiracy of conscience."

Douglass's assertion supports the idea that traveling the Underground Railroad is just the beginning in African Americans' achievement of equality and dignity; if the Underground Railroad were run openly and escapees willingly agreed to legal penalties, it could not have achieved its ends. Only after gaining freedom could African Americans devote themselves to proving slavery unjust, rallying support, and allowing their descendants the freedom to follow in their footsteps. It seems an appropriate exception, then, in the case of the Underground Railroad to exclude openness and acceptance of punishment as requirements for an act of civil disobedience. Hudson, too, points out perilous circumstances and African Americans' patient, determined, and clever reply in a "conspiracy of conscience."

Focusing the Thesis

Once you have completed your research, you should be able to write a very focused thesis that not only indicates the conclusion you have reached but also provides the reasons or main points of support for your assertions. Such a focused thesis also serves as a kind of road map to the organization of your essay, allowing readers to keep track of where they are in the argument.

1. Capital punishment is moral because it is imposed by the rightful authority of the state, it allows for retribution, it safeguards the community, and it provides avenues of appeal.
2. Capital punishment is unfair in its application because members of minorities and the poor who must use public defenders are more likely to receive the death penalty.
3. Capital punishment is moral except in the case of young offenders, those with low IQs, and those found to be legally insane.

Note how the first two claims include the reasons that support them. The third indicates the exceptions. In both cases, readers will expect you to develop each point in the order given.

Planning an Argument: The Outline or Argument in Brief

Write a plan that will help you discover what you think, that will help you focus on the elements of argument you need to include, and that will help you determine if you need additional material. You should include answers to the following questions:

- In light of your topic, what are your values and what assumptions do you make as the **writer?**
- Consider the **audience.** Who are your readers? What views may they already have about your issue? What kinds of values does the audience have? How can you make common ground with them? What will your audience need to know?
- What is your **claim** or thesis?
- Consider **reasons** or **subclaims** that will provide the main framework of your argument. These can provide the main points of an outline or an argument in brief.
- What kinds of **evidence** or **support** will best substantiate your thesis or claim?
- Think about what kinds of **objections** your readers are likely to raise. Forestall them by raising them first. This tactic helps to keep your readers with you. How will you **refute** these objections?

As you focus your thesis and plan your essay, think about the type of argumentative structure best suited for your topic. For example, if you are setting up general principles of a theory of civil disobedience against which you will test a particular action, a deductive framework may work for you. In this case, you might find *The Declaration* a useful model. First write an extended definition of civil disobedience as your major premise; use the body of the essay to demonstrate how a particular action conforms—or fails to conform—to the definition of civil disobedience; and then draw your conclusion from this evidence: The conductors on the Underground Railroad were (or were not) true civil disobedients.

If you wish to focus your essay on what conclusions may be drawn from specific evidence, an inductive approach, you may decide to use Martin Luther King as a model (see paragraph 14, p. 160). Using this approach leads you to collect and present sufficient material about a topic from which you can generalize. After studying a series of personal narratives concerning civil disobedience, for example, you might determine what common elements these narratives have, and then decide which elements are essential to persuade readers of the justice of civil disobedience. The strategies of Rogerian argument may work well if, for example, you want to make an argument that is particularly difficult for an audience to swallow. Here you would look for the common concerns and values that the members of your audience share, and you would take care to illustrate that you understand and accept at least some of the arguments your readers would make.

Another way to proceed is to use the modifications of the syllogism that Toulmin proposes, which we might call the claim/reasons/specific evidence method. Student John Anneken has used this method in his plan for his essay, shown below.

Brief for Argument Paper

Claim: The concept of civil disobedience is sometimes used incorrectly to defend actions.

Warrants for the Claim: The definition on which I base this claim is that civil disobedience must be an open act that breaks an unjust law with full knowledge and acceptance of the punishment as a means of protest.

- According to Fortas, the punishment must be accepted or it will undermine the rule of law.
- According to King, true civil disobedience must be nonviolent.
- My audience (the class and instructor) is familiar with the concept of civil disobedience and has read the seminal texts I'm using.

Reason I: John Brown's raid does not qualify as civil disobedience because it centered on violence, thus violating King's theory.

Specific Evidence: Give background of raid on Harpers Ferry. My audience is probably not familiar with this event.

- Finkelman's preface: narrative of events
- Thoreau on John Brown

Reason II: The 2001 riots in Cincinnati following the police shooting of Timothy Thomas were not civil disobedience because they include looting, random acts of violence, and an outcry for amnesty. The riots violated both Fortas's insistence on accepting punishment and King's proscription of the use of violence.

Specific Evidence: Newspaper accounts of the events. My audience probably is unfamiliar with the riots.

Reason III: The actions of Nathaniel Heathole planting box cutters on airplanes to expose the weakness of airport security was not civil disobedience because there was no unjust law he was protesting, he did not expect punishment, and he was not prepared to take it.

Specific Evidence: News articles about the event. My audience has heard of the event but needs specific information.

Conferring with Your Instructor

If possible, arrange a conference with your instructor to which you bring your bibliography, sources, notes, argument in brief, etc. Be sure to bring your questions as well. Ask for help if you are having problems finding sufficient information, if your thesis is not as focused as it needs to be, or if any part of your paper is giving you particular trouble.

Drafting the Essay

As you write your **introduction,** think about how you are engaging with your sources and your readers in a kind of conversation. How can you interest your readers in your topic? Can you pose a question that demands an answer, write a scenario that engages them emotionally, jolt them with startling or horrifying statistics, or draw them in with a quotation that provides the pith of your argument? How can you let your readers know both what you are arguing and how you will proceed? A carefully crafted thesis can do both, combining your claim and your reasons and thus providing a road map of your argument.

If you find that you are stalled somewhere in your introduction, move on to the body of your paper. For some writers, laying out the evidence is a very helpful way to get started. Then you can return to the introduction, having discovered what you really want to say. Use your outline or plan to guide the writing of the **body** of your draft. For each point turn to your notes, arranging them in the best order to supply the evidence you need to support each reason or subclaim. Keep checking back with your thesis or claim to see whether what you are writing advances it. As you introduce each section of your essay, be sure to use **topic sentences** that relate that section very specifically to your thesis and that show readers where you are in your argument. For example, if your thesis is *Whereas Tolstoy argues that violence will disappear once Christians refuse to participate in a government that is based on violence, Gandhi and King* *understand that violence is a possible outcome of nonviolent resistance,* you might introduce the section on Gandhi as follows: *Like Tolstoy, Gandhi embraces nonviolence, but he recognizes that his followers will encounter violence and trains them accordingly.*

Be careful to introduce your source material accurately, providing parenthetical citations so that you can check later that you have cited material correctly (see Appendix B). Consider whether each quotation, paraphrase, or summary is necessary to make your point. Do not merely drop one into the text but introduce and explain it. Do not allow your text to become a pastiche of quotations. Be true to your sources by presenting them accurately and fairly. Be true to your readers by constantly asking yourself, "What do they need to know? How will they respond to what I have written? How can I show that I respect them even if I suspect they will not be sympathetic to my claim?"

Even if you are not required to submit a draft with your completed paper, do not give in to the temptation to make your first draft your last! You may encounter difficulties or problems that require time to correct. Write a complete draft, including all the support you have gathered from your sources. This is an invaluable step that allows you to see exactly what you have and where you are missing necessary material. When you see gaps or holes in your research, this is a point at which you must return to your sources for additional information or locate new sources. Sometimes you may discover that the organizational structure you proposed in your plan is not working. To clarify the logical progression of your ideas, you may need to try a different order for your reasons or subclaims or even to employ another argumentative strategy.

Many writers find **conclusions** difficult to write. The temptation is to restate the thesis and leave it at that. Certainly you do need to demonstrate that you have proven your thesis or supported your claim. At this point, look back at your introduction to see if you have changed your mind in the course of writing the paper or inadvertently proven a different thesis, and adjust your conclusion accordingly. But a mechanical ending does not do justice to the conversation you have been having with your readers and sources. You might inquire whether the conversation about your topic has really been exhausted. What other questions are left to resolve? What problems remain? Where are you least satisfied with what you have discovered? Where do you think additional research needs to be done?

Revising the Draft

Revision means to see again; it implies re-viewing, re-thinking, and re-writing where necessary. Most likely, you have been revising as you write your draft, catching errors as you see them, and rearranging the order of material in a kind of ongoing, recursive process. Until now, your writing process has probably been rather solitary. Now it is time to seek out what Donald Murray calls a "test reader" in *The Craft of Revision* (Wadsworth). This reader may be a peer-editing partner or group in class or someone you have identified outside of class who can provide responses to your work. Ask this reader to comment on your work as specifically as possible so you can see how a reader responds to what you have written. Of course, you must be willing to do the same for your reader. The following are questions to guide your reader's response. You might also ask your reader to focus on an area with which you have had particular difficulty.

1. Does the introduction grab your readers and draw them into the discussion? What tactic is used? How can it be improved?
2. At the end of the introduction, is there a focused claim that predicts the organization of the essay? What is the claim? Underline it on the draft and write it here. How can it be improved?
3. Does the organization of the essay follow from the thesis? If it deviates from the claim, where does this happen?
4. Does each section of the essay have a topic sentence or subclaim, showing how the section relates to the thesis?
5. Are there transitions that connect sections? Where are transitions needed?
6. Are judiciously chosen quotations included? Are they introduced well and discussed sufficiently, or are they merely dropped into the text?
7. Does the essay include ample, pertinent, and specific support from the sources? Where do you need more information? Where is additional support needed?
8. Are in-text citations present and correct? Is the Works Cited or Reference page properly formatted?
9. What are the most successful parts of the essay? Where would you suggest more work is needed?

Proofreading

Proofread carefully. Remember that this is a different process than revision. Check for spelling, punctuation, and typographical errors because an error-ridden paper is distracting or even insulting to the readers. One helpful technique is to put the paper aside for a few hours or a day so that you can see it with fresh eyes. Then start at the bottom of the page, looking only for errors. Another technique is to keep a list of the errors you make frequently and focus on those. Still another is to read the paper aloud. Often the ear will catch what the eye does not. Many people, including the authors of this text, need to proofread more than once. Check also that you have followed MLA or APA format exactly for both in-text citations and the Works Cited or References page.

Along with your well-edited final essay, submit your annotated bibliography, your argument in brief, copies of your sources, your notes, and your draft. Submit these items in a pocket folder or a manila envelope.

As a guide for your final revision and proofreading, we have also included the kind of checklist many instructors use to evaluate your essay.

Checklist for Argumentative Research Essay

Quality of research
(20 points total) _____
   Authoritative sources (15) _____
     Pertinent
     Ample
     Varied
   Notes (5) _____
     Accuracy
     Documented
     Labeled clearly
     Complete

Success of argument
(50 points total) _____
   Claim (15) _____
     Arguable
     Focused
     Provides major points of support
       or subclaims
     Provides map of argument
   Assumptions clearly
     enunciated (5) _____
   Objections/refutation (5) _____
   Subclaims (20) _____
     Topic sentences
     Complete development
     Necessary definitions
     Specific evidence
   Conclusion (5) _____
     Valid
     Convincing

Documentation
(10 points total) _____
   Acknowledgment of all
     borrowed material
   Accurate quotations
   Complete paraphrasing
   Smooth inclusion in sentence
   In-text citation
   Works Cited page format

Paragraphs
(10 points total) _____
   Effective transition sentences
   Logical order of ideas
   Full development
   Appropriate length

Sentences
(10 points total) _____
   Clear
   Grammatical
   Correct spelling and punctuation
   Exact word usage
   Elimination of unnecessary words
   Smooth transitions

Total: _____

PART TWO

Casebook on
Civil Disobedience

4

Origins

As we begin to think about the issue of civil disobedience, most of us probably summon up famous images: black Americans staging lunch counter sit-ins in the South, draft resisters of the Vietnam War burning their draft cards, peace marchers around the world staging massive protests against the war in Iraq. Images of the Hebrew midwives refusing to kill male children at Pharaoh's behest or of Daniel praying to God when Darius has commanded otherwise may be less likely to spring to mind. Yet both Exodus and Daniel in the Hebrew Bible present dramatic narratives that address very clearly the dilemma of how to behave when the laws of kings contradict the laws of God. The midwives refuse to obey Pharaoh's edict, escaping punishment by subterfuge. Daniel beseeches God, not Darius, and Darius, bound by the implacable law of the Medes and the Persians, is relieved when God delivers Daniel from the lion's den. These narratives speak for themselves; there is no interpretation of their meaning included in the accounts. When the Christian Bible takes up the issue of how to behave when there are two spheres of authority, both Luke and Mark present teachers providing guidelines rather than narratives. John the Baptist addresses the concerns of men working for the secular sphere as tax collectors and soldiers, indicating that they may serve the state without denying the requirements of their baptism. Jesus acknowledges two spheres of authority, that of God and that of Caesar, and commands, "Render therefore to Caesar the things that are Caesar's, and to God the things that are God's." Neither spells out how to recognize when the ruler ventures into God's sphere or how to behave when that happens.

Sophocles' *Antigone* uses the dramatic form to debate the limits of divine and human law, with Antigone and Teiresias defending the duty of piety to family and to God. Creon the king has, of course, a vested interest in standing up for the supremacy of the ruler's edict. Fine dramatist that he is, Sophocles presents multiple views of the issue as seen through the lens of Ismene, Haemon, and the Chorus. We the audience are forced to draw our own conclusions. Interestingly, both Antigone's thinking about where her duty lies and her subsequent behavior have become models for later theorists about civil disobedience and practitioners of the theory.

In both the *Apology* and *Crito*, Plato probes the issue further, using Socrates as his model. Facing the citizens of Athens, Socrates defends himself after being accused both of impiety and of corrupting youth. He argues that he is the "gadfly" sent by the gods to spur his fellow citizens to examine their own behavior. When the state rejects his defense and condemns him to death, he accepts the penalty because although his fealty is to God, he accepts the authority of the state in its proper sphere.

These early voices lay out the parameters of the discussion about civil disobedience. For all of them, the paramount question is whether God's law takes precedence over human law. In the Hebrew Bible, the answer is clear. Both the midwives and Daniel indicate no uncertainty about what God requires, and they do it. In both cases, they are able to avoid harsh penalties either by human ingenuity or God's intervention. The questioners in Matthew and Luke seek guidance, implying that there are areas where they see a conflict between what the state requires and what God requires. Providing another example of civil disobedience, *Antigone* complicates the issue. The heroine remains steadfast throughout, refusing to be swayed by the arguments of those around her; however, these counterclaims undoubtedly muddy the waters for her audience, especially a modern audience. Still more uncomfortable for a modern audience is the linkage of Socrates's belief that he is right to follow what the gods require of him with his acknowledgment that the state has a right to impose a penalty on him for doing so. The problems raised by such apparently contradictory positions will run through the discussions of nineteenth- and twentieth-century theorists and commentators.

The Hebrew Bible: "The Midwives Disobey Pharaoh"

The Bible is the holy book of Jews and Christians and is important to Muslims as well. The Hebrew Bible which is holy to Judaism consists of thirty-nine books divided into three parts: the Five Books of Moses or

Pentateuch, called in Hebrew the Torah; The Prophets; and The Writings. Christians refer to these sections of Scripture as the "Old Testament," but Jews do not, because they do not accept the validity of the Christian "*New* Testament." The Torah, from which the first excerpt is taken, was completed in the form we know it some time between 950 and 450 B.C.E. Exodus, the second book of the Torah, tells the story of Moses and of the Israelites escaping slavery in Egypt under Moses' leadership and God's direction. The passage below comes from the first chapter of Exodus, which continues the story of the descendants of Jacob, also called Israel, from the book of Genesis and sets the scene for Moses' birth. The Israelites have been living in Egypt for four centuries, but the contributions of their ancestor Joseph have been forgotten, and they are enslaved under an especially cruel pharaoh.

For another example of civil disobedience, consult the book of Daniel 6:1–22. It is believed to have been composed about 167–164 B.C.E., during the persecution of the Syrian king Antiochus Epiphanes. The book relates the life of Daniel as well as his apocalyptic visions. In this chapter, Daniel must choose between his faith and his king.

The Midwives Disobey Pharaoh, from Exodus 1:8–22

8: Now there arose a new king over Egypt, who did not know Joseph. *9:* And he said to his people, "Behold, the people of Israel are too many and too mighty for us. *10:* Come, let us deal shrewdly with them, lest they multiply, and, if war befall us, they join our enemies and fight against us and escape from the land." *11:* Therefore they set taskmasters over them to afflict them with heavy burdens; and they built for Pharaoh store-cities, Pithom and Ra-am'ses. *12:* But the more they were oppressed, the more they multiplied and the more they spread abroad. And the Egyptians were in dread of the people of Israel. *13:* So they made the people of Israel serve with rigor, *14:* and made their lives bitter with hard service, in mortar and brick, and in all kinds of work in the field; in all their work they made them serve with rigor. *15:* Then the king of Egypt said to the Hebrew midwives, one of whom was named Shiph'rah and the other Pu'ah, *16:* "When you serve as midwife to the Hebrew women, and see them upon the birthstool, if it is a son, you shall kill him; but if it is a daughter, she shall live." *17:* But the midwives feared God, and did not do as the king of Egypt commanded them, but let the male children live. *18:* So the king of Egypt called the midwives, and said to them, "Why have you done this, and let the male children live?" *19:* The midwives said to Pharaoh, "Because the Hebrew women are not like the Egyptian women; for they are vigorous and are delivered before the midwife comes to them." *20:* So God dealt well with the midwives; and the people multiplied and grew very strong. *21:* And because the midwives feared God he gave them families. *22:* Then Pharaoh commanded all his people, "Every son that is born to the Hebrews you shall cast into the Nile, but you shall let every daughter live."

Questions about the Passages

1. In this passage from Exodus, why do the Egyptians make the lives of the Israelites especially hard?
2. Why do the Hebrew midwives disobey Pharaoh?
3. Why do you think the text states that God rewarded the midwives despite their lie to Pharaoh? What inferences can you draw from God's action about divine and human laws?

Questions about the Arguments

1. Who was the original audience of the Hebrew Bible? Why are the issues raised important to the original audience? Why might they be important to subsequent audiences?
2. How does this passage establish its authority? How effective is it in conveying that authority?
3. This passage implies rather than directly states its message, which can be considered a form of inductive reasoning. Outline the argument that it makes to support its message.

The Christian Bible: "What Shall We Do?" and "Is It Lawful to Pay Taxes to Caesar?"

The Christian Bible includes the Hebrew Bible and the New Testament. The New Testament consists of twenty-seven books, the most important being the four gospels by Matthew, Mark, Luke, and John telling of the life, teachings, death, and resurrection of Jesus. Also included are the Acts of the Apostles, the history of the spread of Christian faith in its first three decades; letters to congregations and individuals written by followers of Jesus, most notably Paul; and the Book of Revelation. Written within the first century after the death of Jesus, the Christian Bible took its final canonical form in the fourth century. Luke's gospel includes an account of John the Baptist's preaching about repentance and his baptism of Jesus. The section below recounts the response of the crowds who came to listen and to be baptized by John. Those who were newly baptized wished to know how they should now live their lives. Luke provides instructions on both the duty of charity and the role of those who serve the state. In the passage included here, Matthew's gospel shows Jesus acknowledging both the authority of the state and the limits of that authority.

What Shall We Do?, from Luke 3:10–14

10: And the multitudes asked him, "What then shall we do?" *11:* And he answered them, "He who has two coats, let him share with him who has none; and he who has food, let him do likewise." *12:* Tax collectors also came to be baptized, and said to him, "Teacher, what shall we do?" *13:* And he said to them, "Collect no more than is appointed you." *14:* Soldiers also asked him, "And we, what shall we do?" And he said to them, "Rob no one by violence or by false accusation, and be content with your wages."

Is It Lawful to Pay Taxes to Caesar?, from Matthew 22:15–22

15: Then the Pharisees went and took counsel how to entangle him in his talk. *16:* And they sent their disciples to him, along with the Hero'di-ans, saying, "Teacher, we know that you are true, and teach the way of God truthfully, and care for no man; for you do not regard the position of men. *17:* Tell us, then, what you think. Is it lawful to pay taxes to Caesar, or not?" *18:* But Jesus, aware of their malice, said, "Why put me to the test, you hypocrites? *19:* Show me the money for the tax." And they brought him a coin. *20:* And Jesus said to them, "Whose likeness and inscription is this?" *21:* They said, "Caesar's." Then he said to them, "Render therefore to Caesar the things that are Caesar's, and to God the things that are God's." *22:* When they heard it, they marveled; and they left him and went away.

Questions about the Passages

1. What guidance do John the Baptist (Luke) and Jesus (Matthew) provide their questioners about living justly? Can you infer from these passages what should be the limits of the civil authorities in determining how one should behave?
2. Why do you think there are no specific rules about how to behave should the civil rulers exceed their authority?

Questions about the Arguments

1. What specific audience does Jesus address? Who are the "multitudes" that John refers to? What expectations and motives does each audience have? Where, specifically, might they differ?
2. How are both Jesus and John depicted here? What can you infer about their ethos, especially their values and their authority as revealed by their words?
3. When Jesus says, "Render therefore to Caesar the things that are Caesar's, and to God the things that are God's," do you think that these are discrete categories—different spheres—or do you think they might partially overlap, or might the one be included within the other? What would be the logical implications, for example, of diagramming this statement as two nonintersecting circles or of placing Caesar's circle within God's circle?

Sophocles, *Antigone*

Sophocles (49?–406) is perhaps the epitome of the Athenian citizen. Multitalented, musically gifted, civic-minded, Sophocles served his city-state in many functions. His public life included posts as ambassador, general, priest, and commissioner of Athens. We know him best for his contributions to the theater. Active in writing, producing, and acting in plays presented during the spring Dionysian festivals, he wrote more than 100 plays, never taking less than second place and often winning first place, even over Aeschylus and Euripides. His eight extant tragedies demonstrate his genius as a dramatist. Though drawing upon stories from Greek myth, Sophocles shapes his material so that he never loses sight of the human dimension. His characters, endowed with real human qualities and beset with flaws, seem like real people, never merely pawns of fate. His tragedies also record his contributions to the development of the dramatic form: He added a third actor, increased the role of the chorus, and made greater use of stage scenery than did his predecessors.

Though we have included *Antigone* for its relevance to our discussion of civil disobedience, it is important not to lose sight of the fact that it is a tragedy. We will examine the debates within the play about the rightness or wrongness of disobeying the gods or the king, but these arguments take place within a tragic plot, which Aristotle argues is the armature on which the whole structure is built. Protagonist and antagonist alike are driven not only by the collision of their values and the logic of their assertions but also by significant flaws that contribute greatly to their downfall. Despite their flaws, these are characters who are neither entirely villainous nor entirely virtuous. They may have higher positions than we do (thus they can fall farther), but they are sufficiently like us that we can experience the tragic effect of pity for unmerited misfortune. We also fear that if they can fall, so can we.

The impact of their arguments is enhanced by what Aristotle calls the magnitude or completeness and unity of the action. We are told the beginning of the dispute as it reaches back into history, as well as its middle stage as the complications increase with the addition of each argumentative voice. We see the change of fortune that Creon experiences. We also see the recognition or realization, the movement from ignorance to understanding—in this case, that the law of the gods takes precedence over his decree—that dawns upon him. This recognition, however, comes too late to avert the tragic end with its seemingly inevitable deaths of so many. The unity of the play, with its events compressed into "a single revolution of the sun," only heightens the impact of each debate and underscores that the debaters are more eager to hasten to a conclusion than to weigh each other's arguments.

The translation of *Antigone* is by C. A. Trypanis. We have added the scene divisions or episodes according to Aristotle's directions: The prologue precedes the entrance of the chorus, providing background; the episodes are dramatic scenes demarcated by the choral odes that surround them; and the exodos is the final scene after which the Chorus leaves the stage.

Prologue

Antigone:　　The horror, the disgrace,
　　　　　　　　The suffering that Oedipus had known
　　　　　　　　Have ripened out to fullness in our lives!
　　　　　　　　Zeus spared us nothing, you and me, Ismene.
　　　　　　　　And now the king's proclamation to the city!
　　　　　　　　Have you not heard? The curse we call upon
　　　　　　　　Our enemies is threatening our friends.

Ismene:	I have heard nothing. Nothing good or bad,
	Antigone, since our brothers killed
	One another with their own hands.
	The Argive army fled into the night . . .
	I have heard nothing else.
Antigone:	I thought so. That is why I called you here,
	To the palace gates, where we can speak alone.
Ismene:	Tell me. Your face is troubled.
Antigone:	Creon has ordered that one of our brothers
	May be buried with all honours—the other
	Must lie uncovered in disgrace.
	Eteocles—so they tell me shall be given
	The proper rites, will be respected among
	the dead.
	But the body of unlucky Polyneices
	Will neither be buried, nor lamented.
	He must lie naked and unwept,
	An easy feast for the searching birds!
	These are the orders of good Creon,
	And he has issued them for you and me,
	I say for me to obey. He will be coming here
	To tell the whole of Thebes himself—
	In case they haven't heard!
	And he considers this a grave matter
	And those who disobey him are to die
	By stoning, a public death.
	Now you know, and now you will be tested,
	If you are noble, worthy of your ancient blood.
Ismene:	But, Antigone, how can I help?
Antigone:	Will you share the danger?
Ismene:	What danger? What is in your mind?
Antigone:	Will you help these hands to carry the dead . . .
Ismene:	But will you bury him? Forbidden to the whole
	of Thebes?
Antigone:	My brother—yes, your brother too . . .
	I will not betray him.
Ismene:	You are talking wildly. Creon has ordered.
Antigone:	What right has Creon! I know my duty.
Ismene:	Remember, Antigone, what a cloud of hate
	And scorn darkened our father's death.
	How he himself uncovered the very sins
	That drove his hands to blind his eyes.

50

How his mother and wife, his wife-mother,
Strangled her life in an angry noose,
And now, how both our brothers found a common
    death,
Shedding their common blood, on the one day.
We two are all that has been left.
Think what a desperate end we shall face
If we defy the King's orders,
Sadder than father, mother or our brothers.
No, no, remember we are women;
We must not fight with men, we must obey;
Now and in the future the stronger will rule.
I beg the dead to forgive me, but I am forced
To obey my master. It is foolish for a woman
To meddle in public matters.

Antigone: I will not force you. Even if you had wished
I would not welcome your help. Be what you will.
But I will bury him—and it is good to die
In doing so. Pure in my crime, he will love me,
When I lie down in death by his side.
My first allegiance must be to the dead,
For I shall be in their world for ever—
The living come after. You, trample on the laws
The gods have made and honoured.

Ismene: I honour them, but how can I insult the state . . .
I haven't the strength.

Antigone: Make these excuses, I will heap
The earth over my brother's body.

Ismene: I fear for you, I fear . . .

Antigone: Don't fear for me—look after your own life.

Ismene: At least tell nobody about your plans . . .
Keep it a secret . . . and so will I.

Antigone: Go, and cry it out to Thebes!
I will hate you more, if you are silent.
Tell them what I will do . . . it will please
Those I should please.

Ismene: You can't succeed. It is impossible.

Antigone: I shall stop when I have no strength left.
Leave me and my madness to suffer.
What could be worse than an infamous death.

Ismene: Go, if you must. You are foolish,
But very dear to those who love you . . .

Choral Ode

Chorus: Shaft of sunlight! Most lovely light
To touch Thebes of the Seven Gates!   100
Golden-eyed day, you rose at last
Over the stream of Dircè,
Driving to headlong flight
The men of Argos.
Armed with bronze shirts and white shields
They marched against us—
Now hands pull sharply at the bridles
Of their horses in retreat!

Like a screeching snow-bright eagle
They came, numberless spears,
Helmets richly plumed,
Led by Polyneices pursuing his quarrel.
They ravened round the seven gates
Thirsting for blood,
But left, before their jaws
Reeked with our gore,
Before the pine-fed flame of Hephaestus
Had licked the crown of our towers.
They could not conquer the sons of the Dragon—
The moan of battle dying in their wake.

Zeus hates the boasting tongue.
And when he saw them coming,
A stream of haughty, clanging gold,
He struck, loosened his thunder's fire
As they were straining to scale the walls
To shout in triumph on our ramparts.

The monster swerved, fell to the ground,
The quick brand burning in his hand.
What storms of fury he had breathed
When he attacked! Great Ares, our strong helper
Has routed many enemies before.

Now the armour of seven captains,
Who charged our seven gates,
Who faced our seven men, is left behind,
An offering to Zeus, the giver of victories.

Only Eteocles and Polyneices,
Those two unlucky men who shared one blood,
Faced one another with the spear
And share a common death.

But victory—great is her name—
Has come! Away from war,
Let us join in the joy of the city,
Visit the temples of Thebes   150
With night-long dance and song.
Let Bacchus lead us,
The Theban earth shudders at his dance!

Chorus: But look, the King is coming.
Creon, the son of Menoeceus, is now our King—
Such was the will of the gods.
Why did he call us here? Why did he summon
The council of elders? What does he mean to do?

Episode I

Creon: Men of Thebes, the gods have saved the city
After they struck it with that bitter storm.
I have called the elders here, because I know
How truly you respected the royalty of Laius,
How loyal you have been to the rule of Oedipus,
And when he perished to his children.
Now both his sons are dead, a brother's blood
Streaked on their hands, and I command the throne.
I was the closest to the dead—my blood was theirs.
Only when you have seen a man's rule,
What laws he sets, can you know his heart.
The King must listen to the best advice,
So I believe, and I despise most of all
The men whose mouths are tight with fear.
Those who will put some other friend
Above their city, are cumberers of the ground!
Zeus who watches all be my witness:
I would never keep silent, if I saw
Disaster coming to this land.
The state is like a ship on which we sail;
Only if she prospers in her journey

Can the passengers make good friends.
This is the spirit in which I will rule,
And that is why I issued my order.
Eteocles fell bravely fighting for Thebes,
He shall be given the honours
That follow the brave to their rest.
But his brother Polyneices,
Who found his way back from exile
To burn down his father's city,
And shatter the temples of her gods   200
And drink his brother's blood,
Dragging those who survived into slavery,
Must we honour him with burial?
No, I have made that clear, no lamentation!
Let his dead flesh be left to the dogs and the birds.
Don't ask me to honour the wicked.
I shall exalt the friends of Thebes
In life and in death.

Chorus: If that is your pleasure, Creon.
You have the power to dispose as you wish—
The living and the dead . . .

Creon: Then you must see my orders are obeyed.

Chorus: That is for younger men, King Creon.

Creon: I have set guards over the body.

Chorus: What do you ask from us?

Creon: Obedience.

Chorus: No one runs after his death.

Creon: Death will be the punishment, But gold lures many
men to their ruin.

Guard: I'm out of breath—not because I was running, Sir.
My thoughts forced me to stop, and stop again,
And turn back on my steps, I said to myself:
You fool, why are you hurrying to your death?
And then: you wretch, why are you stopping?
Some one else will tell King Creon and he will
punish you.
So, talking to myself, I dragged my steps along,
Making a short road long. At last I decided
To come here and tell you—though what I have to tell
Is . . . really . . . nothing. No one escapes his Fate!

Creon:	What is the matter?
Guard:	First I must tell you that I did not do it.
	I mustn't be punished. It isn't right.
Creon:	How well you know your business.
	You fence yourself all round against blame.
	What do you want to tell me?
Guard:	Bad news make you go slowly, Sir.
Creon:	Speak out—and go.
Guard:	Well . . . it is about the corpse . . .

Someone has buried it . . . and disappeared.
He sprinkled dry dust on the body,
And did what they do . . .

Creon: What did you say? Who dared do that?

Guard: I do not know, Sir . . . there was no trace of an axe . . .
No mattock had thrown up the earth . . .   250
The ground was hard and dry, unbroken,
No track of wheels—he left no trace.
When the first day-watchman called us,
The corpse was covered—not in a real grave,
But lightly sprinkled with dust
As by the hand of one who fears a curse.
Not a sign of an animal or a dog was there,
Nothing had touched his flesh.
Uuuuh! Angry words flew fast and hard among us,
Guard was accusing guard. We nearly came to blows,
And there was nobody there to stop us.
Anyone could have done it, but we all swore
We knew nothing—we could blame nobody for certain.
We were ready to grip red-hot iron,
Or walk through fire to prove we told the truth.
We swore by all the gods we knew nothing about it.
When all our searching came to nothing
One of us spoke—but who dared look him in the face?
He was right, how could we say "no"—but "yes"
meant death.
He said we should report the matter to you,
And not keep it a secret. And that seemed the best,
And the lot fell on me—a dangerous prize!
So here I stand, unwelcome and unwilling,
For who wants to bring bad news!

Chorus:	My thoughts were whispering, King Creon,
	Can this be the work of the gods?
Creon:	Stop, before my anger breaks out in a storm.
	You have shown yourself both old and stupid.
	This is intolerable! Why should the gods
	Honour that man's body? To reward his services?
	Because he came to burn down their temples,
	To ravage their holy treasures, to ruin their land
	And scatter their laws to the winds?
	No, the gods do not honour the wicked.
	But I knew there were citizens who muttered against me
	Wagging their heads in the dark,
	Because they hated me and my rule.
	They bribed the man who buried Polyneices
	The greatest evil current among men is silver.
	Silver can shatter their cities,
	Drag them out of their homes; it warps 300
	The honest and lures them to every godless roguery.
	But those who have been bribed will learn
	That they must pay the price—sooner or later.
	By Zeus, whom I honour, I now warn you
	That if you do not bring me the man
	Who buried Polyneices, death will be too easy.
	You will hang alive, until you undo your work
	And that will teach you that all the gold you snatch
	Is worth nothing! Crooked earnings
	Lead to ruin and not to happiness.
Guard:	May I speak? Or shall I turn and go . . .
Creon:	Even your voice offends me.
Guard:	The man who buried him wronged you, I only offend
	your ears . . .
Creon:	You have a sharp tongue.
Guard:	That may be so—till I did not bury him.
Creon:	You have sold your life for a few silver pieces.
Guard:	How dreadful, when the judge is unjust.
Creon:	Say what you like, but if you do not find the criminal,
	You will find sorrow is the reward of those
	Who are bribed into crime.
Guard:	I wish he could be found—but that is a matter of luck!
	However, you won't see me here again.

I owe great thanks to the gods who saved me,
When I wasn't expecting it.

Choral Ode

Chorus: The world is rich with wonders,
Yet none more baffling than man.
Driven by the stormy South
He crosses an ocean white with rage;
He opens a path through the waves
That hunger to engulf him.
He ploughs the old, unwearying earth,
Turning the soil with horses,
Year after year breaking the furrows.
With woven nets he snares the careless birds,
The tribes of savage beasts,
The sea-brood of the deep—
So excellent is his wit.
His cunning controls the animals
That nest in the wilderness,
Or roam across the hills.
He has tamed the rich-maned horse,   350
Putting a yoke upon its neck,
The wild mountain-bull he has conquered.

And he has taught himself to speak,
Trained his wind-swift thoughts
To build an ordered state.
So he escapes the arrows of the frost
When it is hard to sleep under the cold sky,
Under the slanting shafts of rain.
From baffling sickness he has found escape,
Anything he can meet—
Only death he will never master.

How skilfully he comes to evil and to good.
When he honours the laws and the justice
Of Zeus, his cities stand proud and tall;
But he, who rashly sinks into sin,
Is homeless and lost—
May I never share his thoughts.

Chorus: The gods have struck again!
Antigone, it is Antigone!

Unlucky child of an unlucky father—Oedipus.
What does this mean? A prisoner?
Disobeying the orders of the King?
Caught in an act of folly?

Episode II

Guard: She is the one who did it. We caught this girl
As she was burying the body! Where is Creon?

Chorus: He is coming and at the right moment too—

Creon: At the right moment? Why?

Guard: Men should never make promises, King Creon;
When we think again, we change our minds.
I vowed I would never come back to this place.
Your threats had filled me with terror!
But look, here I am. Strange joy
Gives the greatest pleasure, so I broke my oath
To bring this girl whom we caught honouring
The body of Polyneices. This time
There was no casting of lots I found her,
Nobody else can claim the prize.
Now, take her, Sir, question her,
Examine her as you wish. I have the right
To be free, my troubles are all over now.

Creon: But how? Where did you catch her?   400

Guard: She was burying the body—what else can I tell you?

Creon: But are you sure? Is that the truth?

Guard: Yes, Sir, I saw her burying the body,
The one you ordered nobody should honour—

Creon: How did you see her? How was she caught?
The moment she was burying him?

Guard: That's how it was. When your threats drove us back
To that place, we swept away the dust
That covered the corpse. We bared completely
The rotting limbs, and then sat on a ridge of the hill
To windward, so that the smell would not strike us.
Our eyes were wide awake, and we kept our neighbours alert
Cursing and threatening. And so it went,
Until the sun's bright circle touched the centre
Of the sky, and the heat began to burn.

Then suddenly, a whirlwind sucked up from the earth
A storm of dust. The sky was darkened,
And the plain was full! It clawed at the leaves
Of the wood—the whole air was choked.
We closed our eyes stung by that plague of dust.
After a while the storm blew out, and then
We saw the girl. She cried bitterly,
Like a bird that finds her nest stripped of her brood.
When she saw the body was swept clean,
She wailed and called down curses on the men who
    did it.
Then she brought dry dust, lifted a jar
And poured out three libations near the body.
We pounced upon her, taking no chances.
But she was not surprised. We blamed her
For what she had done, but she admitted everything—
I was glad and yet I was sorry . . .
To bring misery to . . . a friend . . .
But most of all I care for my own life.

Creon:	You, you who are looking at the ground,
	Do you deny you did it? or do you admit it?
Antigone:	I deny nothing. I buried him.
Creon:	[To Guard] You can go. You are free.
	[To Antigone] Tell me, but shortly,
	Did you know what my orders were?
Antigone:	Yes, I knew. Everybody knew, they were publicly
	proclaimed.
Creon:	And you dared to break the law?
Antigone:	Yes, that law was not spoken by Zeus,

Nor by Justice of the gods below.   450
Your orders have no power to force
My human will to break the unwritten
And unfailing laws of the gods.
It is a gain for me to die before my time.
If your life like mine was shared with misfortune,
Death would be good. But to leave my brother unburied
I couldn't have borne it . . .
You think me foolish for what I did,
But it could be that I merely look foolish
To the eyes of a fool.

Chorus:	The child is raging with her father's passion.
	She has not learnt to bend before the storm.
Creon:	The stubborn are most often humbled.
	Iron, stiffened to hardness in the fire,
	Is that which snaps and is most easily shivered.
	Yet a little bridle can curb the rage of horses—
	When you are a slave, there is no room for pride.
	Insolent when she disobeyed my orders,
	Now she adds a second insult by her boasting,
	Being proud of what she did!
	If she will go unpunished, she is the man
	Not I. But no, child or no child of my sister,
	The closest of my blood among those who
	worship Zeus
	In my house, she and her sister shall die
	A painful death. For I charge her sister too
	With an equal share in this plot.
	Call her here—I just saw her going to the palace
	Distraught and furtive.
	When men are plotting mischief in the dark
	The mind convicts itself of its own treason.
	What can be worse than to be caught red-handed,
	And then turn your crime into an act of glory?
Antigone:	Then why lose time? There is no pleasure
	In your words—and may there never be—
	And what I say displeases you.
	But as for glory—could there be greater glory
	Than to give burial to my brother?
	All these men standing here would say
	That I was right, but terror has sealed their mouths.
	For sacred royalty has all the power
	To do and say what it wishes.
Creon:	They have different thoughts.
Antigone:	They think as I do—but hold their tongues.
	They are afraid.
Creon:	But did not a brother of yours kill him?
	Why do you treat them both alike?
Antigone:	His brother too, not his slave was killed.
Creon:	Killed fighting against his own city,
	But Eteocles fell defending it.

500

Antigone:	Hades asks for the same rites.
Creon:	Go then to the world of the dead,
	Since it is the dead you love.
Chorus:	Ismene is coming. Look, like a loving
	Sister she is weeping. The cloud over her eyes
	Shadows her flushing face and breaks in raindrops
	On her delicate cheek.
Creon:	You too! Lurking like a viper in my house,
	Secretly drinking my blood. How could I know
	That I was feeding a double enemy
	To my throne!
	Will you confess your part in this burial,
	Or will you say that you know nothing?
Ismene:	Yes, I have done it—if Antigone allows,
	I will share the blame.
Antigone:	No, justice, not I, refuses you.
	You had no part in the burial.
Ismene:	Now that you are caught in this sharp gale, I want to
	sail the sea beside you.
Antigone:	Hades and the dead will witness who did it—You are
	only my friend in words.
Ismene:	Sister, do not insult me. Let me die With you,
	honouring the dead.
Antigone:	You will not share my end. Your hand never touched
	him! He is not yours, And my death is enough.
Ismene:	What is my life to me, when you are gone?
Antigone:	Ask Creon, you cared more for him than for me.
Ismene:	Why are you insulting me? It does not help
	In anything!
Antigone:	As I mock you, I hurt myself.
Ismene:	Is there nothing I can do for you, even now?
Antigone:	Save yourself. I do not grudge your escape.
Ismene:	Aaah! I want to share your death.
Antigone:	You chose to live, and I to die.
Ismene:	But I protested, I didn't agree.
Antigone:	The world of the living finds you wise, But not the
	world of the dead.
Ismene:	We have both offended . . .
Antigone:	You must live—I have given my life To the service
	of the dead.

550

Creon:	Ismene has recently lost her senses, But the other was always mad, crazy.
Ismene:	People lose their reason in great misfortunes . . . I cannot live without her . . .
Creon:	Think of her as already dead.
Ismene:	But your son? Will you kill his promised wife?
Creon:	There are other fields for him to plough.
Ismene:	But never such love as yokes them together.
Creon:	I do not want an evil woman for my son.
Antigone:	Haemon, dearest, Haemon, you have a harsh father . . .
Creon:	Enough, I have had enough of you and your marriage.
Chorus:	Antigone . . . Will you take her from your son?
Creon:	Death himself will forbid their marriage.
Chorus:	He has decided. She must die.
Creon:	No words shall change my mind. Take them away, into the palace, guard them—Even the bravest try to escape When death closes round them.

Choral Ode

Chorus:	Happy the man, whose life has known no sorrow. For, when a house is shaken by the gods, There is no misery that will not follow, And it is handed from father to child. Like swelling waves, hurled by Thracian storms Across the darkness of the sea, They stir the deep black sands To the roar of the wind-thrashed coast.

Sorrow on sorrow in the House of Labdacus!
One generation does not free another,
A god strikes them, there is no end.
And now the last root of the House of Oedipus,
The one lit by hope, is severed again,   600
Because of the blood-stained
Dust we owe to the dead, the folly of speech,
The fury of the heart.

O Zeus, no human wrongs can limit your power.
Neither the wide net of sleep, nor the unsleeping
    seasons
Can overcome your rule. You live in the

Light of Olympus.
As in the past, the law will hold good:
Nothing monstrous can enter the life of man
Without a long shadow, a curse.

Wandering Hope brings comfort to some,
But many it lures to random desires.
Only with the last step into the fire
You learn the price of your folly.
Wise is the famous saying: Evil seems good,
When the gods urge a man to mischief—
But, for little he stands naked of pain.

Look! Here is Haemon, your youngest son;
Sad because of Antigone,
Bitter to be cheated of his bride.

Episode III

Creon: Are you angry with me, Haemon,
Because you heard the woman you chose for a wife
Has been condemned to death? Or are you always
True to your father, no matter what he does?

Haemon: I am yours, father. You taught me how to think,
The laws I must obey. No marriage can shake
The guidance you have given me.

Creon: Follow your father in everything,
Never waver from that. Obedient children
Are a blessing in the home, friends to its friends,
Enemies to its enemies. Evil children
Are ceaseless trouble, a joy to those we hate . . .
No woman should fetter your reason,
No beckoning pleasure. An evil wife   650
Soon dwindles to a cold embrace.
And that is why you should hate this woman,
Consider her an enemy, let her find a husband
In the house of Death! I caught her alone.
Of all the city, openly defying my orders.
But I shall keep my promise—she must die.
Let her appeal—for she will—to Zeus of family
     worship.
If I allow my own flesh and blood to be wicked,
Then the whole city must be corrupt if it chooses.

One can be just to the city, only
If just in one's own home. I do not approve of those
Who ignore the laws, and try to govern their Kings.
When the city chooses a man for its ruler,
He must be obeyed in everything—just or unjust!
Those who have learnt to obey
Are the best subjects and the best rulers;
They stand their ground in battle,
Fearless and loyal by the side of their comrades.
Disobedience ruins home and city,
Breaks the ranks of allies into headlong rout.
We will not allow a woman to defeat us.
If I am to fall, let a man's blow overthrow me,
But I will not be weaker than a woman!

Chorus: The King is right, or I am too old to understand.
Haemon: Father, the greatest gift of the gods is reason.
I am not strong enough to say that you are wrong,
But advice can also be useful. As your son,
I try to hear what people say, how they act,
If they blame you, and this I do for your own sake.
They are afraid to mention in your presence
What might offend you, they fear your royal frown.
But I can hear them muttering in the dark,
And they moan over the death of this young girl.
They say that no woman less deserves such an end,
That she should be honoured, because she did
    not leave
Her brother's body unburied to be torn by the dogs
And the birds. These are the rumours circling in the
    darkness.
My greatest treasure is your happiness, father;
No ornament is greater for a child.
Than the good name of his parents—   700
It is the same for a father and his son.
Change your mind. You must not think that only you
Are right. Those who believe they know everything,
When searched and tested, are often found empty.
It is no shame for a sensible man to listen,
To change his mind. The flexible tree survives
The weight and rush of the winter stream and saves
    its wood;

The stiff-necked perish root and branch.
If a sailor never slackens his sail,
His boat capsizes and floats with an upturned keel.
Father, control your anger, change your mind.
I may be young, but no one is infallible,
Listen to what makes sense.

Chorus: Sir, you should profit from these words;
And you, Haemon, must obey your father,
For you have both spoken well.

Creon: Must men of my age be taught by youngsters like him?

Haemon: Not if what I said was wrong. Look at the force
Of my words, not at the slightness of my years.

Creon: Must the disobedient go unpunished? be honoured?

Haemon: Injustice commands no respect.

Creon: But she has acted unjustly.

Haemon: The whole of Thebes denies it.

Creon: Must Thebes tell the king how to rule?

Haemon: You are speaking now like a green boy.

Creon: And you are under the heel of that woman, Every
word of yours is pleading for her.

Haemon: And for you, and me, and for the gods below

Creon: You will never marry that girl. She must die.   750

Haemon: Her death will destroy another.

Creon: You dare threaten me?

Haemon: I am not threatening—I am fighting your Wrong
decision.

Creon: You have no sense at all. Well, suffering Must teach
you . . .

Haemon: I would say you had no sense at all—But you are
my father . . .

Creon: By the Olympian gods, you shall not go unpunished.
Bring here that creature. She must die Before his
eyes, beside her bridegroom!

Haemon: Not beside me—I shall not be there—You will never
see my face again. Rant on to those, who are weak
enough to listen.

Chorus: He has gone, King Creon, quick with anger. The
young are fierce when stung . . .

Creon: Let him do or say what he likes, But he will not save
those two girls.

Chorus: But will you kill them both?

Creon:	No, you are right. Ismene does not deserve death.
Chorus:	And Antigone?
Creon:	I will have her led where the path is lonely,
	And imprison her alive in the vault of a rock
	With just so much food as piety demands,
	So that the city will avoid the stain of murder.
	There let her pray to Hades for escape—
	Hades the only god she worships. There let her learn
	At last, though late enough, that it is vain and stupid
	To honour the dead.

Choral Ode

Chorus:	Love, destroyer of wealth,
	Unconquered in battle,
	You keep your night-watch
	On the soft cheek of a girl.
	Over the water you wander
	To the lonely dwellings of men.
	There is no escape for god or for man—
	Where you touch, madness seizes.

You warp the mind of the just
To injustice, you drive them to ruin.
It was you who urged these men
Of common blood to fight.
The bright wish kindled by the eyes
Of a graceful bride
Will carry the day;
Harsh as the laws of the gods,
It rules the lives of men—
And mocking Aphrodite smiles,
The goddess none can defeat.

Even I, as I see Antigone moving   800
To the bridal chamber, where all are laid
To rest, even I can feel
My loyalty falter.

Episode IV

Antigone:	Look, my people, look at my last journey,
	The last I will see of the sun.
	Hades, the giver of sleep, is leading me living

To Acheron's shore.
No marriage-feast, no bridal song
Has been chanted for me,
My bride-groom is Death.

Chorus: Honoured by all you move now
To the deep home of the dark.
No wasting sickness touched your limbs,
No wound of the sword.
You alone of the living will pass into Hades,
Because you wished to go.

Antigone: I have heard of the sad death
The daughter of Tantalus suffered
On the Sipylian rock.
How the stone, clinging like ivy,
Embraced her, she hardened to stone.
The slanting rain and the snow—
So they say—still fall on her form
Melting with sorrow.
Beneath the lids of her eyes,
Her ever-weeping eyes,
The streams water the rock.
And I must suffer like her.

Chorus: She was a goddess, the daughter of gods,
And we the children of men.
To share the fate of so godlike a woman
Is a dazzling honour.
You have shared it in life
And in death.

Antigone: Aaah! Aaah! I am being mocked.
Must you insult me to my face?
By our city's gods, wait,
Wait till I have gone.
Land of Thebes, rich in chariots and in men,
Fountain of Dirce, I call on you to witness   850
The laws by which they lead me to my death.
Unhappy and unwept, the hollow prison of a tomb!

Chorus: Your daring drove you to that precipice,
You slipped on the tall steps of Justice,
Deep down you were hurled, my child.
You are punished for the sins of your fathers.

Antigone:	You touch my bitterest thoughts—
	The death of my father, known to all.
	The noble house of Labdacus!
	O horrors of my mother's bed,
	The wretched sleep beside her son—
	This was my miserable birth!
	Unwed and cursed I go to share their home.
	My brother, how ill-starred your marriage,
	Though dead you quicken my death.
Chorus:	You had a sister's love for Polyneices.
	But Kings never forgive
	Those who cross their power.
	Your obstinate temper
	Drove you to ruin.
Antigone:	Naked of friends, my wedding-song not sung
	I am led away. All is prepared
	I shall see the Day-star's holy eye no more . . .
	No friendly tears are falling for this death.
Creon:	Wailing and lamentation would never stop
	If they could fence out death.
	Take her away—and when you lock her
	In that round roof rock, leave her alone to die,
	As I have ordered—or live there a buried life,
	If she chooses that for her home.
	My hands are clean, but she must not live here
	Among us.
Antigone:	My burial chamber! A prison in the empty rock,
	Where I must go to meet my people,
	The many who have gone, and whom Persephone
	Received among her guests. Now I must follow,
	The last and most despairing of them all,
	Before my life has run its course.
	I hope you will welcome me, father,
	And you, my mother, and my brother,
	For I washed and dressed your body with
	these hands
	And poured libations on your graves.
	Polyneices, your death gives this reward . . .
	[And yet I honoured you properly,
	so reasonable men might think.

900

Had I been a mother of children,
Or had I lost a husband,
I would never have done such a thing
Against the will of the people.
Why am I saying all this? By what moral law?
Had I lost a husband,
I could marry again,
I could have had other children
From some other man.
But now, with my mother and father
Hidden in Hades, no brother
Could ever blossom for me again.
By such a law I honoured you first.
But, dear brother, Creon thought I was wrong,
That I was daring terrible things;
And now he leads we away,
A captive in his hands.
I have had no bridal bed, no bridal song,
No joy of marriage, no children to rear.
Unfriended, unhappy, I go living
To the dwellings of the dead.]*
What law of heaven did I break?
But why turn to the gods? What ally can I call,
If piety marks me as a criminal?
When I have died, perhaps I will learn it all.
But if my judges are the guilty ones,
May they meet with a punishment as unjust as mine.

Chorus: The same wild tempest still flooding her heart.

Creon: What are the guards doing? Take her away, Or suffer
for it.

Antigone: Death is near . . . these words tell me . . .
Thebes, city of my fathers,
Gods, oldest of our race,
They are leading me away . . . to death.
Look at me, men of Thebes, the last daughter
Of the house of your kings,
See what I suffer, and from whom . . .
Because I have honoured the gods.

*Lines 904–920 are considered by many scholars spurious.

Choral Ode

Chorus: Even young and slender Danae endured
To change the light of day for brass-bound walls,
A grave-dark room was her prison.
Danae noble of blood, who held the seed of Zeus
That dropped in golden rain,
Fearful the workings of Fate;   950
Neither gold, nor war, nor city walls,
Nor the dark, sea-beaten ships can protect us.

Bonds tamed the angry son of Dryas,
King of the Edonians.
He paid for his frenzied words
Locked in a prison of rock;
Such was the will of Dionysus.
Exuberance of rage died down
And he learnt to know the god,
Whom in madness he had mocked,
Stung to quell the god-possessed women,
The bacchic fires.
He had angered the flute-loving Muses.

The steep shores of Bosphorus
And Thracian Salmydessus rise
By the waters of the Dark Rocks.
There Ares saw the sons of Phineus
Blinded by his fierce wife—
A wound bringing darkness to eyes
Thirsting for revenge.
She struck with a shuttle for a dagger—
Blood leaping on her hands;
She moaned in frenzy over their doom,
She, who could follow her blood
To the house of Erechtheus,
Nursed in solitary caves,
Where her father's storms were raging—
Boreas wild as a stallion across the slanting hills—
A daughter of the gods!
The gray Fates did not spare even her,
My child!

Episode V

Teiresias:	Lords of Thebes, we have come
	By a common path, though only the one
	Of us can see. The blind must walk
	By a guide's hand.
Creon:	What new do you bring, old Teiresias?
Teiresias:	I will tell you, and you must listen To the seer.
Creon:	In the past I followed your advice.
Teiresias:	That is why you steered safely The city's course.
Creon:	I have been helped by you, and I can confirm it.
Teiresias:	Look out, for you are standing On the verge
	of bad luck.
Creon:	What is the matter? I shudder at your words.
Teiresias:	Guided by my art, I must warn you.

When I sat on the old throne of the prophets,   1000
That harbour of all birds, I heard strange voices.
They were screaming in hot anger,
Barbaric cries drowning their language.
With their talons they were tearing one another—
I knew this for the noise of beating wings
Blunted the senses. In terror I turned to sacrifice,
But the flame of the altar would not touch
My offerings—a spluttering moisture trickled
From the thigh-flesh on the smoking embers,
The gall was scattered to the winds,
The streaming thighs lay bare of fat,
My sacrifice had failed. Uselessly I asked for a sign
So this boy tells me who is my guide,
As I am the guide of others.
Creon, what you have done, has brought this sickness
To the city. The altars and the hearths have been
Polluted by the dogs and birds that snatched
Flesh from the defenceless limbs of Polyneices.
The gods will not accept our offerings,
Neither our prayers, nor the flame of meat.
No bird gives signs with a shrill cry,
Now they have tasted the rich blood of the dead.
Think about it, my son. All men run into errors,
But the clever and the blessed are not stubborn,

They heal the damage they have done.
Allow the dead their claims. It is not brave
To strike at the fallen.
I tell you this for your own good.

Creon: You too, old man, like all the others
Are shooting your arrows at me.
But I know you and your art. I have been
Tricked and sold by you too often.
Drive your trade, and gather gains
From the silver of Sardis, or India's gold—
But you shall never bury that man. No,
Not even if the eagles of Zeus
Were to bring the carrion to their master's throne,
Would I allow this burial. For I know far too well
That no mortal can defile the gods.
Old man, the wise fall deeper than the others,
When they mask their plots with beautiful words,
Having been bought.

Teiresias: Alas! does any man know . . .

Creon: Know what? What are these dark mutterings . . .

Teiresias: That good advice is more precious than all the
         gold . . .

Creon: But prophets have always chosen gold.   1050

Teiresias: And tyrants useless gains.

Creon: You are speaking to your King!

Teiresias: But through me that King saved the city.

Creon: You prophesy acutely—but you are no friend of justice.

Teiresias: Don't provoke me, or I will give voice To a dark
         secret . . .

Creon: Speak, if you have not been bought already.

Teiresias: My words can no longer help you . . .
But before the Sun's rapid wheels
Have circled the sky a time or two,
You shall offer one of your own blood to the dead—
Dead body for a dead body . . . And this because
You coldly lodged a living soul in a tomb,
And kept in the daylight unburied and dishonoured
One who belongs to the gods of the dead.
For this the Furies, the avengers, the destroyers,
The barren daughters of Hades and the gods
Lie in ambush, waiting to trap you

In the same desolation . . . Mark my words,
Remember if I have been bribed into speaking.
The wailing of men and women will soon rise
In your house, a tumult of hatred will shake
The cities whose sons were ripped by the dogs
And the wild beasts of prey, birds that carried
To the hearths droppings of flesh, the breath of
    pollution . . .
You have provoked me, so I strike back in anger.
You will not escape the wounds of my arrows.
Boy, lead me home. Let him spend his rage
On younger men, and learn to keep a more temperate
Tongue and a wiser heart in his breast.

Chorus: Teiresias left us, foretelling terrible things . . .
Ever since my hair was dark,
I have always known him speak the truth . . .

Creon: You are right. I am deeply troubled.
This is a hard choice: go back on my word
And free Antigone, bury Polyneices . . .
Or else suffer the death of one of my own blood . . .
A terrible choice . . .

Chorus: Son of Menoeceus, you must be brave And wise.

Creon: What must I do . . . tell me . . . I will follow your
    advice . . .

Chorus: You must go yourself and free Antigone   1100
From her hollow prison, and you must make
    a tomb
For the unburied man.

Creon: Must I do that . . .

Chorus: Yes, King Creon, and lose no time.
For the punishment of the gods
Pounces on man's folly.

Creon: It is hard, but I must revoke my orders.
I will take your advice. It is useless
To wage war on destiny.

Chorus: You must go yourself. Do not send others—

Creon: Yes, I will go. Servants, you there,
Bring your axes and let us go at once.
I must be there to release her myself,
For it was I, who threw her in that prison.
It may be best to keep the ancient laws.

Choral Ode

Chorus: Child of the Cadmian bride,
O god of many names,
Son of loud-thundering Zeus!
You are the master of Italy
And of the sheltered plain of Deô,
Eleusis that welcomes every guest.
Bacchus of Thebes, the mother
Of the bacchants, where soft Ismenus rolls
Over the soil that nursed the Dragon's teeth.
You appear where the flame of torches
Flashes through the smoke,
Over the Sister-Rocks' peaks,
That haunt of Corycian Nymphs,
Near Castalia's water.
From the ivy-decked slopes of Nysa
You come, from shores rich
With clustering vine,
And voices divine escort you
On your journey to Thebes.

For it is Thebes you honour most
Among the cities, you and your mother,
Whom lightning consumed.
Come with healing feet,
For a fierce plague shackles our men,
Come over the rocks of Parnassus,
Across the windy sea.

Master of the night's voices,
The fire-breathing stars in their circles
Rejoice when you come.
Child of Zeus, appear O King
Attended by your Thyiads,
Who all night long dance in frenzy
Before you, giver of good gifts,   1150
Iacchus appear.

Exodus

Messenger: You who have lived in the shadow of Cadmus'
And Amphion's palace should neither praise
Nor blame the life of any man.
Fortune will raise, then humble the living

On the same day—nothing is certain in life.
Creon was happy—what I call happiness.
He saved this land of Cadmus from its enemies,
He was a King, the father of princes.
Now all is lost, for, when you forfeit joy,
You are no better than a living corpse.
Heap up gold in your house, live like a King,
But if no happiness will blossom there,
It is not worth the shadow of a cloud.
Nothing can equal joy.

Chorus: What new horror is here?

Messenger: Death—and the living are to blame.

Chorus: Who died? who killed?

Messenger: Haemon is dead—no stranger killed him.

Chorus: Was it his father? Or did he kill himself?

Messenger: He took his own life—so fierce was his anger
With his father for Antigone's murder.

Chorus: The old prophet was right . . .

Messenger: Now you must think what is to be done in Thebes.

Chorus: Look. Eurydice, Creon's unhappy wife, is coming.
Can she have heard about her son?

Eurydice: Men of Thebes, I have heard all you said,
As I was going to offer prayers to Athene.
I had just loosened the bolt of the door,
When that dreadful message struck my ears;
I fainted into the arms of my attendants.
But tell me, tell me all you know—I shall be calm,
I am no stranger to sorrow.

Messenger: Dear Mistress, I will tell you all I saw.
Why should I comfort you with words
That soon must be found false? Truth is the best.
I led the King to the deepest end of the plain,
Where the body of Polyneices, ripped by the dogs,
Still lay unburied.
We prayed to the Goddess of the Road and Pluto
To be merciful and withhold their anger.   1200
We cleansed the body with holy washings
And with the help of newly-plucked branches
Burnt such relics as there were.
Then we piled a tall mound of Theban earth
Over him, and turned to reach Antigone's prison—

The rocky, hollow palace of the bride of Death.
One of us heard a distant wailing
Coming from that sinister tomb. He ran to tell
    the king.
And as Creon came close, bitter cries floated
    round him,
And then he groaned and cried: "Misery, misery!
Is it true this shadow in my mind,
Is this the saddest road I ever went?
Quickly, my servants, I can hear my son's voice.
Climb through the gap where the stones are loose,
Reach the mouth of the tomb, see if it is Haemon,
Or if my ears are cheated by the gods."
We ran at his command—and found Antigone
    hanging
In the deepest corner of the tomb,
Slung by a halter of twisted linen . . .
And Haemon's hands embraced her round
    the waist,
And he was lamenting the death of his bride,
His father's cruelty, his own unlucky love.
But when Creon saw him he cried out aloud:
"Unhappy son, what have you done?
Has your suffering driven you mad?
Come out, my child—I beg of you, come."
But the boy glared at him with ferocious eyes,
And spat in his face, and silently drew his sword.
His father fell back to escape the blow
And Haemon missed him, and then with mad rage
Leaned with all his weight against the blade,
Driving half the sharp bronze into his side.
And as he swooned he touched the girl in a faint
    embrace,
And gasping stained her pale cheek with a rain
    of blood.
And so they lie, corpse embracing corpse. That was
    his wedding,
The sad young man—not here, in Hades' Halls.

Chorus: The Queen has gone. She did not say a word—
    Good or bad.

Messenger:	Strange! Perhaps she did not wish To show her sorrow in public. In the privacy of her home, among her maids, She will mourn for her son. She is not untaught of discretion.
Chorus:	Strained silence is dangerous, As dangerous as extravagant lamentation. 1250
Messenger:	You are right . . . I must go and see. Some hidden thoughts May have moved her passionate heart . . .
Chorus:	The King is coming. He carries in his hands The proof of his own folly, the body of his son.
Creon:	Oh, oh, sins of a darkened soul! Stubborn sins! Charged with death! Look at us, The father who murdered, the son who was killed! My thoughts were blind, and you died young . . .
Chorus:	You have seen, but too late.
Messenger:	Master, more sorrow is waiting for you In the palace, misery greater Than the one you carry in your hands.
Creon:	Aaaah!
Messenger:	The Queen has just died.
Creon:	Is there no mercy? No sacrifice to soothe The deep waters of Hades? What is this message you bring! You strike a dead man dead. What did you say?
Chorus:	You can see her Creon; she lies there.
Creon:	Aaaaah! My new, my second misery! Is there more to come? First the son, dead here in my arms, 1300 And there the mother!
Messenger:	She stabbed herself at the altar. As her eyes were darkening, she wailed for Megareus, Her son who nobly died before, then for Haemon, The one you hold in your arms, and with her last breath Called down a curse upon you—murderer of her sons.
Creon:	I shudder hearing this. Will no one strike me With a quick sword? A broken man, brimming with misery

The guilt is mine. No one can claim it to acquit me.
I, miserable I, have killed you both—
That is the truth. Lead me away, my servants,
Lead me away, I no longer belong to the living . . .
Death is all that I ask for . . . death is the best.
May I not see the light of tomorrow.

Chorus: The future lies in the hands of the gods.

Creon: All I ask for is in that very prayer.

Chorus: Suffering is ordered by the gods And men cannot
escape.

Creon: Lead me away, I beg you—a rash, foolish man.
I killed you, my son, though against my will,
And you my wife. Where can I look for support?
I feel my misery here, between my arms,
And see it there, lying on the ground . . .

Chorus: Wisdom is the crown of happiness. Honour the Gods.
Words swollen with pride   1350
Are violently punished, strokes that teach
The ageing man how to be wise.

Questions about the Passage

1. Why do you think Sophocles begins the play with the prologue? What does Antigone do and why does she do it? What is Ismene's view of her sister's action? Collect quotations that demonstrate this view. By the end of the scene, which character do you find more appealing? Why?

2. In Episode I, why does Creon provide the history of his coming to the throne and of Polyneices' action? What is Creon's reason for denying his nephew burial? At this point in the play, what is your response both to Creon's reasoning and to the man himself?

3. By the beginning of Episode II, what actions has Antigone undertaken? Does she deny doing them or knowing they have been forbidden? What does she give as her reason for acting? How does Creon react to what she has done? What seems to affect him the most? Why? During their interchange, whose side do you take? Has your initial response to Antigone or Creon changed?

4. In each of his long speeches in Episode III, how does Haemon try to dissuade Creon from punishing Antigone? Why do you think Haemon fails? Why does the latter part of their interchange shift from long speeches to very short lines?

5. In Episode IV, what does Sophocles accomplish dramatically by bringing Antigone back on stage on her way to her punishment? How do you respond to her? To Creon?

6. Why do you think Sophocles introduces Teiresias in Episode V? Why does he succeed in persuading Creon when Haemon does not?

7. At the start of the play, Ismene says, "It is foolish for a woman/To meddle in public matters," and then says of her sister, "You are foolish." Do you think the ending of the play, the Exodos, justifies this epithet? Given the outcome of the play for Antigone, Haemon, Eurydice, and Creon, how can you explain why this ending occurs? For whom do you feel the tragic effect of pity and fear?

8. Why do you think the play is titled *Antigone* when Creon, at least according to Aristotle's view, seems to be the more likely tragic figure? What argument can you make for Antigone as the tragic figure?

Questions about the Argument

1. Think of the prologue as a kind of debate. Identify Antigone's claim and Ismene's counterclaim. What kinds of support does each arguer provide for her claim? How much does each depend on pathos? Look for specific examples. Who wins the debate?

2. In Episode I, what is Creon's claim and how does he justify it?

3. Who are the arguers in Episode II? State each claim. What values or assumptions underlie each claim? Given their assumptions, is there any room for compromise? What role does pathos play in the argument? Can anyone be said to "win" here?

4. In his first speech in Episode III, what argumentative strategies does Haemon use to persuade Creon to change his mind? Do they succeed or fail? Why? What is the reasoning underlying Creon's response? What are Haemon's strategies in his second speech? Do they succeed?

5. In Episode IV, what additional reason does Antigone supply to support her position? Addressing Polyneices, she claims, "I honoured you properly / So reasonable men might think." A few lines later, she cries, "What law of heaven did I break?" Do you agree with her assessment of her position?

6. How does Teiresias' argument in Episode V differ from the others put forth earlier in the play? What is the best evidence that Creon finds it convincing?

7. Do you think Sophocles' original audience would have viewed the play the way you do? Try to infer the objections to each argument that the original audience would have raised. To draw this inference, examine what Ismene says to Antigone and Haemon to Creon, as well as the comments of the Chorus.

8. Many readers see this play as a clash of values: obeying the law of the gods versus obeying the laws of the king. It also seems to be a clash of genders: Antigone asserts the primacy of the family, and Creon refuses to listen to what a woman has to say. There is also a clash of personalities with the flaws of Antigone and Creon contributing to the hardening of their positions. To what extent can you defend each view of the play?

9. Later writers have seen Antigone as a kind of prototype of the civil disobedient. Which elements of her conduct do you think qualify her for this position?

Plato, "Socrates the Gadfly" and "The Sentence of the State"

Plato (423–348/347 B.C.E.) was born in Athens of a distinguished family, descended on his father's side from Codrus, the last king of Athens, and connected on his mother's side with the famous lawmaker Solon. From his boyhood, Plato probably knew Socrates through his family connections. As a young man, Plato most likely had political, not philosophical, aspirations, but he became disenchanted with the Athenian democracy instituted after the fall of the Oligarchy. When Socrates was condemned to death in 399, Plato left Athens and traveled extensively, returning only in 387 to found the Academy. There he brought together those studying philosophy and natural science and remained their mainstay and support until the end of his life. Little is known of Plato as a person, but Aristotle's comment that Plato was a man "whom it was blasphemy in the base even to praise" gives us insight into his personal probity and intellectual gifts.

Plato's writing was primarily dramatic in form, employing dialogues between Socrates and other historical figures to propound questions and explore ethical quandaries. Scholars debate whether Plato is reporting the thought of Socrates or presenting his own ideas or exploring some ideas without making a commitment to them. *The Republic*, Plato's most important work, is his attempt to imagine what the ideal society, based on justice, would look like, thus bringing together both ethics and political philosophy. In the excerpts of the works printed here, Socrates is the primary speaker. In the *Apology* (written some time during the 380s), Socrates defends himself against the charge of impiety that the state has leveled against him, arguing that he performs a crucial function for the state by being its "gadfly." Despite his self-defense, Socrates is convicted of the charge and sentenced to death. While preparing for the sentence to be carried out, Socrates in the final section of *Crito* explains why, even though he feels he has done no wrong, he will not try to evade his punishment.

The passages below are from the Benjamin Jowett translation of Plato.

Socrates the Gadfly, from *Apology*

And now, Athenians, I am not going to argue for my own sake, as you may think, but for yours, that you may not sin against the God by condemning me, who am his gift to you. For if you kill me you will not easily find a successor to me, who, if I may use such a ludicrous figure of speech, am a sort of gadfly, given to the state by God; and the state is great and noble steed who is tardy in his motions owing to his very size, and requires to be stirred into life. I am that gadfly which God has attached to the state, and all day long and in all places am always fastening upon you, arousing and persuading and reproaching you. You will not easily find another like me, and therefore I would advise you to spare me. I dare say that you may feel out of temper (like a person who is suddenly awakened from sleep), and you think that you might easily strike me dead as Anytus advises, and then you would sleep on for the remainder of your lives, unless God in his care of you sent you another gadfly. When I say that I am given to you by God, the proof of my mission is this:—if I had been like other men, I should not have neglected all my own concerns or patiently seen the neglect of them during all these years, and have been doing yours, coming to you individually like a father or elder brother, exhorting you to regard virtue; such conduct, I say, would be unlike human nature. If I had gained anything, or if my exhortations had been paid, there would have been some sense in my doing so; but now, as you will perceive, not even the impudence of my accusers dares to say that I have ever exacted or sought pay of any one; of that they have no witness. And I have a sufficient witness to the truth of what I say—my poverty.

Some one may wonder why I go about in private giving advice and busying myself with the concerns of others, but do not venture to come forward in public and advise the state. I will tell you why. You have heard me speak at sundry times and divers places of an oracle or sign which comes to me, and is the divinity which Meletus ridicules in the indictment. This sign, which is a kind of voice, first began to come to me when I was a child; it always forbids but never commands me to do anything which I am going to do. This is what deters me from being a politician. And rightly, as I think. For I am certain, O men of Athens, that if I had engaged in politics, I should have perished long ago, and done no good either to you or to myself. And do not be offended at my telling you the truth: for the truth is, that no man who goes to war with you or any other multitude, honestly struggling against the many lawless and unrighteous deeds which are done in a state, will save his life; he who will really fight for the right, if he would live even for a brief space, must have a private station and not a public one.

I can give you convincing evidence of what I say, not words only, but what you value far more—actions. Let me relate to you a passage of my own life which will prove to you that I should never have yielded to injustice from any fear of death, and that 'as I should have refused to yield' I must have died at once. I will tell you a tale of the courts, not very interesting perhaps, but nevertheless true. The only office of state which I ever held, O men of Athens, was that of senator: the tribe Antiochis, which is my tribe, had the presidency at the trial of the generals who had not taken up the bodies of the slain after the battle of Arginusae; and you proposed to try them in a body, contrary to law, as you all thought afterwards; but at the time I was the only one of the Prytanes who was opposed to the illegality, and I gave my vote against you; and when the orators threatened to impeach and arrest me, and you called and shouted, I made up my mind that I would run the risk, having law and justice with me, rather than take part in your injustice because I feared imprisonment and death. This happened in the days of the democracy. But when the oligarchy of the Thirty was in power, they sent for me and four others into the rotunda, and bade us bring Leon the Salaminian from Salamis, as they wanted to put him to death. This was a specimen of the sort of commands which they were always giving with the view of implicating as many as possible in their crimes; and then I showed, not in word only but in deed, that, if I may be allowed to use such an expression, I cared not a straw for death, and that my great and only care was lest I should do an unrighteous or unholy thing. For the strong arm of that oppressive power did not frighten me into doing wrong; and when we came out of the rotunda the other four went to Salamis and fetched Leon, but I went quietly home. For which I might have lost my life, had not the power of the Thirty shortly afterwards come to an end. And to this many will witness to my words.

Now do you really imagine that I could have survived all these years, if I had led a public life, supposing that like a good man I had always maintained the right and had made justice, as I ought, the first thing? No indeed, men of Athens, neither I nor any other man. But I have been always the same in all my actions, public as well as private, and never have I yielded any base compliance to those who are slanderously termed my disciples, or to any other. Not that I have any regular disciples. But if anyone likes to come and hear me while I am pursuing my mission, whether he be young or old, he is not excluded. Nor do I converse with those who pay; but any one, whether he be rich or poor, may ask and answer me and listen to my words; and whether he turns out to be a bad man or a good one, neither result can be justly imputed to me; for I never taught him or professed to teach him anything. And if any one says that he has ever learned or heard anything from me in private which all the world has not heard, let me tell you that he is lying.

But I shall be asked, Why do people delight in continually   5
conversing with you? I have told you already, Athenians, the whole truth about this matter: they like to hear the cross-examination of the pretenders to wisdom; there is amusement in it. Now this duty of cross-examining other men has imposed upon me by God; and has been signified to me by oracles, visions, and in every way in which the will of divine power was ever intimated to any one. This is true, O Athenians, or, if not true, would be soon refuted. If I am or have been corrupting the youth, those of them who are now grown up

and have become sensible that I gave them bad advice in the days of their youth should come forward as accusers, and take their revenge; or if they do not like to come themselves, some of their relatives, fathers, brothers, or other kinsmen, should say what evil their families suffered at my hands. Now is their time. Many of them I see in the court. There is Crito, who is of the same age and of the same deme with myself, and there is Critobulus his son, whom I also see. Then again there is Lysanias of Sphettus, who is father of Aeschines—he is present; and also there is Antiphon of Cephisus, who is the father of Epigenes; and there are the brothers of several who have associated with me. There is Nicostratus the son of Theosdotides, and the brother of Theodotus (now Theodotus himself is dead, and therefore he, at any rate, will not seek to stop him); and there is Paralus the son of Demodocus, who had a brother Theages; and Adeimantus the son of Ariston, whose brother Plato is present; and Aeantodorus, who is the brother of Apollodorus, whom I also see. I might mention a great many others, some of whom Meletus should have produced as witnesses in the course of his speech; and let him still produce them, if he has forgotten—I will make way for him. And let him say, if he has any testimony of the sort which he can produce. Nay, Athenians, the very opposite is the truth. For all these are ready to witness on behalf of the corrupter, of the injurer of their kindred, as Meletus and Anytus call me; not the corrupted youth only—there might have been a motive for that—but their uncorrupted elder relatives. Why should they too support me with their testimony? Why, indeed, except for the sake of truth and justice, and because they know that I am speaking the truth, and that Meletus is a liar.

Well, Athenians, this and the like of this is all the defence which I have to offer. Yet a word more. Perhaps there may be some one who is offended at me, when he calls to mind how he himself on a similar, or even a less serious occasion, prayed and entreated the judges with many tears, and how he produced his children in court, which was a moving spectacle, together with a host of relations and friends; whereas I, who am probably in danger of my life, will do none of these things. The contrast may occur to his mind, and he may be set against me, and vote in anger because he is displeased at me on this account. Now if there be such a person among you,—mind, I do not say that there is,—to him I may fairly reply: My friend, I am a man, and like other men, a creature of flesh and blood, and not 'of wood or stone,' as Homer says; and I have a family, yes, and sons. O Athenians, three in number, one almost a man, and two others who are still young; and yet I will not bring any of them hither in order to petition you for an acquittal. And why not? Not from any self-assertion or want of respect for you. Whether I am or am not afraid of death is another question, of which I will not now speak. But, having regard to public opinion, I feel that such conduct would be discreditable to myself, and to you, and to the whole state. One who has reached my years, and who has a name for wisdom, ought not to demean himself. Whether this opinion of me be deserved or not, at any rate the world has decided that Socrates is in some way superior to other men. And if those among you who are said to be superior in wisdom and courage, and any other virtue, demean themselves in this way, how shameful is their conduct! I have seen men of reputation, when they have been condemned, behaving in the strangest manner: they seemed to fancy that they were going to suffer something dreadful if they died, and that they could be immortal if you only allowed them to live; and I think that such are a dishonour to the state, and that any stranger coming in would have said of them that the most eminent men of Athens, to whom the Athenians themselves give honour and command, are no better than women. And I say that these things ought not be done by those of us who have a reputation; and if they are done, you ought not to permit them; you ought rather to show that you are far more disposed to condemn the man who gets up a doleful scene and makes the city ridiculous, that him who holds his peace.

But, setting aside the question of public opinion, there seems to be something wrong in asking a favour of a judge, and thus procuring an acquittal, instead of informing and convincing him. For his duty is, not to make a present of justice, but to give judgment; and he has sworn that he will judge according to the laws, and not according to his own good pleasure; and we ought not to encourage you, nor should you allow yourselves to be encouraged, in this habit of perjury—

there can be no piety in that. Do not then require me to do what I consider dishonourable and impious and wrong, especially now, when I am being tried for impiety on the indictment of Meletus. For if, O men of Athens, by force of persuasion and entreaty I could overpower your oaths, then I should be teaching you to believe that there are no gods, and in defending should simply convict myself of the charge of not believing them. But that is not so—far otherwise. For I do believe that there are gods, and in a sense higher than that in which any of my accusers believe in them. And to you and to God I commit my cause, to be determined by you as is best for you and me.

Questions about the Passage

1. In paragraph 1, Socrates compares himself to a "gadfly" and the state to a "great and noble steed who is tardy in his motions." What is a gadfly, and what does it do? In this analogy, what is Socrates' function vis-à-vis the state? Why should he be considered a "gift of God" to the state?
2. Socrates speaks of an "oracle," or "sign," or "divinity," or "voice" that comes to him (paragraph 2). How do the denotative and connotative meanings of these words differ? Why do you think he uses so many synonyms to explain his meaning? Try to think of another word that a modern audience might understand better. Why does Socrates stress that he is told what not to do rather than what he should do?
3. How does his experience as a senator, his only public office, prove that he would not participate in committing injustice out of fear of death (paragraph 3)?
4. Why is his claim that he has "no regular disciples" a central part of his defense (paragraph 4)?
5. Socrates names many men who know him well and are present in the court; then he challenges Meletus, one of the prosecutors, to call them as witnesses. Why, according to Socrates, will Meletus not do so (paragraph 5)?
6. Why does Socrates choose not to bring forward his family to supplicate for him (paragraph 6)?
7. Why does he consider it wrong "to petition a judge, and thus procuring an acquittal instead of informing and convincing him" (paragraph 7)?

Questions about the Argument

1. Who is Socrates' audience? Are his addresses and references to this audience likely to make them more or less sympathetic to his case? For example, is his analogy of the gadfly and the steed likely to win listeners to his side?
2. What do you learn of Socrates' values and principles from this passage? Is he admirable? In what ways?
3. After answering the questions about the passage, outline the argument Socrates makes in his own defense. What are his main strategies to convince the court that he is innocent of the charges? Does he convince you? Why do you think he does not convince the court?
4. Socrates refuses to use pathos to bolster his argument. Is this a principled position? Is it wise?

The Sentence of the State, from *Crito*

Socrates Then I will proceed to the next step, which may be put in the form of a question: Ought a man to do what he admits to be right, or ought he to betray the right?

Crito He ought to do what he thinks right.

Soc. But if this is true, what is the application? In leaving the prison against the will of the Athenians, do I wrong any? or rather do I not wrong those whom I ought least to wrong? Do I not desert the principles which were acknowledged by us to be just? What do you say?

Cr. I cannot tell, Socrates, for I do not know.

Soc. Then consider the matter in this way: Imagine that I   5 am about to play truant (you may call the proceeding by any name which you like), and the laws and the government come and interrogate me: "Tell us, Socrates," they say; "what are you about? are you going by an act of yours to overturn us—the laws and the whole State, as far as in you lies? Do you imagine that a State can subsist and not be overthrown, in which the decisions of law have no power, but are set aside and overthrown by individuals?" What will be our answer, Crito, to these and the like words? Anyone, and especially a clever rhetorician, will have a good deal to urge about the evil of setting aside the law which requires a sentence to be carried out; and we might reply, "Yes; but the State has injured us and given an unjust sentence." Suppose I say that?

Cr.   Very good, Socrates.

Soc.   "And was that our agreement with you?" the law would say, "or were you to abide by the sentence of the State?" And if I were to express astonishment at their saying this, the law would probably add: "Answer, Socrates, instead of opening your eyes: you are in the habit of asking and answering questions. Tell us what complaint you have to make against us which justifies you in attempting to destroy us and the State? In the first place did we not bring you into existence? Your father married your mother by our aid and begat you. Say whether you have any objection to urge against those of us who regulate marriage?" None, I should reply. "Or against those of us who regulate the system of nurture and education of children in which you were trained? Were not the laws, who have the charge of this, right in commanding your father to train you in music and gymnastic?" Right, I should reply. "Well, then, since you were brought into the world and nurtured and educated by us, can you deny in the first place that you are our child and slave, as your fathers were before you? And if this is true you are not on equal terms with us; nor can you think that you have a right to do to us what we are doing to you. Would you have any right to strike or revile or do any other evil to a father or to your master, if you had one, when you have been struck or reviled by him, or received some other evil at his hands?—you would not say this? And because we think right to destroy you, do you think that you have any right to destroy us in return, and your country as far as in you lies? And will you, O professor of true virtue, say that you are justified in this? Has a philosopher like you failed to discover that our country is more to be valued and higher and holier far than mother or father or any ancestor, and more to be regarded in the eyes of the gods and of men of understanding? also to be soothed, and gently and reverently entreated when angry, even more than a father, and if not persuaded, obeyed? And when we are punished by her, whether with imprisonment or stripes, the punishment is to be endured in silence; and if she leads us to wounds or death in battle, thither we follow as is right; neither may anyone yield or retreat or leave his rank, but whether in battle or in a court of law, or in any other place, he must do what his city and his country order him; or he must change their view of what is just: and if he may do no violence to his father or mother, much less may he do violence to his country." What answer shall we make to this, Crito? Do the laws speak truly, or do they not?

Cr.   I think that they do.

Soc.   Then the laws will say: "Consider, Socrates, if this is true, that in your present attempt you are going to do us wrong. For, after having brought you into the world, and nurtured and educated you, and given you and every other citizen a share in every good that we had to give, we further proclaim and give the right to every Athenian, that if he does not like us when he has come of age and has seen the ways of the city, and made our acquaintance, he may go where he pleases and take his goods with him; and none of us laws will forbid him or interfere with him. Any of you who does not like us and the city, and who wants to go to a colony or to any other city, may go where he likes, and take his goods with him. But he who has experience of the manner in which we order justice and administer the State, and still remains, has entered into an implied contract that he will do as we command him. And he who disobeys us is, as we maintain, thrice wrong: first, because in disobeying us he is disobeying his parents; secondly, because we are the authors of his education; thirdly, because he has made an agreement with us that he will duly obey our commands; and he neither obeys them nor convinces us that our commands are wrong; and we do not rudely impose them, but give him the alternative of obeying or convincing us; that is what we offer and he does neither.

These are the sort of accusations to which, as we were saying, you, Socrates, will be exposed if you accomplish your intentions; you, above all other Athenians." Suppose I ask, why is this? they will justly retort upon me that I above all other men have acknowledged the agreement. "There is clear proof," they will say, "Socrates, that we and the city were not displeasing to you. Of all Athenians you have been the most constant resident in the city, which, as you never leave, you may be supposed to love. For you never went out of the city either to see the games, except once when you went to the Isthmus, or to any other place unless when you were on military service; nor did you travel as other men do. Nor had you any curiosity to know other States or their laws: your affections did not go beyond us and our State; we were your especial favorites, and you acquiesced in our government of you; and this is the State in which you begat your children, which is a proof of your satisfaction. Moreover, you might, if you had liked, have fixed the penalty at banishment in the course of the trial—the State which refuses to let you go now would have let you go then. But you pretended that you preferred death to exile, and that you were not grieved at death. And now you have forgotten these fine sentiments, and pay no respect to us, the laws, of whom you are the destroyer; and are doing what only a miserable slave would do, running away and turning your back upon the compacts and agreements which you made as a citizen. And first of all answer this very question: Are we right in saying that you agreed to be governed according to us in deed, and not in word only? Is that true or not?" How shall we answer that, Crito? Must we not agree?

Cr. There is no help, Socrates.

Soc. Then will they not say: "You, Socrates, are breaking the covenants and agreements which you made with us at your leisure, not in any haste or under any compulsion or deception, but having had seventy years to think of them, during which time you were at liberty to leave the city, if we were not to your mind, or if our covenants

10

appeared to you to be unfair. You had your choice, and might have gone either to Lacedaemon or Crete, which you often praise for their good government, or to some other Hellenic or foreign State. Whereas you, above all other Athenians, seemed to be so fond of the State, or, in other words, of us her laws (for who would like a State that has no laws?), that you never stirred out of her: the halt, the blind, the maimed, were not more stationary in her than you were. And now you run away and forsake your agreements. Not so, Socrates, if you will take our advice; do not make yourself ridiculous by escaping out of the city.

"For just consider, if you transgress and err in this sort of way, what good will you do, either to yourself or to your friends? That your friends will be driven into exile and deprived of citizenship, or will lose their property, is tolerably certain; and you yourself, if you fly to one of the neighboring cities, as, for example, Thebes or Megara, both of which are well-governed cities, will come to them as an enemy, Socrates, and their government will be against you, and all patriotic citizens will cast an evil eye upon you as a subverter of the laws, and you will confirm in the minds of the judges the justice of their own condemnation of you. For he who is a corrupter of the laws is more than likely to be corrupter of the young and foolish portion of mankind. Will you then flee from well-ordered cities and virtuous men? and is existence worth having on these terms? Or will you go to them without shame, and talk to them, Socrates? And what will you say to them? What you say here about virtue and justice and institutions and laws being the best things among men? Would that be decent of you? Surely not. But if you go away from well-governed States to Crito's friends in Thessaly, where there is great disorder and license, they will be charmed to have the tale of your escape from prison, set off with ludicrous particulars of the manner in which you were wrapped in a goatskin or some other disguise, and metamorphosed as the fashion of runaways is—that is very likely; but will there be no one to remind you that in your old age you violated the most sacred laws from a miserable desire of a little more life? Perhaps not, if you keep them in a good temper; but if they are out of temper you will hear many degrading things; you will live, but how?—as the flatterer of all men, and the servant of all men; and doing what?—eating and drinking in Thessaly, having gone abroad in order that you may get a dinner. And where will be your fine sentiments about justice and virtue then? Say that you wish to live for the sake of your children, that you may bring them up and educate them—will you take them into Thessaly and deprive them of Athenian citizenship? Is that the benefit which you would confer upon them? Or are you under the impression that they will be better cared for and educated here if you are still alive, although absent from them; for that your friends will take care of them? Do you fancy that if you are an inhabitant of Thessaly they will take care of them, and if you are an inhabitant of the other world they will not take care of them? Nay; but if they who call themselves friends are truly friends, they surely will.

"Listen, then, Socrates, to us who have brought you up. Think not of life and children first, and of justice afterwards, but of justice first, that you may be justified before the princes of the world below. For neither will you nor any that belong to you be happier or holier or juster in this life, or happier in another, if you do as Crito bids. Now you depart in innocence, a sufferer and not a doer of evil; a victim, not of the laws, but of men. But if you go forth, returning evil for evil, and injury for injury, breaking the covenants and agreements which you have made with us, and wronging those whom you ought least to wrong, that is to say, yourself, your friends, your country, and us, we shall be angry with you while you live, and our brethren, the laws in the world below, will receive you as an enemy; for they will know that you have done your best to destroy us. Listen, then, to us and not to Crito."

	This is the voice which I seem to hear murmuring in my ears, like the sound of the flute in the ears of the mystic; that voice, I say, is humming in my ears, and prevents me from hearing any other. And I know that anything more which you will say will be in vain. Yet speak, if you have anything to say.	
Cr.	I have nothing to say, Socrates.	15
Soc.	Then let me follow the intimations of the will of God. THE END	

Questions about the Passage

1. Socrates uses a series of questions to structure this final part of *Crito*. Working in groups, locate the significant question that is raised in almost every paragraph. How does Socrates answer it? Explain each answer. Report to the class on what you have discovered.

2. In paragraph 7, Socrates notes that the state has regulated the marriage that produced him and the education that trained him; it has also provided him with a share in the goods of the state. What do you think Socrates owes the state in return?

3. Do you agree that Socrates has indeed made "covenants and agreements" with the state (paragraph 11)? If you agree that he has done so, do you think you also have entered into covenants and agreements with the United States? If you think Socrates has not made such a covenant, how would you characterize his relationship with Athens and yours with the United States?

Questions about the Argument

1. What has Crito suggested that Socrates do? Do you think Socrates' response is more than a rejection of a friend's kindly meant suggestion? Whom do you think Plato envisions as the audience for *Crito*?

2. How do the questions that Socrates raises throughout *Crito* serve to build his argument? In addition to his own case, he seems to be making the case for the Athenian state. Is it a convincing case? Why or why not?

3. Does this passage from *Crito* add anything more to your understanding of Socrates' ethos as an arguer than you discovered while analyzing the *Apology*? Based on both readings, what is your assessment of Socrates the man and Socrates the arguer?

Writing Assignments

Conversations

1. Debate the following proposition: Divine law takes precedence over human law. Choose at least three speakers drawn from different readings in this chapter to assist you in defending either the affirmative or the negative position. Consider the midwives, Daniel, Antigone, Creon, Ismene, and/or Plato as possible members of your team. You might conduct this debate in class, with members of the class assuming the different roles. Alternatively, you might write a short paper in which you construct each debater's position.

2. Is Socrates wrong to accept the punishment of the state? Meet with a group of your classmates to discuss this issue. Explain Socrates' position to them. What reasons do they give for approving or disapproving of what he does? Which of their reasons do you find most convincing? Then write up your discussion and present it to the class.

Writing Sequence One: Putting Your Life on the Line?

1. Would you be willing to put your life on the line to defend a moral or religious principle? Do you admire characters or people who are willing to do so? Explore the convictions that you might hold strongly enough to justify such a stand. Under what circumstances might you be willing actually to take such a stand?

2. In a 1–2 page paper, explain the case made either by Socrates or Antigone to defend the actions he or she is taking. Do you accept the argument?

3. Writing as either Crito or Creon, raise the objections to the case you made in question 2.

4. Now write a 4–6 page argumentative essay in which you defend either Socrates or Antigone's position. In addition to providing a strong claim, good reasons for it, and specific support from the text, be sure to refute the objections that other readers or characters from the play might raise.

Writing Sequence Two: Drama as Debate

1. Examine carefully the following scenes of Antigone as if they were debates: Prologue, Episodes II, III, and V. For each scene, write a well-developed paragraph in which you explain the claims made by each pair of debaters: Antigone and Ismene, Antigone and Creon, Creon and Haemon, and Creon and Teiresias.

2. Explore the ethos of each pair. As arguers, what credentials do they have? What are the convictions and values that underlie their claims? What authorities do they call on in support of their position?

3. How does each make use of pathos?

4. Now draw this material together to write a 4–6 page essay in which you determine which character makes the best argument. Be sure to set up the criteria by which you will evaluate this argument.

CHAPTER

5

Classics

Henry David Thoreau, who begins this chapter, lived 2,000 years after Socrates and 1,750 years after the compilation of the Christian Bible. Though we include a few writings from those intervening years elsewhere in the casebook, we need to remember the numerous civil disobedients of this long period. Thousands of Christian martyrs, as well as Jewish rebels, refused to acknowledge the authority of Roman rulers to legislate which God they should worship, and they went to their deaths rather than follow the law. Sir Thomas More refused to submit to Henry VIII when to do so went against his conscience. Nonconformists in many countries refused to pay taxes designated for a particular established church. Quakers and Mennonites, committed pacifists, refused to take up arms even in defense of their country.

Thoreau's essay, "Civil Disobedience," coined the term that describes the actions taken by so many dissidents in refusing to obey unjust commands. Many would agree with Thoreau that his only obligation was "to do what I think is right" when he refused to pay a poll tax supporting the Mexican-American War (1846–1848). Others, including Socrates, might find that he discounts too much what he owes to the state that nurtured him.

Count Leo Tolstoy builds a bridge between the ideas of Thoreau and Mohandas K. Gandhi. Tolstoy admires Thoreau for refusing to support a government that tolerates slavery and wages an unjust war, but Thoreau does not share Tolstoy's pacifism. Making clear his own commitment to nonviolence based on the teachings of Jesus, Tolstoy identifies with Gandhi's absolute adherence to pacifism. A seminal thinker who firmly joined nonviolence to resistance in his theory of *satyagraha* ("soul force" or "truth force"), Gandhi profoundly influenced all civil disobedience thinkers after him. In his successful opposition to British rule in India, he demonstrated the power of peaceful mass opposition to wrongful authority.

One man who was deeply moved by Gandhi's ideas was Martin Luther King, Jr. His "Letter from Birmingham Jail" is a fine example of how the history of ideas can create a chain of reasoning over time, or, as T. S. Eliot puts it, an example of how one writer stands on the shoulders of those who have gone before. The "Letter" is a powerful document that traces the development of the doctrine of civil disobedience, legitimizes it by the stature of those who preach it, and defends it against its attackers. Ultimately, it stands as a very compelling, though not universally accepted, argument for the necessity and legitimacy of the actions taken to assure civil rights for all Americans.

Henry David Thoreau, "Civil Disobedience"

Schoolmaster. Pencil maker. Surveyor. Naturalist. Reclusive builder of a cabin on Walden Pond. Friend of Ralph Waldo Emerson and Bronson Alcott and member of their Transcendental Club. Author of dozens of books. All of these titles are accurate denominators of Henry David Thoreau (1817–1862). His active and varied career never took him far from Concord, Massachusetts, where his easygoing father and social activist mother had settled their family. Thoreau left Concord long enough to graduate from Harvard (1837), after which he founded a school with his brother John. A stint of tutoring for a Staten Island family and visits to New York left a bad taste in his mouth, and he quickly returned to Concord. After returning, he worked in the family pencil-making business and made several improvements in his product. He traveled with his brother along the Chesapeake River, lectured in Salem, and explored the Maine wilderness with a friend, but he was always drawn back to Concord and to Walden Pond, a mile-and-a-half walk from the town.

Walden; or Life in the Woods (1854), Thoreau's most famous work, compresses more than two years' experiences at Walden Pond into a single yearlong cycle. Noting the passing of the seasons becomes a means of meditating on subjects ranging from thrift to slavery and on activities as diverse—and related—as reading and hoeing beans. His cyclical arrangement also allows him to sing the beauties of nature.

"Civil Disobedience" (1848) originated in a specific time and place—as Henry David Thoreau's opposition to the Mexican War (1846–1848) and the existence of slavery in the United States. In July 1846, Thoreau refused to pay the poll tax because it supported unjust government laws and actions; he was arrested and served one night in jail. Since its publication over 150 years ago, it has been an important text to resisters of all kinds—famously, to Mahatma Gandhi and Dr. Martin Luther King, Jr.—but also to people all over the world, including the Danish resistance movement in the 1940s and to those fighting apartheid in South Africa.

Thoreau argues that it is a person's duty to work to eradicate wrongs or, at the very least, not to support wrongs. He addresses us as individuals and demands that we think about our failure to take action against unjust laws and policies. In "Civil Disobedience," Thoreau confronts his readers with fundamental questions about the individual's responsibility for his or her government's actions—questions that are never out of date.

> I heartily accept the motto, "That government is best which governs least"; and I should like to see it acted up to more rapidly and systematically. Carried out, it finally amounts to this, which also I believe—"That government is best which governs not at all"; and when men are prepared for it, that will be the kind of government which they will have. Government is at best but an expedient; but most governments are usually, and all governments are sometimes, inexpedient. The objections which have been brought against a standing army, and they are many and weighty, and deserve to prevail, may also at last be brought against a standing government. The standing army is only an arm of the standing government. The government itself, which is only the mode which the people have chosen to execute their will, is equally liable to be abused and perverted before the people can act through it. Witness the present Mexican war, the work of comparatively a few individuals using the standing government as their tool; for in the outset, the people would not have consented to this measure.
>
> This American government—what is it but a tradition, though a recent one, endeavoring to transmit itself unimpaired to posterity, but each instant losing some of its integrity? It has not the vitality and force of a single living man; for a single man can bend it to his will. It is a sort of wooden gun to the people themselves. But it is not the less necessary for this; for the people must have some complicated machinery or other, and hear its din, to satisfy that idea of government which they

have. Governments show thus how successfully men can be imposed upon, even impose on themselves, for their own advantage. It is excellent, we must all allow. Yet this government never of itself furthered any enterprise, but by the alacrity with which it got out of its way. *It* does not keep the country free. *It* does not settle the West. *It* does not educate. The character inherent in the American people has done all that has been accomplished; and it would have done somewhat more, if the government had not sometimes got in its way. For government is an expedient, by which men would fain succeed in letting one another alone; and, as has been said, when it is most expedient, the governed are most let alone by it. Trade and commerce, if they were not made of India-rubber, would never manage to bounce over obstacles which legislators are continually putting in their way; and if one were to judge these men wholly by the effects of their actions and not partly by their intentions, they would deserve to be classed and punished with those mischievious persons who put obstructions on the railroads.

But, to speak practically and as a citizen, unlike those who call themselves no-government men, I ask for, not at once no government, but *at once* a better government. Let every man make known what kind of government would command his respect, and that will be one step toward obtaining it.

After all, the practical reason why, when the power is once in the hands of the people, a majority are permitted, and for a long period continue, to rule is not because they are most likely to be in the right, nor because this seems fairest to the minority, but because they are physically the strongest. But a government in which the majority rule in all cases can not be based on justice, even as far as men understand it. Can there not be a government in which the majorities do not virtually decide right and wrong, but conscience?—in which majorities decide only those questions to which the rule of expediency is applicable? Must the citizen ever for a moment, or in the least degree, resign his conscience to the legislator? Why has every man a conscience then? I think that we should be men first, and subjects afterward. It is not desirable to cultivate a respect for the law, so much as for the right. The only obligation which I have a right to assume is to do at any time what I think right.

It is truly enough said that a corporation has no conscience; but a corporation of conscientious men is a corporation *with* a conscience. Law never made men a whit more just; and, by means of their respect for it, even the well-disposed are daily made the agents of injustice. A common and natural result of an undue respect for the law is, that you may see a file of soldiers, colonel, captain, corporal, privates, powder-monkeys, and all, marching in admirable order over hill and dale to the wars, against their wills, ay, against their common sense and consciences, which makes it very steep marching indeed, and produces a palpitation of the heart. They have no doubt that it is a damnable business in which they are concerned; they are all peaceably inclined. Now, what are they? Men at all? or small movable forts and magazines, at the service of some unscrupulous man in power? Visit the Navy Yard, and behold a marine, such a man as an American government can make, or such as it can make a man with its black arts—a mere shadow and reminiscence of humanity, a man laid out alive and standing, and already, as one may say, buried under arms with funeral accompaniment, though it may be,

"Not a drum was heard, not a funeral note,
   As his corse to the rampart we hurried;
Not a soldier discharged his farewell shot
   O'er the grave where our hero was buried."

The mass of men serve the State thus, not as men mainly, but as machines, with their bodies. They are the standing army, and the militia, jailers, constables, *posse comitatus*, etc. In most cases there is no free exercise whatever of the judgment or of the moral sense; but they put themselves on a level with wood and earth and stones; and wooden men can perhaps be manufactured that will serve the purpose as well. Such command no more respect than men of straw or a lump of dirt. They have the same sort of worth only as horses and dogs. Yet such as these even are commonly esteemed good citizens. Others—as most legislators, politicians, lawyers, ministers, and office-holders—serve the State chiefly with their heads; and, as they rarely make any moral distinctions, they are as likely to serve the devil, without intending it, as God. A very few—as heroes, patriots, martyrs, reformers in the great sense, and *men*—serve the State with their consciences also, and so necessarily resist it for the most part; and they are commonly treated as enemies by it. A wise man will only be useful as a man, and will not submit to be "clay," and "stop a hole to keep the wind away," but leave that office to his dust at least:

"I am too high born to be propertied,
To be a secondary at control,
Or useful serving-man and instrument
To any sovereign state throughout the world."

He who gives himself entirely to his fellow men appears to them useless and selfish; but he who gives himself partially to them is pronounced a benefactor and philanthropist.

How does it become a man to behave toward the American government today? I answer, that he cannot without disgrace be associated with it. I cannot for an instant recognize that political organization as *my* government which is the *slave's* government also.

All men recognize the right of revolution; that is, the right to refuse allegiance to, and to resist, the government, when its tyranny or its inefficiency are great and unendurable. But almost all say that such is not the case now. But such was the case, they think, in the Revolution of '75. If one were to tell me that this was a bad government because it taxed certain foreign commodities brought to its ports, it is most probable that I should not make an ado about it, for I can do without them. All machines have their friction; and possibly this does enough good to counter-balance the evil. At any rate, it is a great evil to make a stir about it. But when the friction comes to have its machine, and oppression and robbery are organized, I say, let us not have such a machine any longer. In other words, when a sixth of the population of a nation which has undertaken to be the refuge of liberty are slaves, and a whole country is unjustly overrun and conquered by a foreign army, and subjected to military law, I think that it is not too soon for honest men to rebel and revolutionize. What makes this duty the more urgent is the fact that the country so overrun is not our own, but ours is the invading army.

Paley, a common authority with many on moral questions, in his chapter on the "Duty of Submission to Civil Government," resolves all civil obligation into expediency; and he proceeds to say that "so long as the interest of the whole society requires it, that it, so long as the established government cannot be resisted or changed without public inconveniencey, it is the will of God . . . that the established government be obeyed—and no longer. This principle being admitted, the justice of every particular case of resistance is reduced to a computation of the quantity of the danger and grievance on the one side, and of the probability and expense of redressing it on the other." Of this, he says, every man shall judge for himself. But Paley appears never to have contemplated those cases to which the rule of expediency does not apply, in which a people, as well as an individual, must do justice, cost what it may. If I have unjustly wrested a plank from a drowning man, I must restore it to him though I drown myself. This, according to Paley, would be inconvenient. But he that would save his life, in such a case, shall lose it. This people must cease to hold slaves, and to make war on Mexico, though it cost them their existence as a people.

In their practice, nations agree with Paley; but does anyone   10
think that Massachusetts does exactly what is right at the present crisis?

"A drab of state, a cloth-o'-silver slut,
To have her train borne up, and her soul trail in the dirt."

Practically speaking, the opponents to a reform in Massachusetts are not a hundred thousand politicians at the South, but a hundred thousand merchants and farmers here, who are more interested in commerce and agriculture than they are in humanity, and are not prepared to do justice to the slave and to Mexico, *cost what it may.* I quarrel not with far-off foes, but with those who, near at home, co-operate with, and do the bidding of, those far away, and without whom the latter would be harmless. We are accustomed to say, that the mass of men are unprepared; but improvement is slow, because the few are not as materially wiser or better than the many. It is not so important that many should be good as you, as that there be some absolute goodness somewhere; for that will leaven the whole lump. There are thousands who are *in opinion* opposed to slavery and to the war, who yet in effect do nothing to put an end to them; who, esteeming themselves children of Washington and Franklin, sit down with their hands in their pockets, and say that they know not what to do, and do nothing; who even postpone the question of freedom to the question of free-trade, and quietly read the prices-current along with the latest advices from Mexico, after dinner, and, it may be, fall asleep over them both. What is the price-current of an honest man and patriot today? They hesitate, and they regret, and sometimes they petition; but they do nothing in earnest and with effect. They will wait, well disposed, for others to remedy the evil, that they may no longer have it to regret. At most, they give up only a cheap vote, and a feeble countenance and God-speed, to the right, as it goes by them. There are nine hundred and ninety-nine patrons of virtue to one virtuous man. But it is easier to deal with the real possessor of a thing than with the temporary guardian of it.

All voting is a sort of gaming, like checkers or backgammon, with a slight moral tinge to it, a playing with right and wrong, with moral questions; and betting naturally accompanies it. The character of the voters is not staked. I cast my vote, per-chance, as I think right; but I am not vitally concerned that that right should prevail. I am willing to leave it to the majority. Its obligation, therefore, never exceeds that of expediency. Even voting *for the right* is *doing* nothing for it. It is only expressing to men feebly your desire that it should prevail. A wise man will not leave the right to the mercy of chance, nor wish it to prevail through the power of the majority. There is but little virtue in the action of masses of men. When the majority shall at length vote for the abolition of slavery, it will be because they are indifferent to slavery, or because there is but little slav-ery left to be abolished by their vote. *They* will then be the only slaves. Only *his* vote can hasten the abolition of slavery who asserts his own freedom by his vote.

I hear of a convention to be held at Baltimore, or elsewhere, for the selection of a candidate for the Presidency, made up chiefly of editors, and men who are politicians by profession; but I think, what is it to any independent, intelligent, and respectable man what decision they may come to? Shall we not have the advantage of this wisdom and honesty, nevertheless? Can we not count upon some independent votes? Are there not many individuals in the country who do not attend conven-tions? But no: I find that the respectable man, so called, has immediately drifted from his position, and despairs of his country, when his country has more reasons to despair of him. He forthwith adopts one of the candidates thus selected as the only *available* one, thus proving that he is himself *available* for any purposes of the demagogue. His vote is of no more worth than that of any unprincipled foreigner or hireling native, who may have been bought. O for a man who is a *man*, and, as my neighbor says, has a bone in his back which you cannot pass your hand through! Our statistics are at fault: the population has been returned too large. How many *men* are there to a square thousand miles in the country? Hardly one. Does not America offer any inducement for men to settle here? The American has dwindled into an Odd Fellow—one who may be known by the development of his organ of gregariousness, and a manifest lack of intellect and cheerful self-reliance; whose first and chief concern, on coming into the world, is to see that the almshouses are in good repair; and, before yet he has lawfully donned the virile garb, to collect a fund to the support of the widows and orphans that may be; who, in short, ventures to live only by the aid of the mutual insurance company, which has promised to bury him decently.

It is not a man's duty, as a matter of course, to devote himself to the eradication of any, even the most enormous, wrong; he may still properly have other concerns to engage him; but it is his duty, at least, to wash his hands of it, and, if he gives it no thought longer, not to give it practically his support. If I devote myself to other pursuits and contemplations, I must first see, at least, that I do not pursue them sitting upon another man's shoulders. I must get off him first, that he may pursue his contemplations too. See what gross inconsistency is tolerated. I have heard some of my townsmen say, "I should like to have them order me out to help put down an insurrection of the slaves, or to march to Mexico—see if I would go"; and yet these very men have each, directly by their allegiance, and so indirectly, at least, by their money, furnished a substitute. The soldier is applauded who refuses to serve in an unjust war by those who do not refuse to sustain the unjust government which makes the war; is applauded by those whose own act and authority he disregards and sets at naught; as if the State were penitent to that degree that it hired one to scourge it while it sinned, but not to that degree that it left off sinning for a moment. Thus, under the name of Order and Civil Government, we are all made at last to pay homage to and support our own meanness. After the first blush of sin comes its indifference; and from immoral it becomes, as it were, *un*moral, and not quite unnecessary to that life which we have made.

The broadest and most prevalent error requires the most disinterested virtue to sustain it. The slight reproach to which the virtue of patriotism is commonly liable, the noble are most likely to incur. Those who, while they disapprove of the character and measures of a government, yield to it their allegiance and support are undoubtedly its most conscientious supporters, and so frequently the most serious obstacles to reform. Some are petitioning the State to dissolve the Union, to disregard the requisitions of the President. Why do they not dissolve it themselves—the union between themselves and the State—and refuse to pay their quota into its treasury? Do not they stand in the same relation to the State that the State does to the Union? And have not the same reasons prevented the State from resisting the Union which have prevented them from resisting the State?

How can a man be satisfied to entertain and opinion merely,   15
and enjoy *it?* Is there any enjoyment in it, if his opinion is that he is aggrieved? If you are cheated out of a single dollar by your neighbor, you do not rest satisfied with knowing you are cheated, or with saying that you are cheated, or even with petitioning him to pay you your due; but you take effectual steps at once to obtain the full amount, and see to it that you are never cheated again. Action from principle, the perception and the performance of right, changes things and relations; it is essentially revolutionary, and does not consist wholly with anything which was. It not only divides states and churches, it divides families; aye, it divides the *individual*, separating the diabolical in him from the divine.

Unjust laws exist: shall we be content to obey them, or shall we endeavor to amend them, and obey them until we have succeeded, or shall we transgress them at once? Men, generally, under such a government as this, think that they ought to wait until they have persuaded the majority to alter them. They think that, if they should resist, the remedy would be worse than the evil. But it is the fault of the government itself that the remedy is worse than the evil. *It* makes it worse. Why is it not more apt to anticipate and provide for reform? Why does it not cherish its wise minority? Why does it cry and resist before it is hurt? Why does it not encourage its citizens to put out its faults, and do better than it would have them? Why does it always crucify Christ and excommunicate Copernicus and Luther, and pronounce Washington and Franklin rebels?

One would think, that a deliberate and practical denial of its authority was the only offense never contemplated by its government; else, why has it not assigned its definite, its suitable and proportionate, penalty? If a man who has no property refuses but once to earn nine shillings for the State, he is put in prison for a period unlimited by any law that I know, and determined only by the discretion of those who put him there; but if he should steal ninety times nine shillings from the State, he is soon permitted to go at large again.

If the injustice is part of the necessary friction of the machine of government, let it go, let it go: perchance it will wear smooth—certainly the machine will wear out. If the injustice has a spring, or a pulley, or a rope, or a crank, exclusively for itself, then perhaps you may consider whether the remedy will not be worse than the evil; but if it is of such a nature that it requires you to be the agent of injustice to another, then I say, break the law. Let your life be a counter-friction to stop the machine. What I have to do is to see, at any rate, that I do not lend myself to the wrong which I condemn.

As for adopting the ways which the State has provided for remedying the evil, I know not of such ways. They take too much time, and a man's life will be gone. I have other affairs to attend to. I came into this world, not chiefly to make this a good place to live in, but to live in it, be it good or bad. A man has not every thing to do, but something; and because he cannot do *every thing*, it is not necessary that he should do *something* wrong. It is not my business to be petitioning the Governor or the Legislature any more than it is theirs to petition me; and if they should not hear my petition, what should I do then? But in this case the State has provided no way: its very Constitution is the evil. This may seem to be harsh and stubborn and unconciliatory; but it is to treat with the utmost kind-

ness and consideration the only spirit that can appreciate or
deserves it. So is all change for the better, like birth and death,
which convulse the body.

I do not hesitate to say, that those who call themselves Abo-   20
litionists should at once effectually withdraw their support,
both in person and property, from the government of Massachusetts, and not wait till they constitute a majority of one,
before they suffer the right to prevail through them. I think
that it is enough if they have God on their side, without waiting for that other one. Moreover, any man more right than his
neighbors constitutes a majority of one already.

I meet this American government, or its representative, the
State government, directly, and face to face, once a year—no
more—in the person of its tax-gatherer; this is the only mode
in which a man situated as I am necessarily meets it; and it
then says distinctly, Recognize me; and the simplest, the most
effectual, and, in the present posture of affairs, the indispens-
ablest mode of treating with it on this head, of expressing
your little satisfaction with and love for it, is to deny it then. My
civil neighbor, the tax-gatherer, is the very man I have to deal
with—for it is, after all, with men and not with parchment that
I quarrel—and he has voluntarily chosen to be an agent of the
government. How shall he ever know well that he is and does
as an officer of the government, or as a man, until he is obliged
to consider whether he will treat me, his neighbor, for whom
he has respect, as a neighbor and well-disposed man, or as a
maniac and disturber of the peace, and see if he can get over
this obstruction to his neighborliness without a ruder and more
impetuous thought or speech corresponding with his action? I
know this well, that if one thousand, if one hundred, if ten men
whom I could name—if ten *honest* men only—aye, if *one* HON-
EST man, in this State of Massachusetts, *ceasing to hold slaves,*
were actually to withdraw from this co-partnership, and be
locked up in the county jail therefore, it would be the abolition
of slavery in America. For it matters not how small the beginning may seem to be: what is once well done is done forever.
But we love better to talk about it: that we say is our mission.
Reform keeps many scores of newspapers in its service, but not
one man. If my esteemed neighbor, the State's ambassador,
who will devote his days to the settlement of the question of

human rights in the Council Chamber, instead of being threatened with the prisons of Carolina, were to sit down the prisoner of Massachusetts, that State which is so anxious to foist the sin of slavery upon her sister—though at present she can discover only an act of inhospitality to be the ground of a quarrel with her—the Legislature would not wholly waive the subject the following winter.

Under a government which imprisons unjustly, the true place for a just man is also a prison. The proper place today, the only place which Massachusetts has provided for her freer and less desponding spirits, is in her prisons, to be put out and locked out of the State by her own act, as they have already put themselves out by their principles. It is there that the fugitive slave, and the Mexican prisoner on parole, and the Indian come to plead the wrongs of his race should find them; on that separate but more free and honorable ground, where the State places those who are not *with* her, but *against* her—the only house in a slave State in which a free man can abide with honor. If any think that their influence would be lost there, and their voices no longer afflict the ear of the State, that they would not be as an enemy within its walls, they do not know by how much truth is stronger than error, nor how much more eloquently and effectively he can combat injustice who has experienced a little in his own person. Cast your whole vote, not a strip of paper merely, but your whole influence. A minority is powerless while it conforms to the majority; it is not even a minority then; but it is irresistible when it clogs by its whole weight. If the alternative is to keep all just men in prison, or give up war and slavery, the State will not hesitate which to choose. If a thousand men were not to pay their tax bills this year, that would not be a violent and bloody measure, as it would be to pay them, and enable the State to commit violence and shed innocent blood. This is, in fact, the definition of a peaceable revolution, if any such is possible. If the tax-gatherer, or any other public officer, asks me, as one has done, "But what shall I do?" my answer is, "If you really wish to do anything, resign your office." When the subject has refused allegiance, and the officer has resigned from office, then the revolution is accomplished. But even suppose blood should flow. Is there not a sort of blood shed when the conscience is wounded?

Through this wound a man's real manhood and immortality flow out, and he bleeds to an everlasting death. I see this blood flowing now.

I have contemplated the imprisonment of the offender, rather than the seizure of his goods—though both will serve the same purpose—because they who assert the purest right, and consequently are most dangerous to a corrupt State, commonly have not spent much time in accumulating property. To such the State renders comparatively small service, and a slight tax is wont to appear exorbitant, particularly if they are obliged to earn it by special labor with their hands. If there were one who lived wholly without the use of money, the State itself would hesitate to demand it of him. But the rich man— not to make any invidious comparison—is always sold to the institution which makes him rich. Absolutely speaking, the more money, the less virtue; for money comes between a man and his objects, and obtains them for him; it was certainly no great virtue to obtain it. It puts to rest many questions which he would otherwise be taxed to answer; while the only new question which it puts is the hard but superfluous one, how to spend it. Thus his moral ground is taken from under his feet. The opportunities of living are diminished in proportion as that are called the "means" are increased. The best thing a man can do for his culture when he is rich is to endeavor to carry out those schemes which he entertained when he was poor. Christ answered the Herodians according to their condition. "Show me the tribute-money," said he—and one took a penny out of his pocket—if you use money which has the image of Caesar on it, and which he has made current and valuable, that is, *if you are men of the State,* and gladly enjoy the advantages of Caesar's government, then pay him back some of his own when he demands it. "Render therefore to Caesar that which is Caesar's and to God those things which are God's"—leaving them no wiser than before as to which was which; for they did not wish to know.

When I converse with the freest of my neighbors, I perceive that, whatever they may say about the magnitude and seriousness of the question, and their regard for the public tranquillity, the long and the short of the matter is, that they cannot spare the protection of the existing government, and they dread the

consequences of disobedience to it to their property and families. For my own part, I should not like to think that I ever rely
on the protection of the State. But, if I deny the authority of the
State when it presents its tax bill, it will soon take and waste all
my property, and so harass me and my children without end.
This is hard. This makes it impossible for a man to live honestly,
and at the same time comfortably, in outward respects. It will
not be worth the while to accumulate property; that would be
sure to go again. You must hire or squat somewhere, and raise
but a small crop, and eat that soon. You must live within yourself, and depend upon yourself always tucked up and ready for
a start, and not have many affairs. A man may grow rich in
Turkey even, if he will be in all respects a good subject of the
Turkish government. Confucius said: "If a State is governed by
the principles of reason, poverty and misery are subjects of
shame; if a State is not governed by the principles of reason,
riches and honors are subjects of shame." No: until I want the
protection of Massachusetts to be extended to me in some distant Southern port, where my liberty is endangered, or until I
am bent solely on building up an estate at home by peaceful
enterprise, I can afford to refuse allegiance to Massachusetts,
and her right to my property and life. It costs me less in every
sense to incur the penalty of disobedience to the State, than it
would to obey. I should feel as if I were worth less in that case.

Some years ago, the State met me in behalf of the Church, and   25
commanded me to pay a certain sum toward the support of a
clergyman whose preaching my father attended, but never I
myself. "Pay," it said, "or be locked up in the jail." I declined to
pay. But, unfortunately, another man saw fit to pay it. I did not
see why the schoolmaster should be taxed to support the priest,
and not the priest the schoolmaster; for I was not the State's
schoolmaster, but I supported myself by voluntary subscription. I did not see why the lyceum should not present its tax bill,
and have the State to back its demand, as well as the Church.
However, at the request of the selectmen, I condescended to
make some such statement as this in writing: "Know all men
by these presents, that I, Henry Thoreau, do not wish to be
regarded as a member of any society which I have not joined."
This I gave to the town clerk; and he has it. The State, having

thus learned that I did not wish to be regarded as a member of that church, has never made a like demand on me since; though it said that it must adhere to its original presumption that time. If I had known how to name them, I should then have signed off in detail from all the societies which I never signed on to; but I did not know where to find such a complete list.

I have paid no poll tax for six years. I was put into a jail once on this account, for one night; and, as I stood considering the walls of solid stone, two or three feet thick, the door of wood and iron, a foot thick, and the iron grating which strained the light, I could not help being struck with the foolishness of that institution which treated me as if I were mere flesh and blood and bones, to be locked up. I wondered that it should have concluded at length that this was the best use it could put me to, and had never thought to avail itself of my services in some way. I saw that, if there was a wall of stone between me and my townsmen, there was a still more difficult one to climb or break through before they could get to be as free as I was. I did not for a moment feel confined, and the walls seemed a great waste of stone and mortar. I felt as if I alone of all my townsmen had paid my tax. They plainly did not know how to treat me, but behaved like persons who are underbred. In every threat and in every compliment there was a blunder; for they thought that my chief desire was to stand the other side of that stone wall. I could not but smile to see how industriously they locked the door on my meditations, which followed them out again without let or hindrance, and *they* were really all that was dangerous. As they could not reach me, they had resolved to punish my body; just as boys, if they cannot come at some person against whom they have a spite, will abuse his dog. I saw that the State was half-witted, that it was timid as a lone woman with her silver spoons, and that it did not know its friends from its foes, and I lost all my remaining respect for it, and pitied it.

Thus the State never intentionally confronts a man's sense, intellectual or moral, but only his body, his senses. It is not armed with superior wit or honesty, but with superior physical strength. I was not born to be forced. I will breathe after my own fashion. Let us see who is the strongest. What force has a multitude? They only can force me who obey a higher law than

I. They force me to become like themselves. I do not hear of *men* being *forced* to live this way or that by masses of men. What sort of life were that to live? When I meet a government which says to me, "Your money or your life," why should I be in haste to give it my money? It may be in a great strait, and not know what to do: I cannot help that. It must help itself; do as I do. It is not worth the while to snivel about it. I am not responsible for the successful working of the machinery of society. I am not the son of the engineer. I perceive that, when an acorn and a chestnut fall side by side, the one does not remain inert to make way for the other, but both obey their own laws, and spring and grow and flourish as best they can, till one, perchance, overshadows and destroys the other. If a plant cannot live according to nature, it dies; and so a man.

The night in prison was novel and interesting enough. The prisoners in their shirtsleeves were enjoying a chat and the evening air in the doorway, when I entered. But the jailer said, "Come, boys, it is time to lock up"; and so they dispersed, and I heard the sound of their steps returning into the hollow apartments. My room-mate was introduced to me by the jailer as "a first-rate fellow and clever man." When the door was locked, he showed me where to hang my hat, and how he managed matters there. The rooms were whitewashed once a month; and this one, at least, was the whitest, most simply furnished, and probably neatest apartment in town. He naturally wanted to know where I came from, and what brought me there; and, when I had told him, I asked him in my turn how he came there, presuming him to be an honest man, of course; and as the world goes, I believe he was. "Why," said he, "they accuse me of burning a barn; but I never did it." As near as I could discover, he had probably gone to bed in a barn when drunk, and smoked his pipe there; and so a barn was burnt. He had the reputation of being a clever man, had been there some three months waiting for his trial to come on, and would have to wait as much longer; but he was quite domesticated and contented, since he got his board for nothing, and thought that he was well treated.

He occupied one window, and I the other; and I saw that if one stayed there long, his principal business would be to look out the window. I had soon read all the tracts that were left there, and examined where former prisoners had broken out, and where a grate had been sawed off, and heard the history of the various occupants of that room; for I found that even here there was a history and a gossip which never circulated beyond the walls of the jail. Probably this is the only house in the town where verses are composed, which are afterward printed in a circular form, but not published. I was shown quite a long list of young men who had been detected in an attempt to escape, who avenged themselves by singing them.

I pumped my fellow-prisoner as dry as I could, for fear I   30 should never see him again; but at length he showed me which was my bed, and left me to blow out the lamp.

It was like travelling into a far country, such as I had never expected to behold, to lie there for one night. It seemed to me that I never had heard the town clock strike before, nor the evening sounds of the village; for we slept with the windows open, which were inside the grating. It was to see my native village in the light of the Middle Ages, and our Concord was turned into a Rhine stream, and visions of knights and castles passed before me. They were the voices of old burghers that I heard in the streets. I was an involuntary spectator and auditor of whatever was done and said in the kitchen of the adjacent village inn—a wholly new and rare experience to me. It was a closer view of my native town. I was fairly inside of it. I never had seen its institutions before. This is one of its peculiar institutions; for it is a shire town. I began to comprehend what its inhabitants were about.

In the morning, our breakfasts were put through the hole in the door, in small oblong-square tin pans, made to fit, and holding a pint of chocolate, with brown bread, and an iron spoon. When they called for the vessels again, I was green enough to return what bread I had left, but my comrade seized it, and said that I should lay that up for lunch or dinner. Soon after he was let out to work at haying in a neighboring field, whither he went every day, and would not be back till noon; so he bade me good day, saying that he doubted if he should see me again.

When I came out of prison—for some one interfered, and paid that tax—I did not perceive that great changes had taken place on the common, such as he observed who went in a youth and emerged a gray-headed man; and yet a change had come to my eyes come over the scene—the town, and State, and country, greater than any that mere time could effect. I saw yet more distinctly the State in which I lived. I saw to what extent the people among whom I lived could be trusted as good neighbors and friends; that their friendship was for summer weather only; that they did not greatly propose to do right; that they were a distinct race from me by their prejudices and superstitions, as the Chinamen and Malays are; that, in their sacrifices to humanity, they ran no risks, not even to their property; that, after all they were not so noble but they treated the thief as he had treated them, and hoped, by a certain outward observance and a few prayers, and by walking in a particular straight though useless path from time to time, to save their souls. This may be to judge my neighbors harshly; for I believe that many of them are not aware that they have such an institution as the jail in their village.

It was formerly the custom in our village, when a poor debtor came out of jail, for his acquaintances to salute him, looking through their fingers, which were crossed to represent the jail window, "How do ye do?" My neighbors did not thus salute me, but first looked at me, and then at one another, as if I had returned from a long journey. I was put into jail as I was going to the shoemaker's to get a shoe which was mended. When I was let out the next morning, I proceeded to finish my errand, and, having put on my mended shoe, joined a huckleberry party, who were impatient to put themselves under my conduct; and in half an hour—for the horse was soon tackled—was in the midst of a huckleberry field, on one of our highest hills, two miles off, and then the State was nowhere to be seen.

This is the whole history of "My Prisons."   35

I have never declined paying the highway tax, because I am as desirous of being a good neighbor as I am of being a bad subject; and as for supporting schools, I am doing my part to educate my fellow countrymen now. It is for no particular item in the tax bill that I refuse to pay it. I simply wish to refuse allegiance to the State, to withdraw and stand aloof from it effectually. I do not care to trace the course of my dollar, if I could, till it buys a man a musket to shoot one with— the dollar is innocent—but I am concerned to trace the effects of my allegiance. In fact, I quietly declare war with the State, after my fashion, though I will still make use and get what advantages of her I can, as is usual in such cases.

If others pay the tax which is demanded of me, from a sympathy with the State, they do but what they have already done in their own case, or rather they abet injustice to a greater extent than the State requires. If they pay the tax from a mistaken interest in the individual taxed, to save his property, or prevent his going to jail, it is because they have not considered wisely how far they let their private feelings interfere with the public good.

This, then, is my position at present. But one cannot be too much on his guard in such a case, lest his actions be biased by obstinacy or an undue regard for the opinions of men. Let him see that he does only what belongs to himself and to the hour.

Questions about the Passage

1. What does Thoreau think of the American government? What does he think of the idea of majority rule?
2. What does he mean when he says in paragraph 7: "I cannot for an instant recognize that political organization as *my* government which is the *slave's* government also"?
3. What is Paley's argument, and how does Thoreau refute it (paragraph 9)?
4. Why doesn't Thoreau think voting will change the government?
5. In what way do those who do not serve in the army against Mexico or own slaves still support the government policies of war and slavery, according to Thoreau (paragraph 10)?
6. What is Thoreau's argument for not paying his poll taxes? Why does he pay his highway taxes?
7. What does Thoreau mean when he writes, "Under a government which imprisons any unjustly, the true place for a just man is also a prison" (paragraph 22)?

Questions about the Argument

1. Democracy is supposed to be governed by the rule of the majority, but Thoreau says that his only obligation is "to do at any time what I think is right" (paragraph 4). How do you respond to this

assertion? Do you think that the two principles—majority rule and individual conscience—are compatible or mutually incompatible? Why?

2. We find the heart of Thoreau's argument in paragraph 16. Answer the following questions about this paragraph:

   a. Thoreau gives us three choices in dealing with unjust laws. We can obey them. We can try to change them while continuing to obey them. We can break the laws right now. Are these really the only options citizens have when faced with an unjust law?

   b. Why does Thoreau say that in a government such as ours, which is ruled by the majority, citizens think they should "wait until they have persuaded the majority" to change the law rather than disobey it? Do you think he is right? Can you think of any examples of people obeying unjust laws even as they work to repeal or amend them?

   c. Thoreau claims that people hesitate to disobey unjust laws because they believe that "the remedy would be worse than the evil." What does he mean? He even blames the government for deliberately making it difficult for people to persuade the majority to alter unjust laws. Is this a fair criticism?

   d. Locate all the questions in the paragraph. What is the impact on the reader of the series of questions? Why doesn't Thoreau directly answer the questions?

   e. Why does Thoreau mention Christ, Copernicus, Luther, Washington, and Franklin all in one question? What do these men have in common? What do you think of Thoreau for associating himself with them?

3. What do you think of Thoreau's brief stay in jail? How does he describe the experience? Why does he select the details he does? What impact do these tactics have on you?

Leo Tolstoy, "Nonviolence as a Life Principle" and "A Letter from Tolstoy to Gandhi"

Count Leo Tolstoy (1828–1910) was born into an aristocratic Russian family. Educated in language and law at the University of Kazan, he returned home to administer the family estates at Yasnaya Polyana. He followed his brother into the Russian army in 1852 and served at the siege of Sevastopol during the Crimean War. This army experience pro-40 vided the germ for many short stories. After traveling abroad in 1857, he returned to his estates to found a school for peasants. He again traveled abroad to study educational practices in other countries. In 1862, he married Sonya Beris, with whom he had thirteen children. The next seventeen years were his greatest period of artistic productivity with the serial publication of *War and Peace* (1865–1869) and *Anna Karenina* (1875–1877). These works reveal both his talent as a novelist, specifically his realistic style, and his commitment to moral principles and to a didactic purpose. Happily married, successful, and very wealthy, he nonetheless experienced a spiritual crisis in 1879. Searching for meaning in his life, he re-examined his beliefs, rejecting church authority but embracing the teachings of Jesus. Eventually, he adopted a kind of Christian anarchism in which he opposed organized government, private property, paying taxes, and serving in the army. He simplified his life. His writing subsequent to his conversion concentrated on explaining his views about religion and society and morality and art. These writings, which led to his excommunication by the Orthodox Church in 1901, also attracted followers who attempted to live a communitarian life in accordance with Tolstoy's "commandments": to avoid anger and lust, to refuse to take oaths, to practice nonresistance to evil, and to love both the just and unjust.

Though Tolstoy is best known to American readers as the brilliant Russian novelist, his letters printed below establish him as an important link between Thoreau and Gandhi, clearly demonstrating his credentials to join the conversation about civil disobedience.

Nonviolence as a Life Principle

You write to me that people seem quite unable to understand that to serve the government is incompatible with Christianity.

In just the same way people were long unable to see that indulgences, inquisitions, slavery, and tortures were incompatible with Christianity. But a time came when it was comprehensible; and a time will come when men will understand the incompatibility with Christianity, first of war service (that already is beginning to be felt), and then of service to government in general.

It is now fifty years since a not widely known, but very remarkable, American writer—Thoreau—not only clearly expressed that incompatibility in his admirable essay on "Civil Disobedience," but gave a practical example of such disobedience. Not wishing to be an accomplice or supporter of a government which legalized slavery, he declined to pay a tax demanded of him, and went to prison for it.

Thoreau refused to pay taxes to government, and evidently the same motives as actuated him would prevent men from serving a government. As, in your letter to the minister, you have admirably expressed it: you do not consider it compatible with your moral dignity to work for an institution which represents legalized murder and robbery.

Thoreau was, I think, the first to express this view. People   5
paid scant attention to either his refusal or his article fifty years ago—the thing seemed so strange. It was put down to his eccentricity. Today your refusal attracts some attention, and, as is always the case when new truth is clearly expressed, it evokes a double surprise—first, surprise that a man should say such queer things, and then, surprise that I had not myself discovered what this man is saying; it is so certain and so obvious.

Such a truth as that a Christian must not be a soldier—*i.e.* a murderer—and must not be the servant of an institution maintained by violence and murder, is so certain, so clear and irrefutable, that to enable people to grasp it, discussion, proof, or eloquence are not necessary. For the majority of men to hear and understand this truth, it is only needful that it should be constantly repeated.

The truth that a Christian should not take part in murdering, or serve the chiefs of the murderers for a salary collected from the poor by force, is so plain and indisputable that those who hear it cannot but agree with it. And if a man continues to act contrary to these truths after hearing them, it is only because he is accustomed to act contrary to them, and it is difficult to break the habit. Moreover, as long as most people act as he does, he will not, by acting contrary to the truth, lose the regard of the majority of those who are most respected.

The case is the same as it is with the question of vegetarianism. "A man can live and be healthy without killing animals for food; therefore, if he eats meat, he participates in taking animal life merely for the sake of his appetite. And to act so is immoral." It is so simple and indubitable that it is impossible not to agree with it. But because most people do eat meat, people, on hearing the case stated, admit its justice, and then, laughing, say; "But a good beefsteak is a good thing all the same; and I shall eat one at dinner today with pleasure."

Just in the same way officers in the army, and officials employed in the civil service, treat statements of the incompatibility of Christianity and humanitarianism with military and civil service. "Yes, of course, it's true," says such a man, "but, all the same, it is nice to wear a uniform and epaulets, which serve as an introduction anywhere, and which people respect; and it is still better to know that, whatever happens, your salary will be paid punctually and accurately on the first of each month. So that though your statement of the case is correct, I am nevertheless bent on getting a rise of salary and securing a pension."

The position is admitted to be indubitable; but, in the first   10 place, one need not oneself kill an ox to get beefsteaks. It has already been killed. And one need not oneself collect taxes or murder. The taxes are already collected, and the army already exists. And, secondly, most people have not yet heard this view of things, and do not know that it is wrong to do these things. So that, for the present, one need not refuse a well-cooked beefsteak, or a uniform, and all its advantages, or medals and orders; or, above all, a secure monthly salary; "and as for the future, we shall see when the time comes."

At the root of the matter lies the fact that people have not yet heard the injustice and wickedness of such a way of life stated. And, therefore, it is necessary continually to repeat "Carthago delenda est," and Carthage will certainly fall.

I do not say that government and its power will be destroyed. It will not fall to pieces quickly; there are still too many gross elements among the people to support it. But the Christian support of government will be destroyed—*i.e.* those who do violence will cease to find support for their authority in the sanctity of Christianity. Those who employ violence will be simply violators, and nothing else. And when that is so—when they can no longer cloak themselves with pseudo-Christianity— then the end of all violence will be near.

Let us seek to hasten that end. "Carthago delenda est." Government is violence, Christianity is meekness, nonresistance, love. And, therefore, government cannot be Christian, and a man who wishes to be a Christian must not serve government. Government cannot be Christian. A Christian cannot serve government. Government cannot . . . and so on.

Questions about the Passage

1. How does Tolstoy connect the claim that "to serve the government is incompatible with Christianity" with the thought of Thoreau?
2. Do you agree with Tolstoy that this statement does not need discussion or proof: "A Christian must not be a soldier—*i.e.* a murderer—and must not be the servant of an institution maintained by violence and murder is so certain, so clear and irrefutable"?
3. Do you agree that "the case is the same" for vegetarianism? Is it "simple and indubitable"?

Questions about the Argument

1. Why do you think Tolstoy chooses not to make an argument, that is, supply proof? Is it sufficient to reiterate a claim several times?
2. Is such a proofless claim sufficient for his correspondent? Will it work for a wider audience?
3. In what way does Tolstoy use Thoreau as an authority?
4. Does Tolstoy's parallel claim about the immorality of vegetarianism weaken or strengthen his argument about the immorality of violence?

A Letter from Tolstoy to Gandhi
To Mohandas Gandhi
Kochety, 7 September 1910

I got your journal *Indian Opinion,* and was glad to learn all that was written there about those who practise non-resistance.[1] I also wanted to tell you the thoughts that reading it aroused in me.

The longer I live, and especially now when I feel keenly the nearness of death, I want to tell others what I feel so particularly keenly about, and what in my opinion is of enormous importance, namely what is called non-resistance, but what is essentially nothing other than the teaching of love undistorted by false interpretations. The fact that love, i.e. the striving of human souls towards unity and the activity resulting from such striving, is the highest and only law of human life is felt and known by every person in the depth of his soul (as we see most clearly

---

1   This letter was published in Gandhi's Transvaal newspaper *Indian Opinion* on 26 November 1910 (English translation by Chertkov).

of all with children)—known by him until he is ensnared by the false teachings of the world. This law has been proclaimed by all the world's sages, Indian, Chinese, Jewish, Greek and Roman. I think it has been expressed most clearly of all by Christ who even said frankly that on this alone hang all the Law and the prophets. Furthermore, foreseeing the distortion to which this law is subject or may be subject, he pointed frankly to the danger of its distortion which comes naturally to people who live by worldly interests, namely the danger of allowing themselves to defend these interests by force, i.e. as he said, returning blow for blow, taking back by force objects which have been appropriated, etc., etc. He knows, as every reasonable person is bound to know, that the use of violence is incompatible with love as the basic law of life, that once violence is tolerated in any cases whatsoever, the inadequacy of the law of love is recognised and therefore the law itself is repudiated. The whole of Christian civilisation, so brilliant on the surface, grew up on this obvious, strange, sometimes conscious but for the most part unconscious misunderstanding and contradiction.

Essentially speaking, once resistance was tolerated, side by side with love, there no longer was or could be love as a law of life, and there was no law of love except violence, i.e. the power of the stronger. For 19 centuries Christian mankind has lived in this way. True, people at all times have been guided by violence alone in organising their lives. The difference between the lives of Christian peoples and all others is merely the fact that in the Christian world, the law of love was expressed so clearly and definitely, as it hasn't been expressed in any other religious teaching, and that people in the Christian world solemnly accepted this law but at the same time allowed themselves to use violence and built their lives on violence. And so the whole life of Christian peoples is an outright contradiction between what they profess and what they build their lives on; a contradiction between love, recognised as the law of life, and violence recognised even as a necessity in various forms such as the power of rulers, courts and armies—recognised and extolled. This contradiction kept growing with the advancement of the peoples of the Christian world and has recently reached the ultimate degree. The question now obviously amounts to one of two things—either we recognise that we don't recognise any religious and moral teaching and are guided in the organisation of our lives only by the power of the strong, or that all our taxes collected by force, our judicial and police institutions and above all our armies must be abolished.

This spring, at a scripture examination at one of the women's institutes in Moscow, the scripture teacher, and then a bishop who was present, asked the girls about the commandments and particularly the sixth one. When the correct answer was given about the commandment, the bishop usually asked a further question: is killing always and in all cases forbidden by the scriptures, and the unfortunate girls, corrupted by their mentors, had to answer and did answer—not always; that killing is permitted in war and in executing criminals. However, when one of these unfortunate girls (what I am telling you is not fiction but a fact, reported to me by an eyewitness), after giving her answer, was asked the usual question: is killing always sinful? She blushed nervously and gave the firm answer that it always was, and she answered all the bishop's usual sophisms with the firm conviction that killing was always forbidden, that killing was forbidden even in the Old Testament and that not only was killing forbidden by Christ but also any evil against one's brother. And despite all his grandeur and art of eloquence, the bishop fell silent and the girl went away victorious.

Yes, we may talk in our papers about the successes of avia-   5
tion, about complicated diplomatic relations, about various clubs, discoveries, alliances of every kind, of so-called works of art, and still pass over in silence what this girl said; but we oughtn't to do so, because every person in the Christian world feels it—feels it more or less vaguely, but still feels it. Socialism, communism, anarchism, the Salvation Army, the growth of crime, unemployment among the population, the growth of the insane luxury of the rich and the destitution of the poor, the terrible growth in the number of suicides—all these things are signs of this internal contradiction which ought to and must be solved—and, of course, solved in the sense of recognising the law of love and renouncing all violence. And so your work in the Transvaal, at the other end of the world as it seems to us, is the most central and most important of all tasks now being done in the world, and not only Christian peoples, but peoples of the whole world will inevitably take part in it. I think you

will be pleased to know that this work is also rapidly developing in Russia in the form of refusals to do military service, of
which there are more and more every year. However insignificant may be the number of your people who practise nonresistance and of our people in Russia who refuse military service, both can boldly say that God is with them. And God is
more powerful than men.

In recognising Christianity, even in the distorted form in
which it is professed among Christian peoples, and in recognising at the same time the necessity for armies and arms to kill
in wars on the most enormous scale, there is such an obvious
and crying contradiction that sooner or later, probably very
soon, it will be exposed and will put an end either to the acceptance of the Christian religion which is necessary to maintain
power, or to the existence of an army and any violence supported by it, which is no less necessary to maintain power. This
contradiction is felt by all governments, your British as well as
our Russian, and from a natural feeling of self-preservation is
prosecuted more vigorously than any other antigovernment
activity, as we see in Russia and as is seen from the articles in
your journals. Governments know where their main danger
lies, and in this question are keeping a careful eye not only on
their own interests, but on the question: to be or not to be.

With the utmost respect,
Leo Tolstoy

Questions about the Passage

1. In paragraph 1, what is Tolstoy's purpose in writing to Gandhi?
   How does Tolstoy define love?
2. Tolstoy develops his ideas about the "inherent contradiction" of
   Christianity in paragraph 2 and develops the thought in paragraph 3. Explain what he means by the term.
3. Why is the response the student gives in paragraph 4 so important to Tolstoy?
4. In paragraph 5, he lists a series ranging from socialism to suicide
   as signs of internal contradiction. Be sure you understand each
   term, and then examine each one to determine how the term
   might qualify as such a sign.

5. Why does Tolstoy think that governments like Great Britain and Russia find Christianity and violence necessary to maintain power? Do you agree that they recognize the contradiction? From your vantage point in history, living nearly a century later than Tolstoy, did these countries do away with either violence or Christianity to resolve this contradiction?

Questions about the Argument

1. How does Tolstoy support the validity of his definition of love?
2. He states an either/or proposition at the end of paragraph 3. What is it? Do you accept its validity, or can you locate some kind of intermediate position?
3. What claim does Tolstoy's example in paragraph 4 support?
4. Tolstoy includes in paragraph 5 the statement, "And so your work in the Transvaal . . . is the most central and most important of all the tasks now being done in the world." What has Tolstoy said previously in the letter to justify this conclusion? Explain what the connection is to Gandhi's work.
5. Paragraph 6 includes another either/or proposition. Can you think of any other choices governments might have?

Mohandas K. Gandhi, "On Satyagraha, Nonviolence, and Civil Disobedience"

Mohandas Karamchand Gandhi (1869–1948), called the Mahatma ("Great Soul"), is widely considered one of the great leaders of the twentieth century. Not only did he successfully lead the nonviolent struggle to end Britain's imperial rule of his native India, but he also developed a philosophy of nonviolent resistance and civil disobedience campaigns that continues to be used to protest and change the unjust exercise of authority throughout the world. In addition, the example of his own life of devotion to his people and country, to truth, to nonviolence, and to self-sacrifice in these causes made him millions of admirers.

An English-trained lawyer, Gandhi moved to Natal, South Africa, early in his career. To protest the country's policies of racial discrimination, he founded the Natal Indian Congress in 1894 and then began to develop his concept of *satyagraha*: nonviolent, but sometimes illegal, resistance to illegitimate authority. *Satyagraha* was first put into practice in mass civil disobedience in South Africa, and Gandhi brought it back to India when he returned there in 1914. In 1915 he founded his first religious community, called the Satyagraha Ashram, in his native district of Gujarat. After World War I ended, Gandhi began organizing mass non-violent demonstrations and other acts of civil disobedience aimed at repressive colonial laws and, ultimately, at forcing the British to grant Indian Home Rule. Gandhi was arrested, convicted, and imprisoned for seditious conspiracy in 1922. He continued to speak, write, and lead the movement for Home Rule in the 1920s, 1930s, and 1940s. In the 1947 Partition, India and Pakistan were created as independent states, dividing the Hindu and Muslim majority populations. During the violence that broke out between the two populations at Partition, Gandhi, who had opposed the two-state model, began a fast to protest the bloodshed and to work for peace and understanding. During this fast, a Hindu fanatic, enraged by Gandhi's words of brotherhood, assassinated him on January 30, 1948.

A. Civil Disobedience and Mass Satyagraha, 1919

It is not without sorrow that I feel compelled to advise the temporary suspension of civil disobedience. I give this advice not because I have less faith now in its efficacy, but because I have, if possible, greater faith than before. It is my perception of the law of *satyagraha* which impels me to suggest the suspension. I am sorry, when I embarked upon a mass movement, I underrated the forces of evil and I must now pause and consider how best to meet the situation. But whilst doing so, I wish to say that from a careful examination of the tragedy at Ahmedabad and Viramgam, I am convinced that *satyagraha* had nothing to do with the violence of the mob and that many swarmed round the banner of mischief raised by the mob, largely because of their affection for Anasuyabai and myself. Had the Government in an unwise manner not prevented me from entering Delhi and so compelled me to disobey their order, I feel certain that Ahmedabad and Viramgam would have remained free from the horrors of the past week. In other words, *satyagraha* has neither been the cause nor the occasion of the upheaval. If anything, the presence of *satyagraha* has acted as a check even so slight upon the previously existing lawless elements. As regards events in the Punjab, it is admitted that they are unconnected with the *satyagraha* movement.

In the course of the *satyagraha* struggle in South Africa, several thousands of indentured Indians had struck work. This was a *satyagraha* strike and therefore entirely peaceful and voluntary. Whilst the strike was going on, a strike of European miners, railway employees, etc., was declared. Overtures were made to me to make common cause with the European strikers. As a *satyagrahi*, I did not require a moment's consideration to decline to do so. I went further and for fear of our strike being classed with the strike of Europeans in which methods of violence and use of arms found a prominent place, ours was suspended and *satyagraha* from that moment came to be recognized by the Europeans of South Africa as an honourable and honest movement—in the words of General Smuts, a constitutional movement. I can do no less at the present critical moment. I would be untrue to *satyagraha*, if I allowed it by any action of mine to be used as an occasion for feeding violence for embittering relations between the English and the Indians. Our *satyagraha* must therefore now consist in ceaselessly helping the authorities in all the ways available to us as *satyagrahis* to restore order and to curb lawlessness. We can turn the tragedies going on before us to good account if we could but succeed in gaining the adherence of the masses to the fundamental principles of *satyagraha*.

Satyagraha is like a banyan tree with innumerable branches. Civil disobedience is one such branch, *satya* (truth) and *ahimsa* (non-violence) together make the parent trunk from which all innumerable branches shoot out. We have found by bitter experience that whilst in an atmosphere of lawlessness, civil disobedience found ready acceptance. *Satya* and *ahimsa*, from which alone civil disobedience can worthily spring, have commanded little or no respect. Ours then is a Herculean task, but we may not shirk it. We must fearlessly spread the doctrine of *satya* and *ahimsa* and then, and not till then, shall we be able to undertake mass *satyagraha*.

My attitude towards the Rowlatt legislation remains unchanged. Indeed, I do feel that the Rowlatt legislation is one of the many causes of the present unrest. But in a surcharged atmosphere, I must refrain from examining these causes. The main and only purpose of this letter is to advise all *satyagrahis* to temporarily suspend civil disobedience, to give Government effective co-operation in restoring order and by preaching and practice to gain adherence to the fundamental principles mentioned above.

Press Statement on Suspension of Civil Disobedience
The Hindu, 21 Apr. 1919

B. Definition of Terms, 1921

Satyagraha, Civil Disobedience, Passive Resistance, Non-co-operation—
It is often my lot to answer knotty questions on all sorts of topics arising out of this great movement of national purification. A company of collegiate Non-co-operators asked me to define for them the terms which I have used as heading for this note. And even at this late day, I was seriously asked whether Satyagraha did not at times warrant resistance by violence, as for instance, in the case of a sister whose virtue might be in danger from a desperado. I ventured to suggest that it was the completest defence without irritation, without being ruffled, to interpose one-self between the victim and the victimizer, and to face death. I added that this (for the assailant) novel method of defence would, in all probability, exhaust his passion and he will no longer want to ravish an innocent woman, but would want to flee from her presence for very shame, and that, if he did not, the act of personal bravery on the part of her brother would steel her heart for putting up an equally brave defence and resisting the lust of man, turned brute for the while. And I thought I clinched my argument by saying that if, inspite of all the defence, the unexpected happened, and the physical force of the tyrant overpowered his victim, the disgrace would not be that of the woman, but of her assailant, and that both she and her brother, who died in the attempt to defend her virtue, would stand well before the Throne of Judgment. I do not warrant that my argument convinced my listener or that it would convince the reader. The world I know will go on as before. But it is well at this moment of self-examination to understand and appreciate the implications of the powerful movement of non-violence. All religions have emphasised the highest ideal, but all have more or less permitted departures as so many concessions to human weaknesses.

I now proceed to summarise the explanations I gave of the   5
various terms. It is beyond my capacity to give accurate and terse definitions.

Satyagraha, then, is literally holding on to Truth and it means, therefore Truth-force. Truth is soul or spirit. It is, therefore, known as soul-force. It excludes the use of violence because man is not capable of knowing the absolute truth and, therefore, not competent to punish. The word was coined in South Africa to distinguish the non-violent resistance of the Indians of South Africa from the contemporary 'passive resistance' of the suffragettes and others. It is not conceived as a weapon of the weak.

Passive resistance is used in the orthodox English sense and covers the suffragette movement as well as the resistance of the Non-conformists. Passive resistance has been conceived and is regarded as a weapon of the weak. Whilst it avoids violence, being not open to the weak, it does not exclude its use if, in the opinion of the passive resister, the occasion demands it. However, it has always been distinguished from armed resistance, and its application was at one time confined to Christian martyrs.

Civil Disobedience is civil breach of unmoral statutory enactments. The expression was, so far as I am aware, coined by Thoreau to signify his own resistance to the laws of a slave state. He has left a masterly treatise on the duty of Civil Disobedience. But Thoreau was not perhaps an out and out champion of non-violence. Probably, also, Thoreau limited his breach of statutory laws to the revenue law, *i.e.,* payment of taxes, whereas the term Civil Disobedience, as practised in 1919, covered a breach of any statutory and unmoral law. It signified the resister's outlawry in a civil, *i.e.,* non-violent manner. He invoked the sanctions of the law and cheerfuly suffered imprisonment. It is a branch of Satyagraha.

Non-co-operation predominantly implies withdrawing of Co-operation from the State that in the Non-co-operator's view has become corrupt and excludes Civil Disobedience of the fierce type described above. By its very nature, Non-co-operation is even open to children of understanding and can be safely practised by the masses. Civil Disobedience presupposes the habit of willing obedience to laws without fear of their sanctions. It can therefore be practised only as a last resort and by a select few in the first instance at any rate. Non-co-operation, too, like Civil Disobedience is a branch of Sathyagraha which includes all non-violent resistance for the vindication of Truth.—M. K. G. in *Young India* of 21st March, 1921.

Co-operation and Non-co-operation defined—It is no small thing   10
for the country, that Dwijendranath Tagore fondly known as
Bada Dada by his friends, follows with keen attention even in his
old age and in his seclusion at Shantiniketan all that is going on
in the country. Mr. Andrews has circulated a free translation of
his latest thoughts on Non-co-operation. Although the whole of
it is published in the daily press, I cannot resist reproducing his
definitions of Co-operation and Non-co-operation; they are so
true and telling. Writing of the former, he says, "Our rulers, in
order to hide their despotic measures from the world's eye,
dressed up a puppet show in the form of Legislative Councils, in
which a few platform orators have been invited to co-operate.
Our rulers believe that, by doing so, they have placed us under
an eternal debt of gratitude, but in reality they have only added
insult to injury. These Councils cling to us now, and threaten
to choke us like the old man in the story of Sindbad, the sailor."
"If this is the meaning of co-operation," proceeds Bada Dada,
"according to our English rulers, then it is no very difficult matter to understand what Non-co-operation means to us. We shall
never accept, even if it costs us our lives to refuse it, anything that
will bring evil upon our country. That is Non-co-operation."—
Young India of 14th July, 1920.

C. Some Rules of Satyagraha, 1930
Satyagraha literally means insistence on truth. This insistence
arms the votary with matchless power. This power or force is
connoted by the word *satyagraha*. . . .

Such a universal force necessarily makes no distinction
between kinsmen and strangers, young and old, man and
woman, friend and foe. The force to be so applied can never be
physical. There is in it no room for violence. The only force of
universal application can, therefore, be that of *ahimsa* or love.
In other words, it is soul-force.

Love does not burn others, it burns itself. Therefore, a *satyagrahi*, i.e., a civil resister, will joyfully suffer even unto death.

As an Individual
1. A *satyagrahi*, i.e., a civil resister, will harbour no anger.
2. He will suffer the anger of the opponent.
3. In so doing he will put up with assaults from the opponent,
   never retaliate; but he will not submit, out of fear of punishment or the like, to any order given in anger.

4. When any person in authority seeks to arrest a civil resister, he will voluntarily submit to the arrest, and he will not resist the attachment or removal of his own property, if any, when it is sought to be confiscated by authorities. . . .

As a Prisoner   15

10. As a prisoner, a civil resister will behave courteously towards prison officials, and will observe all such discipline of the prison as is not contrary to self-respect; . . .
11. A civil resister will make no distinction between an ordinary prisoner and himself, will in no way regard himself as superior to the rest, nor will he ask for any conveniences that may not be necessary for keeping his body in good health and condition. He is entitled to ask for such conveniences as may be required for his physical or spiritual well-being. . . .

As a Unit

13. A civil resister will joyfully obey all the orders issued by the leader of the corps, whether they please him or not.
14. . . . He is free before joining to determine the fitness of the corps to satisfy him, but after he has joined it, it becomes a duty to submit to its discipline, irksome or otherwise. If the sum total of the energy of the corps appears to a member to be improper or immoral, he has a right to sever his connection, but being within it, he has no right to commit a breach of its discipline. . . .
   How much more, then, should such be the case in *satyagraha*? It is the universal experience that in such times hardly anybody is left to starve.

. . .

'Some Rules of *Satyagraha*' (G.)
Navajivan, 23 Feb. 1930
Young India, 27 Feb. 1930

D. The Danger of Civil Disobedience, 1930

There is danger in civil disobedience only because it is still only a partially tried remedy and has always to be tried in an atmosphere surcharged with violence. For when tyranny is rampant much rage is generated among the victims. It remains latent because of their weakness and bursts in all its fury on the slightest pretext. Civil disobedience is a sovereign method of transmuting this undisciplined life-destroying latent energy into disciplined life-saving energy whose use ensures absolute success. The attendant risk is nothing compared to the result promised. When the world has become familiar with its use and when it has had a series of demonstrations of its successful working, there will be less risk in civil disobedience than there is in aviation, in spite of that science having reached a high stage of development.

'Duty of Disloyalty'
Young India, 27 Mar. 1930

E. Satyagraha in the Face of Hooliganism, 1946

A friend has gently posed the question as to what a *satyagrahi* should do to prevent looting by *goondas*. If he had understood the secret of *satyagraha*, he would not have put it.

To lay down one's life, even alone, for what one considers to be right, is the very core of *satyagraha*. More no man can do. If a man is armed with a sword, he might lop off a few heads but ultimately he must surrender to superior force or else die fighting. The sword of the *satyagrahi* is love and the unshakeable firmness that comes from it. He will regard as brothers the hundreds of *goondas* that confront him and instead of trying to kill them he will choose to die at their hands and thereby live.

This is straight and simple. But how can a solitary *satyagrahi*   20
succeed in the midst of a huge population? Hundreds of hooligans were let loose on the city of Bombay for arson and loot. A solitary *satyagrahi* will be like a drop in the ocean. Thus argues the correspondent.

My reply is that a *satyagrahi* may never run away from danger, irrespective of whether he is alone or in the company of many. He will have fully performed his duty, if he dies fighting. The same holds good in armed warfare. It applies with greater force in *satyagraha*. Moreover the sacrifice of one will evoke the sacrifice of many and may possibly produce big results. There is always this possibility. But one must scrupulously avoid the temptation of a desire for results. Here I am indicating only a possibility. May no one regard results as a temptation.

I believe that every man and woman should learn the art of self-defence in this age. This is done through arms in the West. Every adult man is conscripted for army training for a definite period. The training for *satyagraha* is meant for all, irrespective of age or sex. The more important part of the training here is mental, not physical. There can be no compulsion in mental training. The surrounding atmosphere no doubt acts on the mind but that cannot justify compulsion.

It follows that shopkeepers, traders, mill-hands, labourers, farmers, clerks, in short everyone ought to consider it his or her duty to get the necessary training in *satyagraha*.

Satyagraha is always superior to armed resistance. This can only be effectively proved by demonstration, not by argument. It is the weapon that adorns the strong. It can never adorn the weak. By weak is meant the weak in mind and spirit, not in body. That limitation is a quality to be prized and not a defect to be deplored.

One ought also to understand one of its other limitations. It   25
can never be used to defend a wrong cause.

Satyagraha brigades can be organized in every village and in every block of buildings in the cities. Each brigade should be composed of those persons who are well-known to the organizers. In this respect *satyagraha* differs from armed defence. For the latter the State impresses the service of everybody. For a *satyagraha* brigade only those are eligible who believe in *ahimsa* and *satya*. Therefore an intimate knowledge of the persons enlisted is necessary for the organizers.

'*Satyagraha* in Face of Hooliganism' (G.)
Harijan, 17 Mar. 1946

Questions about the Passages

    A. 1. Why does Gandhi suspend civil disobedience?
       2. Why does Gandhi not think *satyagraha* has caused violence?
       3. Gandhi likens *satyagraha* to a banyan tree. How does he use this simile to explain the relationship of civil disobedience to *satyagraha*?

B. 1. At various times, Gandhi calls *satyagraha* "truth-force," "soul-force," and "insistence on truth." Why does such a reliance on truth not allow humans to punish; that is, why must they rely on nonviolence?

2. How does Gandhi define *satyagraha* and distinguish it from the passive resistance of the suffragettes and non-conformists?

3. What is Gandhi's definition of "civil disobedience"? How does he distinguish his usage from Thoreau's?

4. Gandhi sees both civil disobedience and noncooperation as branches of *satyagraha*. How do the terms differ in meaning?

C. Read the rules for *satyagraha* carefully. Which do you find most compelling? Which are most puzzling? Try to think of the reasons underlying these rules. Which might be most difficult to follow? Do you think anyone can abide by all of these rules?

D. Do you agree with Gandhi that civil disobedience rather than provoking violence will transform it into "life-saving energy"?

E. 1. What is the core of *satyagraha*?

2. How does Gandhi answer the objection of a correspondent who says that a solitary *satyagrahi* will be "like a drop in the ocean" among a sea of hooligans?

3. Gandhi says that every man and woman should learn the art of self-defense. How does Gandhi distinguish self-defense, as understood by the West, from his meaning?

Questions about the Arguments

1. Having looked at the development over time of Gandhi's thinking, what are his values and assumptions? How would you evaluate his ethos? How is he qualified to speak about civil disobedience? What is his reputation? What authorities does he cite?

2. To what extent can you determine the audience for each of Gandhi's writings included above? What clues do you find in these pieces?

3. Looking back, which piece makes the strongest case for civil disobedience? Defend your answer.

Mohandas K. Gandhi and Judah L. Magnes, "How Should the German Jews Respond to Nazi Persecution?"

In 1938, Gandhi responded to requests from friends and supporters to speak out about the rise of Hitler and anti-Semitism in Germany. Gandhi condemned the racism of the Nazis, which he believed was similar to the racial and religious discrimination and oppression he had experienced and fought throughout his life. In his *Harijan* article of November 26, 1938, published only a few weeks after the state-sponsored German pogrom against the Jews known as *Kristalnacht*, he recommends that the Jews adopt *satyagraha* to combat persecution.

In response to this letter, several prominent Jewish leaders wrote public letters to Gandhi. Martin Buber, the Austrian-born religious philosopher (1878–1965), replied at length. Buber wrote from Palestine, where he had recently fled from Nazi Germany. He criticized the analogy Gandhi drew between the Jews of Germany and the Indians of South Africa. Another response came from Judah L. Magnes (1877–1948), the president of Hebrew University in Jerusalem. Magnes was born in San Francisco and became a prominent Reform Jewish rabbi and social activist. He embraced pacifism during World War I and spoke at antiwar rallies in 1917. When he moved to Palestine after the war, he worked for Arab-Jewish reconciliation and eventually advocated a binational state. Magnes writes to Gandhi on February 26, 1939, with admiration for his ideas and work but with reservations and questions about his understanding of the Jews' plight in Nazi Germany.

M. K. Gandhi, "The Jews"

Several letters have been received by me asking me to declare my views about the persecution of the Jews in Germany. It is not without hesitation that I venture to offer my views on this very difficult question.

My sympathies are all with the Jews. I have known them intimately in South Africa. Some of them became lifelong companions. Through these friends I came to learn much of their age-long persecution. They have been the untouchables of Christianity. The parallel between their treatment by Christians and the treatment of untouchables by Hindus is very close. Religious sanction has been invoked in both cases for the justification of the inhuman treatment meted out to them. Apart from the friendships, therefore, there is the more common universal reason for my sympathy for the Jews.

The German persecution of the Jews seems to have no parallel in history. The tyrants of old never went so mad as Hitler seems to have gone. And he is doing it with religious zeal. For, he is propounding a new religion of exclusive and militant nationalism in the name of which any inhumanity becomes an act of humanity to he rewarded here and hereafter. The crime of an obviously mad but intrepid youth is being visited upon his whole race with unbelievable ferocity. If there ever could be a justifiable war in the name of and for humanity, a war against Germany, to prevent the wanton persecution of a whole race, would be completely justified. But I do not believe in any war. A discussion of the pros and cons of such a war is, therefore, outside my horizon or province.

But if there can be no war against Germany, even for such a crime as is being committed against the Jews, surely there can be no alliance with Germany. How can there be alliance between a nation which claims to stand for justice and democracy and one which is the declared enemy of both? Or is England drifting towards armed dictatorship and all it means?

Germany is showing to the world how efficiently violence can   5
be worked when it is not hampered by any hypocrisy or weakness masquerading as humanitarianism. It is also showing how hideous, terrible and terrifying it looks in its nakedness.

Can the Jews resist this organized and shameless persecution? Is there a way to preserve their self-respect, and not to feel helpless, neglected and forlorn? I submit there is. No person who has faith in a living God need feel helpless or forlorn. Jehovah of the Jews is a God more personal than the God of the Christians, the Mussalmans or the Hindus, though as a matter of fact, in essence, He is common to all and one without a second and beyond description. But as the Jews attribute personality to God and believe that He rules every action of theirs, they ought not to feel helpless. If I were a Jew and were born in Germany and earned my livelihood there, I would claim Germany as my home even as the tallest gentile German might, and challenge him to shoot me or cast me in the dungeon; I would refuse to be expelled or to submit to discriminating treatment. And for doing this I should not wait for the fellow Jews to join me in civil resistance, but would have confidence that in the end the rest were bound to follow my example. If one Jew or all the Jews were to accept the prescription here offered, he or they cannot be worse off than now. And suffering voluntarily undergone will bring them an inner strength and joy which no number of resolutions of sympathy passed in the world outside Germany can. Indeed, even if Britain, France and America were to declare hostilities against Germany, they can bring no inner joy, no inner strength. The calculated violence of Hitler may even result in a general massacre of the Jews by way of his first answer to the declaration of such hostilities. But if the Jewish mind could be prepared for voluntary suffering, even the massacre I have imaged could be turned into a day of thanksgiving and joy that Jehovah had wrought deliverance of the race even at the hands of the tyrant. For to the God-fearing, death has no terror. It is a joyful sleep to be followed by a waking that would be all the more refreshing for the long sleep.

It is hardly necessary for me to point out that it is easier for the Jews than for the Czechs to follow my prescription. And they have in the Indian Satyagraha campaign in South Africa an exact parallel. There the Indians occupied precisely the same place that the Jews occupy in Germany. The persecutions had also a religious tinge. President Kruger used to say that the white Christians were the chosen of God and Indians were inferior beings created to serve the whites. A fundamental clause in the Transvaal constitution was that there should be no equality between the whites and colored races including Asiatics. There too the Indians were consigned to ghettos described as locations. The other disabilities were almost of the same type as those of the Jews in Germany. The Indians, a mere handful, resorted to Satyagraha without any backing from the world outside or the Indian Government. Indeed the British officials tried to dissuade the satyagrahis from their contemplated step. World opinion and the Indian Government came to their aid after eight years of fighting. And that too was by way of diplomatic pressure, not of a threat of war.

But the Jews of Germany can offer Satyagraha under infinitely better auspices than the Indians of South Africa. The Jews are a compact, homogeneous community in Germany. They are far more gifted than the Indians of South Africa. And they have organized world opinion behind them. I am convinced that, if someone with courage and vision can arise among them to lead them in non-violent action, the winter of their despair can in the twinkling of an eye be turned into the summer of hope. And what has today become a degrading man-hunt can he turned into a calm and determined stand offered by unarmed men and women possessing the strength of suffering given to them by Jehovah. It will be then a truly religious resistance offered against the godless fury of a dehumanized man. The German Jews will score a lasting victory over the German gentiles in the sense that they will have converted the latter to an appreciation of human dignity. They will have rendered service to fellow-Germans and proved their title to be the real Germans as against those who are today dragging, however unknowingly, the German name into the mire. . . .

Judah L. Magnes, "A Letter to Gandhi"

What you have said recently about the Jews is the one statement I have yet seen which needs to be grappled with fundamentally. Your statement is a challenge, particularly to those of us who had imagined ourselves your disciples.

I am sure you must be right in asserting the Jews of Germany can offer Satyagraha to the "godless fury of their dehumanized oppressors."

But how and when? You do not give the answer. You may say that you are not sufficiently acquainted with the German persecution to outline the practical technique of Satyagraha for use by the German Jews. But one of the great things about you and your doctrine has been that you have always emphasized the chance of practical success, if Satyagraha be offered. Yet to the German Jews you have not given the practical advice which only your unique experience could provide, and I wonder if it is helpful merely in general terms to call upon the Jews of Germany to offer Satyagraha. I have heard that many a Jew of Germany has asked himself how and when Satyagraha must be offered without finding the answer. Conditions in Germany are radically different from those that have prevailed in South Africa and in India. Those of us who are outside Germany must, I submit, think through most carefully the advice

we proffer the unfortunates who are caught in the claws of the
Hitler beast. . . .

If ever a people was a people of nonviolence through century after century, it was the Jews. I think they need learn but
little from anyone in faithfulness to their God and in their
readiness to suffer while they sanctify His Name.

What is new and great about you has seemed to me this, that   5
you have exalted nonviolence into the dominant principle of
all of life, both religious, social and political; and that you have
made it into a practical technique both of communing with the
divine and of battling for a newer world, which would respect
the human personality of even the most insignificant outcast.
You exhort the German Jew to add "the surpassing contribution of non-violent action" to the precious contribution he has
already made to mankind. But you could be of much greater
help by showing how the technique of Satyagraha could be of
practical use to the German Jews.

You would have the right to say that some Jew should point
this technique out. But we have no one comparable to you as
religious and political leader.

There are, as I am aware, other elements besides nonviolence
in Satyagraha. There is non-cooperation, and the renunciation
of property, and the disdain of death.

The Jews are a people who exalt life, and they can hardly be
said to disdain death. Leviticus 18:5 reads: "My Judgments,
which if a man do he shall live in them," and the interpretation
adds, as a principle of Jewish life, "and not die through them."
For this reason I have often wondered if we Jews are fit subjects
for Satyagraha. As to property, it is but natural that Jews should
want to take along with them a minimum of their property from
Germany or elsewhere, so as not to fall a burden upon others. It
would, I am sure, give you satisfaction to see how large numbers of refugees, who in Germany were used to wealth, comfort,
culture, have, without too much complaint and very often
cheerfully, buckled down to a new life in Palestine, many of
them in the fields or in menial employment in the cities.

It is in the matter of non-cooperation that I have a question
of importance to put to you.

A plan is being worked out between the Evian Refugee   10
Committee and the German Government which appears to me

to be nothing short of devilish. The details are not yet known. But it seems to amount to this: The German Government is to confiscate all German Jewish property, and in exchange for increased foreign trade and foreign currency which Jews are to bring them, they will permit a limited number of Jews to leave Germany annually for the next several years. The scheme involves the sale of millions of pounds of debentures to be issued by a Refugee or Emigration Bank to be created. Whether Governments are to subscribe to these debentures, I do not know. But certainly the whole Jewish world will be called upon to do so.

Here is the dilemma: If one does not subscribe, no Jews will be able to escape from this prison of torture called Germany. If one does subscribe, one will be cooperating with that Government, and be dealing in Jewish flesh and blood in a most modern and up-to-date slave market. I see before me here in Jerusalem a child who is happy, now that he is away from the torment there; and his brother, or parent, or grandparent. One of the oldest of Jewish sayings is: "Who saves a single soul in Israel is as if he had saved a whole world." Not to save a living soul? And yet to cooperate with the powers of evil and darkness? Have you an answer?

You touch upon a vital phase of the whole subject when you say that, "if there ever could be a justifiable war in the name of and for humanity, a war against Germany, to prevent the wanton persecution of a whole race, would be completely justified. But I do not believe in any war. A discussion of the pros and cons of such a war is therefore outside my horizon and province."

But it is on "the pros and cons of such a war" that I would ask your guidance. The question gives me no rest, and I am sure there are many like myself. Like you, I do not believe in any war. I have pledged myself never to take part in a war. I spoke up for pacifism in America during the World War [I], alongside of many whose names are known to you. That war brought the "peace" of Versailles and the Hitlerism of today. But my pacifism, as I imagine the pacifism of many others, is passing through a pitiless crisis. I ask myself: Suppose America, England, France are dragged into a war with the Hitler bestiality, what am I to do and what am I to teach? This war may destroy the life of a large part of the youth of the world, and force those who remain alive to lead the lives of savages. Yet I know I would pray with all my heart for the defeat of the Hitler inhumanity; and am I then to stand aside and let others do the fighting? During the last war I prayed for a peace without defeat or victory.

The answer given by Romain Rolland in his little book, *Par la révolution la paix* (1935), seems to be that while he himself as an individual continues to refuse to bear arms, he will do everything he can to help his side (at that time, Russia) to win the war. That is hardly a satisfying answer.

I ask myself how I might feel if I were not a Jew. Is the Hitler   15 iniquity really as profound as I imagine? I recall that during the last war the arguments against Germany were much the same as those of today. I took no stock in those arguments then. Perhaps it is the torture of my own people that enrages me unduly? Yet it is my conviction that, being a Jew, my sense of outrage at injustice may, perhaps, be a bit more alive than the average, and therefore more aware of the evils which the Hitler frenzy is bringing upon all mankind. The Jew, scattered as he is, is an outpost, bearing the brunt earlier of an action against mankind, and bearing it longest. For a dozen reasons, he is a convenient scapegoat. I say this in order to make the point that if the Jew is thoroughly aroused about an evil such as the Hitler madness, his excitement and indignation are apt to be based not only on personal hurt, but on a more or less authentic appraisal of the evil that must be met.

If you will take the trouble of looking at the little pamphlet I am sending, *Fellowship in War* (1936), you will see that I have an ineradicable belief that no war whatsoever can be a righteous war. The war tomorrow for the "democracies" or for some other noble slogan will be just as unrighteous or as fatuous as was the "war to save democracy" yesterday. Moreover, to carry on the war, the democracies will perforce become totalitarian. Not even a war against the ghastly Hitler savagery can be called righteous, for we all of us have sinned, conquerors and conquered alike, and it is because of our sins, because of our lack of generosity and of the spirit of conciliation and renunciation, that the Hitler beast has been enabled to raise its head. Even on the pages of the Nuremberg *Memorbuch* we find the words "Because of our many sins" this and that massacre took place. There can be no war for something good. That is a contradiction in terms. The good is to be achieved through totally different means.

But a war against something evil? If the Hitler cruelty launches a war against you, what would you do, what will you do? Can you refrain from making a choice? It is a choice of evils—a choice between the capitalisms, the imperialisms, the militarisms of the western democracies, and between the Hitler religion. Can one hesitate as to which is the lesser of these two evils? Is not a choice therefore imperative? I am all too painfully conscious that I am beginning to admit that if Hitler hurls his war upon us, we must resist. For us it would thus become not a righteous war, nor, to use your term, a justifiable war, but a necessary war, not for something good, but, because no other choice is left us, against the greater evil. Or do you know of some other choice? . . .

1939

Questions about the Passages

1. Why might Gandhi begin with his sympathy for the Jews and his comparison of them to the untouchables within Hinduism?
2. Gandhi implicitly criticizes England in paragraph 4 for the Munich Agreement of October 1938, which Neville Chamberlain had just negotiated a few months before. What is the basis of Gandhi's objection to England's "alliance" with Germany?
3. What is the connection, according to Gandhi, between belief in God and nonviolent resistance or *satyagraha?* What advantages does Gandhi believe the Jews have over the Czechs, who had been forced to cede the Sudetenland to Germany in September 1938?
4. Magnes finds Gandhi's view not fully convincing. In what ways?
5. What aspect of Jewish belief does Magnes think might make Jews poor practitioners of *satyagraha?*
6. Why does Magnes ask Gandhi's guidance about a possible war with Nazi Germany? What case does Magnes make to fight Hitler?

Questions about the Arguments

1. Gandhi asserts several assumptions, notably in paragraphs 2, 3, 6, 7, and 8. What are they? Does he provide any evidence to support these assumptions? How does he use them in his argument?

2. Evaluate Gandhi's arguments by analogy. Do you find them convincing? Why or why not?
3. On what authority does he base his argument? How does his ethos contribute to the effectiveness of his argument?
4. How does Magnes's opening praise of Gandhi work as part of his response to Gandhi's suggestions?
5. Why does Magnes insist upon his pacifist credentials by sending Gandhi his pamphlet?
6. Would you characterize Magnes as opposed to Gandhi's suggestion to German Jews to practice *satyagraha*? Be prepared to defend your answer.

Martin Luther King, Jr., "Letter from Birmingham Jail"

Martin Luther King, Jr., was born in Atlanta in 1929 into a middle-class black family. The son of a clergyman, he changed his name from Michael to Martin to reflect his father's name and calling as a Protestant minister. During his childhood he had little direct experience of racism, but at the age of 14, he was returning to Atlanta after winning a speech contest when the bus driver insisted that he and his teacher surrender their seats to white passengers. When he wanted to protest this treatment, his teacher said to obey the law. As they stood in the aisle of the bus for the ninety-mile trip, King was angrier than he had ever been before.

After receiving his B.A. in 1948 from Morehouse College in Atlanta, King attended Crozier Theological Seminary (M. Div., 1951) and Boston University (Ph.D., 1955, and D.Div., 1959). In the course of his seminary training, King was attracted to the work of Protestant theologians who considered that the church should be actively engaged in remedying social injustice. He was also influenced by Mahatma Gandhi's writings on nonviolent resistance as a means of countering unjust treatment.

Ordained a minister in 1947 at his father's church, the Dexter Avenue Baptist Church, King was pastor there from 1954 to 1960. From 1960 to 1968, he was co-pastor with his father at the Ebenezer Baptist Church. At the same time, King became an active participant and leader in the struggle for civil rights. In 1957, he founded and then directed the Southern Christian Leadership Congress until his death in 1968.

Though King had been active in civil rights causes and demonstrations throughout the 1950s, 1963 was a peak year for his activism. He participated in the mass demonstrations and arrests in Birmingham, Alabama, to protest the refusal of Bull Connor, the police chief, to enforce the law mandating integration. Follow-up demonstrations expressed outrage at Connor's actions in turning police dogs and fire hoses on large crowds, many of whom were children. King was arrested during these demonstrations and used scraps of paper to write "Letter from Birmingham Jail" as he awaited trial. Later the same year he helped organize the March to Washington in which an interracial group of 200,000 participated. In front of the Lincoln Memorial, he delivered his famous "I Have a Dream" speech to that crowd. Historians credit these demonstrations as crucial to the passage of the Civil Rights Act of 1964. Also testaments of King's importance to the civil rights movement are the awards he was given in 1963 and 1964: *Time*'s Man of the Year and the Nobel Prize for Peace.

King's allegiance to nonviolence continued throughout his life, but others were impatient with the rate of progress toward civil rights. Black militant groups espoused violent solutions, and the Watts riots erupted in 1965. To reinforce support for his movement, King joined his cause to that against the war in Vietnam in a speech given at Riverside Church in New York. Some civil rights activists, however, felt this linkage would weaken the civil rights movement.

In April 1968, King traveled to Montgomery, Alabama, to assist striking sanitation workers. There he was shot by James Earl Ray, a white segregationist, and died on April 4. In the years following his death, King received both criticism—for personal and scholarly failings—and widespread praise for his important contributions to the civil rights movement and to both the theory and practice of civil disobedience. To assess his achievements for ourselves, we can turn to his writings, especially *Why We Can't Wait* (1964) and *Where Do We Go from Here: Chaos or Community?* (1968). In 1983, Congress declared January 15, the birthday of Martin Luther King, Jr., a national holiday, thereby recognizing his legacy to American society as a whole.

During the Birmingham demonstrations, on April 12, 1963, eight Alabama clergymen published a letter addressed to Dr. King. In it, they5 expressed their consternation at King's presence and tactics. They were particularly disturbed that the demonstrations were "led in part by outsiders" and were "unwise and untimely." The writers feared that the demonstrations could lead to "hatred and violence." They praised the "calm manner" in which police handled the demonstrators, and they urged their "own Negro community" to work toward negotiation and to refuse participation in civil disobedience. (If you would like to read the clergymen's letter for yourself, it can be found on the world wide web and in many collections about the civil rights movement.) King responded to the clergymen's fears and accusations in his "Letter from Birmingham Jail," written on April 16, 1963.

"Letter from Birmingham Jail," April 16, 1963

My Dear Fellow Clergymen:

While confined here in the Birmingham city jail, I came across your recent statement calling present activities "unwise and untimely." Seldom do I pause to answer criticism of my work and ideas. If I sought to answer all the criticisms that cross my desk, my secretaries would have little time for anything other than such correspondence in the course of the day, and I would have no time for constructive work. But since I feel that you are men of genuine good will and that your criticisms are sincerely set forth, I want to try to answer your statement in what I hope will be patient and reasonable terms.

I think I should indicate why I am here in Birmingham, since you have been influenced by the view which argues against "outsiders coming in." I have the honor of serving as President of the Southern Christian Leadership Conference, an organization operating in every southern state, with headquarters in Atlanta, Georgia. We have some eighty-five affiliated organizations across the South, and one of them is the Alabama Christian Movement for Human Rights. Frequently we share staff, educational and financial resources with our affiliates. Several months ago the affiliate here in Birmingham asked us to be on call to engage in a nonviolent direct-action program if such were deemed necessary. We readily consented, and when the hour came we lived up to our promise. So I, along with several members of my staff, am here because I was invited here. I am here because I have organizational ties here.

But more basically, I am in Birmingham because injustice is here. Just as the prophets of the eighth century B.C. left their villages and carried their "thus saith the Lord" far beyond the boundaries of their home towns, and just as the Apostle Paul left his village of Tarsus and carried the gospel of Jesus Christ to the far corners of the Greco-Roman world, so am I compelled to carry the gospel of freedom beyond my own home town. Like Paul, I must constantly respond to the Macedonian call for aid.

Moreover, I am cognizant of the interrelatedness of all communities and states. I cannot sit idly in Atlanta and not be concerned about what happens in Birmingham. Injustice anywhere is a threat to justice everywhere. We are caught in an inescapable network of mutuality, tied in a single garment of destiny. Whatever affects one directly, affects all indirectly. Never again can we afford to live with the narrow, provincial "outside agitator" idea. Anyone who lives inside the United States can never be considered an outsider anywhere within its bounds.

You deplore the demonstrations taking place in Birmingham.   5 But your statement, I am sorry to say, fails to express a similar concern for the conditions that brought about the demonstrations. I am sure that none of you would want to rest content with the superficial kind of social analysis that deals merely with effects and does not grapple with underlying causes. It is unfortunate that demonstrations are taking place in Birmingham, but it is even more unfortunate that the city's white power structure left the Negro community with no alternative.

In any nonviolent campaign there are four basic steps: collection of the facts to determine whether injustices exist; negotiation; self-purification; and direct action. We have gone through all these steps in Birmingham. There can be no gain saying the fact that racial injustice engulfs this community. Birmingham is probably the most thoroughly segregated city in the United States. Its ugly record of brutality is widely known. Negroes have experienced grossly unjust treatment in the courts. There have been more unsolved bombings of Negro homes and churches in Birmingham than in any other city in the nation. These are the hard, brutal facts of the case. On the basis of these conditions, Negro leaders sought to negotiate with the city fathers. But the latter consistently refused to engage in good-faith negotiation.

Then, last September, came the opportunity to talk with leaders of Birmingham's economic community. In the course of the negotiations, certain promises were made by the merchants—for example, to remove the stores' humiliating racial signs. On the basis of these promises, the Reverend Fred Shuttlesworth and the leaders of the Alabama Christian Movement for Human Rights agreed to a moratorium on all demonstrations. As the weeks and months went by, we realized that we were the victims of a broken promise. A few signs, briefly removed, returned; the others remained.

As in so many past experiences, our hopes had been blasted, and the shadow of deep disappointment settled upon us. We had no alternative except to prepare for direct action, whereby we would present our very bodies as a means of laying our case before the conscience of the local and the national community. Mindful of the difficulties involved, we decided to undertake a process of self-purification. We began a series of workshops on nonviolence, and we repeatedly asked ourselves: "Are you able to accept blows without retaliation?" "Are you able to endure the ordeal of jail?" We decided to schedule our direct-action program for the Easter season, realizing that except for Christmas, this is the main shopping period of the year. Knowing that a strong economic withdrawal program would be the by-product of direct action, we felt that this would be the best time to bring pressure to bear on the merchants for the needed change.

Then it occurred to us that Birmingham's mayoralty election was coming up in March, and we speedily decided to postpone action until after election day. When we discovered that the Commissioner of Public Safety, Eugene "Bull" Connor, had piled up enough votes to be in the run-off, we decided again to postpone action until the day after the run-off so that the demonstrations could not be used to cloud the issues. Like many others, we waited to see Mr. Connor defeated, and to this end we endured postponement after postponement. Having aided in this community need, we felt that our direct-action program could be delayed no longer.

You may well ask: "Why direct action? Why sit-ins, marches, and so forth? Isn't negotiation a better path?" You are quite right in calling for negotiation. Indeed, this is the very purpose of direct action. Nonviolent direct action seeks to create such a crisis and foster such a tension that a community which has constantly refused to negotiate is forced to confront the issue. It seeks so to dramatize the issue that it can no longer be ignored. My citing the creation of tension as part of the work of the nonviolent-resister may sound rather shocking. But I must confess that I am not afraid of the word "tension." I have earnestly opposed violent tension, but there is a type of constructive, nonviolent tension which is necessary for growth. Just as Socrates felt that it was necessary to create a tension in the mind so that individuals could rise from the bondage of myths and halftruths to the unfettered realm of creative analysis and objective appraisal, so must we see the need for nonviolent gadflies to create the kind of tension in society that will help men rise from the dark depths of prejudice and racism to the majestic heights of understanding and brotherhood.

The purpose of our direct-action program is to create a situation so crisis-packed that it will inevitably open the door to negotiation. I therefore concur with you in your call for negotiation. Too long has our beloved Southland been bogged down in a tragic effort to live in monologue rather than dialogue.

One of the basic points in your statement is that the action that I and my associates have taken in Birmingham is untimely. Some have asked: "Why didn't you give the new city administration time to act?" The only answer that I can give to this query is that the new Birmingham administration must be prodded about as much as the outgoing one, before it will act. We are sadly mistaken if we feel that the election of Albert Boutwell as mayor will bring the millennium to Birmingham. While Mr. Boutwell is a much more gentle person than Mr. Connor, they are both segregationists, dedicated to maintenance of the status quo. I have hoped that Mr. Boutwell will be reasonable enough to see the futility of massive resistance to desegregation. But he will not see this without pressure from devotees of civil rights. My friends, I must say to you that we have not made a single gain in civil rights without determined legal and nonviolent pressure. Lamentably, it is an historical fact that privileged groups seldom give up their privileges voluntarily. Individuals may see the moral light and voluntarily give up their unjust posture; but as Reinhold Niebuhr has reminded us, groups tend to be more immoral than individuals.

We know through painful experience that freedom is never voluntarily given by the oppressor; it must be demanded by the oppressed. Frankly, I have yet to engage in a direct-action campaign that was "well timed" in view of those who have not suffered unduly from the disease of segregation. For years now I have heard the word "wait!" It rings in the ear of every Negro with piercing familiarity. This "Wait" has almost always meant "Never." We must come to see, with one of our distinguished jurists, that "justice too long delayed is justice denied."

We have waited for more than 340 years for our constitutional and God-given rights. The nations of Asia and Africa are moving with jetlike speed toward gaining political independence, but we still creep at horse-and-buggy pace toward gaining a cup of coffee at a lunch counter. Perhaps it is easy for those who have never felt the stinging darts of segregation to say, "Wait." But when you have seen vicious mobs lynch your mothers and fathers at will and drown your sisters and brothers at whim; when you have seen hate-filled policemen curse, kick, and even kill your black brothers and sisters; when you see the vast majority of your twenty million Negro brothers smothering in an airtight cage of poverty in the midst of an affluent society; when you suddenly find your tongue twisted and your speech stammering as you seek to explain to your six-year-old daughter why she can't go to the public amusement park that has just been advertised on television, and see tears welling up in her eyes when she is told that Funtown is closed to colored children, and see ominous clouds of inferiority beginning to form in her little mental sky, and see her beginning to distort her personality by developing an unconscious bitterness toward white people; when you have to concoct an answer for a five-year-old son who is asking, "Daddy, why do white people treat colored people so mean?"; when you take a cross-country drive and find it necessary to sleep night after night in the uncomfortable corners of your automobile because no motel will accept you; when you are humiliated day in and day out by nagging signs reading "white" and "colored"; when your first name becomes "Nigger," your middle name becomes "boy" (however old you are) and your last name becomes "John," and your wife and mother are never given the respected title "Mrs."; when you are harried by day and haunted by night by the fact that you are a Negro, living constantly at tiptoe stance, never quite knowing what to expect next, and are plagued with inner fears and outer resentments; when you are forever fighting a degenerating sense of "nobodiness" then you will understand why we find it difficult to wait. There comes a time when the cup of endurance runs over, and men are no longer willing to be plunged into the abyss of despair. I hope, sirs, you can understand our legitimate and unavoidable impatience.

You express a great deal of anxiety over our willingness to   15
break laws. This is certainly a legitimate concern. Since we so diligently urge people to obey the Supreme Court's decision of 1954 outlawing segregation in the public schools, at first glance it may seem rather paradoxical for us consciously to break laws. One may ask: "How can you advocate breaking some laws and obeying others?" The answer lies in the fact that there are two types of laws: just and unjust. I would be the first to advocate obeying just laws. One has not only a legal but a moral responsibility to obey just laws. Conversely, one has a moral responsibility to disobey unjust laws. I would agree with St. Augustine that "an unjust law is no law at all."

Now, what is the difference between the two? How does one determine whether a law is just or unjust? A just law is a man-made code that squares with the moral law or the law of God. An unjust law is a code that is out of Harmony with the moral law. To put it in the terms of St. Thomas Aquinas: An unjust law is a human law that is not rooted in eternal law and natural law. Any law that uplifts human personality is just. Any law that degrades human personality is unjust. All segregation statutes are unjust because segregation distorts the soul and damages the personality. It gives the segregator a false sense of superiority and the segregated a false sense of inferiority. Segregation, to use the terminology of the Jewish philosopher Martin Buber, substitutes an "I-it" relationship for an "I-thou" relationship and ends up relegating persons to the status of things. Hence segregation is not only politically, economically and sociologically unsound, it is morally wrong and sinful. Paul Tillich has said that sin is separation. Is not segregation an existential expression of man's tragic separation, his awful estrangement, his terrible sinfulness? Thus is it that I can urge men to obey the 1954 decision of the Supreme Court, for it is morally right; and I can urge them to disobey segregation ordinances, for they are morally wrong.

Let us consider a more concrete example of just and unjust laws. An unjust law is a code that a numerical or power majority group compels a minority group to obey but does not make binding on itself. This is difference made legal. By the same token, a just law is a code that a majority compels a minority to follow and that it is willing to follow itself. This is sameness made legal.

Let me give another explanation. A law is unjust if it is inflicted on a minority that, as a result of being denied the right to vote, had no part in enacting or devising the law. Who can say that the legislature of Alabama which set up that state's segregation laws was democratically elected? Throughout Alabama all sorts of devious methods are used to prevent Negroes from becoming registered voters, and there are some counties in which, even though Negroes constitute a majority of the population, not a single Negro is registered. Can any law enacted under such circumstances be considered democratically structured?

Sometimes a law is just on its face and unjust in its application. For instance, I have been arrested on a charge of parading without a permit. Now, there is nothing wrong in having an ordinance which requires a permit for a parade. But such an ordinance becomes unjust when it is used to maintain segregation and to deny citizens the First-Amendment privilege of peaceful assembly and protest.

I hope you are able to see the distinction I am trying to point   20
out. In no sense do I advocate evading or defying the law, as would the rabid segregationist. That would lead to anarchy. One who breaks an unjust law must do so openly, lovingly, and with a willingness to accept the penalty. I submit that an individual who breaks a law that conscience tells him is unjust, and who willingly accepts the penalty of imprisonment in order to arouse the conscience of the community over its injustice, is in reality expressing the highest respect for law.

Of course, there is nothing new about this kind of civil disobedience. It was evidenced sublimely in the refusal of Shadrach, Meshach, and Abednego to obey the laws of Nebuchadnezzar, on the ground that a higher moral law was at stake. It was practiced superbly by the early Christians, who were willing to face hungry lions and the excruciating pain of chopping blocks rather than submit to certain unjust laws of the Roman Empire. To a degree, academic freedom is a reality today because Socrates practiced civil disobedience. In our own nation, the Boston Tea Party represented a massive act of civil disobedience.

We should never forget that everything Adolf Hitler did in Germany was "legal" and everything the Hungarian freedom fighters did in Hungary was "illegal." It was "illegal" to aid and comfort a Jew in Hitler's Germany. Even so, I am sure that, had I lived in Germany at the time, I would have aided and comforted my Jewish brothers. If today I lived in a Communist country where certain principles dear to the Christian faith are suppressed, I would openly advocate disobeying that country's anti-religious laws.

I must make two honest confessions to you, my Christian and Jewish brothers. First, I must confess that over the past few years I have been gravely disappointed with the white moderate. I have almost reached the regrettable conclusion that the Negro's great stumbling block in his stride toward freedom is not the White Citizen's Councilor or the Ku Klux Klanner, but the white moderate, who is more devoted to "order" than to justice; who prefers a negative peace which is the absence of tension to a positive peace which is the presence of justice; who constantly says, "I agree with you in the goal you seek, but I cannot agree with your methods of direct action"; who paternalistically believes he can set the timetable for another man's freedom; who lives by a mythical concept of time and who constantly advises the Negro to wait for a "more convenient season." Shallow understanding from people of good will is more frustrating than absolute misunderstanding from people of ill will. Lukewarm acceptance is much more bewildering than outright rejection.

I had hoped that the white moderate would understand that law and order exist for the purpose of establishing justice and that when they fail in this purpose they become the dangerously structured dams that block the flow of social progress. I had hoped that the white moderate would understand that the present tension in the South is a necessary phase of the transition from an obnoxious negative peace, in which the Negro passively accepted his unjust plight, to a substantive and positive peace, in which all men will respect the dignity and worth of human personality. Actually, we who engage in nonviolent direct action are not the creators of tension. We merely bring to the surface the hidden tension that is already alive. We bring it out in the open, where it can be seen and dealt with. Like a boil that can never be cured so long as it is covered up but must be opened with all its ugliness to the natural medicines of air and light, injustice must be exposed with all the tension its exposure creates, to the light of human conscience and the air of national opinion, before it can be cured.

In your statement you assert that our actions, even though   25
peaceful, must be condemned because they precipitate violence. But is this a logical assertion? Isn't this like condemning a robbed man because his possession of money precipitated the evil act of robbery? Isn't this like condemning Socrates because his unswerving commitment to truth and his philosophical inquiries precipitated the act by the misguided populace in which they made him drink hemlock? Isn't this like condemning Jesus because his unique God-consciousness and never-ceasing devotion to God's will precipitated the evil act of crucifixion? We must come to see that, as the federal courts have consistently affirmed, it is wrong to urge an individual to cease his efforts to gain his basic constitutional rights because the quest may precipitate violence. Society must protect the robbed and punish the robber.

I had also hoped that the white moderate would reject the myth concerning time in relations to the struggle for freedom. I have just received a letter from a white brother in Texas. He writes: "All Christians know that the colored people will receive equal rights eventually, but it is possible that you are in too great a religious hurry. It has taken Christianity almost two thousand years to accomplish what it has. The teachings of Christ take time to come to earth." Such an attitude stems from a tragic misconception of time, from the strangely irrational notion that there is something in the very flow of time will inevitably cure all ills. Actually, time itself is neutral; it can be used either destructively or constructively. More and more I feel that the people of ill will have used time much more effectively than have the people of good will. We will have to repent in the generation not merely for the hateful words and actions of the bad people, but for the appalling silence of the good people. Human progress never rolls in on wheels of inevitability; it comes through the tireless efforts of men willing to be coworkers with God, and without this hard work, time itself becomes an ally of the forces of stagnation. We must use time creatively, in the knowledge that the time is always ripe to do right. Now is the time to make real the promise of democracy and transform our pending national elegy into a creative psalm of brotherhood. Now is the time to lift our national policy from the quicksand of racial injustice to the solid rock of human dignity.

You speak of our activity in Birmingham as extreme. At first I was rather disappointed that fellow clergymen would see my nonviolent efforts as those of an extremist. I began thinking about the fact that I stand in the middle of two opposing forces in the Negro community. One is a force of complacency, made up in part of Negroes who, as a result of long years of oppression, are so drained of self-respect and a sense of "somebodiness" that they have adjusted to segregation; and in part of a few middle-class Negroes who, because of a degree of academic and economic security and because in some ways they profit by segregation, have become insensitive to the problems of the masses. The other force is one of bitterness and hatred, and it comes perilously close to advocating violence. It is expressed in the various black nationalist groups that are springing up across the nation, the largest and best-known being Elijah Muhammad's Muslim movement. Nourished by the Negro's frustration over the continued existence of racial discrimination, this movement is made up of people who have lost faith in America, who have absolutely repudiated Christianity, and who have concluded that the white man is an incorrigible "devil."

I have tried to stand between these two forces, saying that we need emulate neither the "do-nothingism" of the complacent nor the hatred and despair of the black nationalist. For there is the more excellent way of love and nonviolent protest. I am grateful to God that, through the influence of the Negro church, the way of nonviolence became an integral part of our struggle.

If this philosophy had not emerged, by now many streets of the South would, I am convinced, be flowing with blood. And I am further convinced that if our white brothers dismiss as "rabble-rousers" and "outside agitators" those of us who employ nonviolent direct action, and if they refuse to support our nonviolent efforts, millions of Negroes will, out of frustration and despair, seek solace and security in black-nationalist ideologies—a development that would inevitably lead to a frightening racial nightmare.

Oppressed people cannot remain oppressed forever. The   30
yearning for freedom eventually manifests itself, and that is what has happened to the American Negro. Something within has reminded him of his birthright of freedom, and something without has reminded him that it can be gained. Consciously or unconsciously, he has been caught up by the Zeitgeist, and with his black brothers of Africa and his brown and yellow brothers of Asia, South America, and the Caribbean, the United States Negro is moving with a sense of great urgency toward the promised land of racial justice. If one recognizes this vital urge that has engulfed the Negro community, one should readily understand why public demonstrations are taking place. The Negro has many pent-up resentments and latent frustrations, and he must release them. So let him march; let him make prayer pilgrimages to the city hall; let him go on freedom rides—and try to understand why he must do so. If his repressed emotions are not released in nonviolent ways, they will seek expression through violence; this is not a threat but a fact of history. So I have not said to my people, "Get rid of your discontent." Rather, I have tried to say that this normal and healthy discontent can be channeled into the creative outlet of nonviolent direct action. And now this approach is being termed extremist.

But though I was initially disappointed at being categorized as an extremist, as I continued to think about the matter I gradually gained a measure of satisfaction from the label. Was not Jesus an extremist for love: "Love your enemies, bless them that curse you, do good to them that hate you, and pray for them which despitefully use you, and persecute you." Was not Amos an extremist for justice: "Let justice roll down like waters and righteousness like an ever-flowing stream." Was not Paul an extremist for the Christian gospel: "I bear in my body the marks of the Lord Jesus." Was not Martin Luther an extremist: "Here I stand; I cannot do otherwise, so help me God." And John Bunyan: "I will stay in jail to the end of my days before I make a butchery of my conscience." And Abraham Lincoln: "This nation cannot survive half slave and half free." And Thomas Jefferson: "We hold these truths to be self-evident, that all men are created equal. . . ." So the question is not whether we will be extremists, but what kind of extremists we will be. Will we be extremists for hate or for love? Will we be extremists for the preservation of injustice or for the extension of justice? In that dramatic scene on Calvary's hill three men were crucified. We must never forget that all three were crucified for the same crime—the crime of extremism. Two were extremists for immorality, and thus fell below their environment. The other, Jesus Christ, was an extremist for love, truth, and goodness, and thereby rose above his environment. Perhaps the South, the nation, and the world are in dire need of creative extremists.

I had hoped that the white moderate would see this need. Perhaps I was too optimistic; perhaps I expected too much. I suppose I should have realized that few members of the oppressor race can understand the deep groans and passionate yearnings of the oppressed race, and still fewer have the vision to see that injustice must be rooted out by strong, persistent, and determined action. I am thankful, however, that some of our white brothers in the South have grasped the meaning of this social revolution and committed themselves to it. They are still all too few in quantity, but they are big in quality. Some—such as Ralph McGill, Lillian Smith, Harry Golden, James McBride Dabbs, Ann Braden, and Sarah Patton Boyle—have written about our struggle in eloquent and prophetic terms. Others have marched with us down nameless streets of the South. They have languished in filthy, roach-infested jails, suffering the abuse and brutality of policemen who view them as "dirty nigger-lovers." Unlike so many of their moderate brothers and sisters, they have recognized the urgency of the moment and sensed the need for powerful "action" antidotes to combat the disease of segregation.

Let me take note of my other major disappointment. I have been so greatly disappointed with the white church and its leadership. Of course, there are some notable exceptions. I am not unmindful of the fact that each of you has taken some significant stands on this issue. I commend you, Reverend Stallings, for your Christian stand on this past Sunday, in welcoming Negroes to your worship service on a nonsegregated basis. I commend the Catholic leaders of this state for integrating Spring Hill College several years ago.

But despite these notable exceptions, I must honestly reiterate that I have been disappointed with the church. I do not say this as one of those negative critics who can always find something wrong with the church. I say this as a minister of the gospel, who loves the church; who was nurtured in its bosom; who has been sustained by its spiritual blessings and who will remain true to it as long as the cord of life shall lengthen.

When I was suddenly catapulted into the leadership of the   35
bus protest in Montgomery, Alabama, a few years ago, I felt we would be supported by the white church. I felt that the ministers, priests, and rabbis of the South would be among our strongest allies. Instead, some have been outright opponents, refusing to understand the freedom movement and misrepresenting its leaders; all too many others have been more cautious than courageous and have remained silent behind the anesthetizing security of stained-glass windows.

In spite of my shattered dreams, I came to Birmingham with the hope that the white religious leadership of this community would see the justice of our cause and, with deep moral concern, would serve as the channel through which our just grievances could reach the power structure. I had hoped that each of you would understand. But again I have been disappointed.

I have heard numerous southern religious leaders admonish their worshipers to comply with a desegregation decision because it is the law, but I have longed to hear white ministers declare: "Follow this decree because integration is morally right and because the Negro is your brother." In the midst of blatant injustices inflicted upon the Negro, I have watched white churchmen stand on the sideline and mouth pious irrelevancies and sanctimonious trivialities. In the midst of a mighty struggle to rid our nation of racial and economic injustice, I have heard many ministers say: "Those are social issues, with which the gospel has no real concern." And I have watched many churches commit themselves to a completely otherworldly religion which makes a strange, un-Biblical distinction between body and soul, between the sacred and the secular.

I have traveled the length and breadth of Alabama, Mississippi, and all the other southern states. On sweltering summer days and crisp autumn mornings I have looked at the South's beautiful churches with their lofty spires pointing heavenward.

I have beheld the impressive outlines of her massive religious-education buildings. Over and over I have found myself asking: "What kind of people worship here? Who is their God? Where were their voices when the lips of Governor Barnett dripped with words of interposition and nullification? Where were they when Governor Wallace gave a clarion call for defiance and hatred? Where were their voices of support when bruised and weary Negro men and women decided to rise from the dark dungeons of complacency to the bright hills of creative protest?"

Yes, these questions are still in my mind. In deep disappointment I have wept over the laxity of the church. But be assured that my tears have been tears of love. Yes, I love the church. How could I do otherwise? I am in the rather unique position of being the son, the grandson, and the great-grandson of preachers. Yes, I see the church as the body of Christ. But, oh! How we have blemished and scarred that body through social neglect and through fear of being nonconformists.

There was a time when the church was very powerful—in the time when the early Christians rejoiced at being deemed worthy to suffer for what they believed. In those days the church was not merely a thermometer that recorded the ideas and principles of popular opinion; it was a thermostat that transformed the mores of society. Whenever the early Christians entered a town, the people in power became disturbed and immediately sought to convict the Christians for being "disturbers of the peace" and "outside agitators." But the Christians pressed on, in the conviction that they were "a colony of heaven," called to obey God rather than man. Small in number, they were big in commitment. They were too God-intoxicated to be "astronomically intimidated." By their effort and example they brought an end to such ancient evils as infanticide and gladiatorial contests.

Things are different now. So often the contemporary church is a weak, ineffectual voice with an uncertain sound. So often it is an archdefender of the status quo. Far from being disturbed by the presence of the church, the power structure of the average community is consoled by the church's silent—and often even vocal—sanction of things as they are.

But the judgment of God is upon the church as never before. If today's church does not recapture the sacrificial spirit of the early church, it will lose its authenticity, forfeit the loyalty of millions, and be dismissed as an irrelevant social club with no meaning for the twentieth century. Every day I meet young people whose disappointment with the church has turned into outright disgust.

Perhaps I have once again been too optimistic. Is organized religion too inextricably bound to the status quo to save our nation and the world? Perhaps I must turn my faith to the inner spiritual church, the church within the church, as the true *ekklesia* and the hope of the world. But again I am thankful to God that some noble souls from the ranks of organized religion have broken loose from the paralyzing chains of conformity and joined us as active partners in the struggle for freedom. They have left their secure congregations and walked the streets of Albany, Georgia, with us. They have gone down the highways of the South on tortuous rides for freedom. Yes, they have gone to jail with us. Some have been dismissed from their churches, have lost the support of their bishops and fellow ministers. But they have acted in the faith that right defeated is stronger than evil triumphant. Their witness has been the spiritual salt that has preserved the true meaning of the gospel in these troubled times. They have carved a tunnel of hope through the dark mountain of disappointment.

I hope the church as a whole will meet the challenge of this decisive hour. But even if the church does not come to the aid of justice, I have no despair about the future. I have no fear about the outcome of our struggle in Birmingham, even if our motives are at present misunderstood. We will reach the goal of freedom in Birmingham and all over the nation, because the goal of America if freedom. Abused and scorned though we may be, our destiny is tied up with America's destiny. Before the pilgrims landed at Plymouth, we were here. For more than two centuries our forebears labored in this country without wages; they made cotton king; they built the homes of their masters while suffering gross injustice and shameful humiliation—and yet out of bottomless vitality they continued to thrive and develop. If the inexpressible cruelties of slavery could not stop us, the opposition we now face will surely fail. We will win our freedom because the sacred heritage of our nation and the eternal will of God are embodied in our echoing demands.

Before closing I feel impelled to mention one other point in   45
your statement that has troubled me profoundly. You warmly

commended the Birmingham police force for keeping "order" and "preventing violence." I doubt that you would so quickly commend the policemen if you were to observe their ugly and inhumane treatment of Negroes here in the city jail; if you were to watch them push and curse old Negro women and young Negro girls; if you were to see them slap and kick Negro men and young boys; if you were to observe them, as they did on two occasions, refuse to give us food because we wanted to sing our grace together. I cannot join you in your praise of the Birmingham police department.

It is true that the police have exercised a degree of discipline in handling the demonstrations. In this sense they have conducted themselves rather "nonviolently" in public. But for what purpose? To preserve the evil system of segregation. Over the past few years I have consistently preached that nonviolence demands that the means we use must be as pure as the ends we seek. I have tried to make clear that it is wrong to use immoral means to attain moral ends. But now I must affirm that it is just as wrong, or perhaps even more so, to use moral means to preserve immoral ends. Perhaps Mr. Connor and his policemen have been rather nonviolent in public, as was Chief Pritchett in Albany, Georgia, but they have used the moral means of nonviolence to maintain the immoral end of racial injustice. As T. S. Eliot has said, "The last temptation is the greatest treason: To do the right deed for the wrong reason."

I wish you had commended the Negro sit-inners and demonstrators of Birmingham for their sublime courage, their willingness to suffer, and their amazing discipline in the midst of great provocation. One day the South will recognize its real heroes. They will be the James Merediths, with the noble sense of purpose that enables them to face jeering and hostile mobs, and with the agonizing loneliness that characterizes the life of the pioneer. They will be old, oppressed, battered Negro women, symbolized in a seventy-two-year-old woman in Montgomery, Alabama, who rose up with a sense of dignity and when her people decided not to ride segregated buses, and who responded with ungrammatical profundity to one who inquired about her weariness: "My feets is tired, but my soul is at rest." They will be the young high school and college students, the young ministers of the gospel and a host of their elders, courageously and nonviolently sitting in at lunch counters and willingly going to jail for conscience' sake. One day the South will know that when these disinherited children of God sat down at lunch counters, they were in reality standing up for what is best in the American dream and for the most sacred values in our Judaeo-Christian heritage, thereby bringing our nation back to those great wells of democracy which were dug deep by the founding fathers in their formulation of the Constitution and the Declaration of Independence.

Never before have I written so long a letter. I'm afraid it is much too long to take your precious time. I can assure you that it would have been much shorter if I had been writing from a comfortable desk, but what else can one do when he is alone in a narrow jail cell, other than write long letters, think long thoughts, and pray long prayers?

If I have said anything in this letter that overstates the truth and indicates an unreasonable impatience, I beg you to forgive me. If I have said anything that understates the truth and indicates my having a patience that allows me to settle for anything less than brotherhood, I beg God to forgive me.

I hope this letter finds you strong in the faith. I also hope that circumstances will soon make it possible for me to meet each   50 of you, not as an integrationist or a civil-rights leader but as a fellow clergyman and a Christian brother. Let us all hope that the dark clouds of racial prejudice will soon pass away and the deep fog of misunderstanding will be lifted from our fear-drenched communities, and in some not too distant tomorrow the radiant stars of love and brotherhood will shine over our great nation with all their scintillating beauty.

Yours for the cause of Peace and Brotherhood,

Martin Luther King, Jr.

Questions about the Passage

1. What are the four steps characterizing a nonviolent campaign? Why do you think King explains them so thoroughly?
2. In paragraphs 2, 5, 12, 25, 27, and 45, King introduces points from the Clergymen's Letter that he wishes to refute. Locate and state each of these points and briefly summarize (one or two sentences) his answer to each criticism.

3. Examine carefully the lengthy periodic sentence in paragraph 14. Which examples do you find most powerful? Why? Determine the principle by which King orders these examples. How does the order in which he arranges them contribute to their effectiveness?

4. How does King define just and unjust laws? How does he distinguish between them?

5. How does King describe the civil disobedient? Why do you think he chooses the particular historical examples he uses?

6. Note the following word usage: in paragraph 23 King confesses he is "gravely disappointed in the white moderate"; in paragraph 27 he is "rather disappointed" in his fellow clergymen; and in paragraph 33 he is "so greatly disappointed with the white church." Explain the reasons for the disappointment in each case. Why do you think he chooses the adverbs he does?

7. In paragraph 31 King lists multiple examples of extremists. Identify each of them and decide why King included them. Can you think of any other extremists he might also have included?

8. Working in groups, decide how to outline this document. Divide it into its main parts and name each section. Then subdivide each section as appropriate. Finally, justify your outline to the rest of the class.

Questions about the Argument

1. How does King demonstrate his ethos as an arguer? What kind of person does he reveal himself to be? Look beyond his rhetorical strategies to infer what qualities of mind and heart he possesses, what values he espouses. Examine the "Letter" carefully to collect examples of the various ways he uses other authorities to bolster his assertions.

2. How has King's reputation changed over time? To answer this question, you might look at responses to his letter from the time he wrote it, at evaluations of his contributions immediately after his death (editorials, articles), and at current estimations of his contribution (for example, editorials written for Martin Luther King Day).35

3. King clearly identifies his initial audience by labeling this a letter in response to the clergymen's letter. What rhetorical and argumentative moves does he make to appeal to this audience? What evidence is there that he also had a wider audience in mind?

4. Paragraph 14 is often cited as an excellent example of pathos. Is it? Why? Do you think the appeal to pathos is a legitimate way of convincing an audience? What other examples of pathos do you find in this letter?

5. This letter is also a treasure trove of logical strategies: Collect all the examples of induction, deduction, argument by analogy, use of definition and distinctions to underpin an argument, and refutation that you can find. Explain why you think each strategy is or is not effective. Which had the most impact on you?

Writing Assignments

Conversations

1. Imagine that you are the host of an issues-dominated news program (like the Lehrer News Hour) known for wide-ranging discussion. Your topic is civil disobedience, and you have snared Sophocles, Thoreau, and Martin Luther King as your discussants. Your role is to lay out the issue for the audience at the start of the program, to ask the essential questions that allow for a thorough and orderly exploration of the issues, to get the discussants interacting with one another, to keep the discussion on track, to probe, to challenge the participants, and to sum up when necessary, especially at the end. Some questions you might want to ask are: What kinds of laws and situations warrant civil disobedience? What are the guidelines for properly undertaking civil disobedience?

2. Suppose you are moderating another discussion, this time in the weeks following *Kristalnacht*, November 9, 1938. Your audience consists of German Jews, who listen to speakers who advocate different responses—some violent and some nonviolent resistance to Nazi persecution. Because it is 1938, your audience does not know about the death camps, although so-called concentration and labor camps already exist. Two speakers are Mahatma Gandhi and Rabbi Magnes. Another speaker urges the audience to take up arms against the Nazis. Report what Gandhi and Magnes each say in response to one another and in response to the advocate of violent resistance. Also allow Gandhi and Magnes to answer a few questions from the audience.

3. Imagine Thoreau, Tolstoy, and Gandhi meeting over coffee. They have never met in person before, but Tolstoy and Gandhi have corresponded, and they both know Thoreau's work. You're

sitting at the next table and cannot avoid hearing what they have to say. What current event gets them talking about civil disobedience? Who takes the lead in the conversation? What positions do they take? Where do they agree and disagree with each other? Do they come to any conclusions?

Writing Sequence One: The Case For or Against Nonviolent Civil Disobedience

1. In a two-page paper, explore your own thinking about civil disobedience. What do you find attractive about it? What might you find worrisome about it? To what extent do you think it is likely to work? Can you think of historical examples where civil disobedience has had a real impact?

2. Using Gandhi's writings on *satyagraha* printed in this chapter, construct an extended definition of civil disobedience as Gandhi would define it. What is its formal definition? What are its assumptions? How is it related to *satyagraha, ahimsa,* and noncooperation? What is it *not*? What are examples of it? What is its purpose? Can it achieve its purpose?

3. How has Martin Luther King, Jr., adopted Gandhi's thinking about civil disobedience and nonviolence? Compare and contrast Gandhi's rules for the *satyagrahi* and King's steps for nonviolent direct action in "Letter from Birmingham Jail."

4. Now make your own case for or against civil disobedience, drawing on both Gandhi and King as your sources. You may also find Tolstoy helpful. Be sure to have a strong claim, good reasons to support the claim, and very specific examples to back up each reason.

Writing Sequence Two: A Serious Debate

1. Prepare for a debate on Gandhi's proposition that "Satyagraha is always superior to armed resistance" (*Harijan,* 17 March 1946). First research the affirmative position by reviewing Gandhi's analysis of the meaning of *satyagraha* and King's defense of nonviolent demonstrations, as well as historical instances from India and the United States. Write a two-page argument in brief to summarize the position.

2. Next consider the contrary position. You might look at the clergymen's letter, Gandhi's own reasons for suspending the anti-Rowlatt action and his reasoning about protecting a sister against rape, and Magnes's objection to Gandhi's position on Hitler. Again write up your argument in brief.

3. Now write the debate, taking care to present each position fairly and making sure to rebut the points made by each side. If you are an experienced debater, you might want to follow the rules of formal debate.

6

The Abolitionist Movement

We begin this chapter on the great American abolitionist movement with the *Declaration of Independence*. The abolitionists looked to the *Declaration* as a model and inspiration. The United States should be a nation that did not merely proclaim that "all men are created equal" but that also observed this idea in law. And some abolitionists as well as slaves believed that if government could not be changed by peaceful means, then revolution would be once again justified.

The *Declaration* did not condone slavery, but the Constitution clearly kept slavery as a legal system. By 1830, there were 2 million slaves out of an American population of 12,500,000. A few Americans had opposed slavery from its very beginnings; Quakers had been active in renouncing slavery since the early eighteenth century. But the powerful reform abolitionist movement really dates from the 1820s. An important early manifesto of the movement is William Lloyd Garrison's declaration of the American Anti-Slavery Society. To Garrison and his followers, it was clear that God's law and American law as laid out in the Constitution were at odds.

Garrison's gifted follower, the former slave Frederick Douglass, broke with his mentor as he came to believe in political action to end slavery. During the 1840s, Douglass and many other abolitionists, both white and black, aided escaping slaves to reach freedom. With the passage of the Fugitive Slave Act of 1850, Douglass and others were confronted with a harsh federal law that authorized federal marshals to aid masters in tracking and capturing their escaped slaves, substituted special federal commissioners for juries to hear the cases of alleged fugitives, and made it a federal crime to help slaves flee. Every time a slave was helped to Canada on the Underground Railroad, abolitionist "conductors" were breaking federal law.

Like other reform movements in the United States and around the world, abolitionism embraced a variety of opinion. At one end of the spectrum, abolitionists relied upon preaching, rallies, and writing to change the moral atmosphere of the country. At the other end, John Brown's 1859 seizure of a federal arsenal at Harpers Ferry, Virginia, represented the belief that only violent opposition could end the immorality of slavery. Between the two extremes lie various acts of civil disobedience undertaken to help individual slaves and to bring an end to the "peculiar institution" of American slavery.

Thomas Jefferson, *The Declaration of Independence*

The Declaration of Independence, approved July 4, 1776, as "The Unanimous Declaration of the Thirteen United States of America" by the Second Continental Congress, announced the formal separation of the colonies from Great Britain. Thomas Jefferson (1743–1826), John Adams, Benjamin Franklin, Roger Sherman, and Robert R. Livingston made up the drafting committee, but Jefferson wrote the initial draft, which was revised once by Franklin, Adams, and Jefferson before it went to Congress and then was revised a second time in Congress. The document established the new revolutionary government and allowed it to seek aid from foreign countries in its war with Great Britain. *The Declaration* draws on ideas of the Enlightenment, especially those of John Locke, and puts them into political practice as well as justifying, through a series of grievances, the break with British rule. Since its proclamation, *The Declaration* has influenced and inspired revolutionary movements throughout the world.

IN CONGRESS, July 4, 1776.

The Unanimous Declaration of the Thirteen United States of America,
When in the Course of human events, it becomes necessary for one people to dissolve the political bands which have connected them with another, and to assume among the powers of the earth, the separate and equal station to which the Laws of Nature and of Nature's God entitle them, a decent respect to

the opinions of mankind requires that they should declare the causes which impel them to the separation.

We hold these truths to be self-evident, that all men are created equal, that they are endowed by their Creator with certain unalienable Rights, that among these are Life, Liberty and the pursuit of Happiness.—That to secure these rights, Governments are instituted among Men, deriving their just powers from the consent of the governed,—That whenever any Form of Government becomes destructive of these ends, it is the Right of the People to alter or to abolish it, and to institute new Government, laying its foundation on such principles and organizing its powers in such form, as to them shall seem most likely to effect their Safety and Happiness. Prudence, indeed, will dictate that Governments long established should not be changed for light and transient causes; and accordingly all experience hath shewn, that mankind are more disposed to suffer, while evils are sufferable, than to right themselves by abolishing the forms to which they are accustomed. But when a long train of abuses and usurpations, pursuing invariably the same Object evinces a design to reduce them under absolute Despotism, it is their right, it is their duty, to throw off such Government, and to provide new Guards for their future security.—Such has been the patient sufferance of these Colonies; and such is now the necessity which constrains them to alter their former Systems of Government. The history of the present King of Great Britain is a history of repeated injuries and usurpations, all having in direct object the establishment of an absolute Tyranny over these States. To prove this, let Facts be submitted to a candid world.

He has refused his Assent to Laws, the most wholesome and necessary for the public good.

He has forbidden his Governors to pass Laws of immediate and pressing importance, unless suspended in their operation till his Assent should be obtained; and when so suspended, he has utterly neglected to attend to them.

He has refused to pass other Laws for the accommodation of large districts of people, unless those people would relinquish the right of Representation in the Legislature, a right inestimable to them and formidable to tyrants only.

He has called together legislative bodies at places unusual, uncomfortable, and distant from the depository of their public Records, for the sole purpose of fatiguing them into compliance with his measures.

He has dissolved Representative Houses repeatedly, for opposing with manly firmness his invasions on the rights of the people.

He has refused for a long time, after such dissolutions, to cause others to be elected; whereby the Legislative powers, incapable of Annihilation, have returned to the People at large for their exercise; the State remaining in the mean time exposed to all the dangers of invasion from without, and convulsions within.

He has endeavoured to prevent the population of these States; for that purpose obstructing the Laws for Naturalization of Foreigners; refusing to pass others to encourage their migrations hither, and raising the conditions of new Appropriations of Lands.

He has obstructed the Administration of Justice, by refusing his Assent to Laws for establishing Judiciary powers.

He has made Judges dependent on his Will alone, for the tenure of their offices, and the amount and payment of their salaries.

He has erected a multitude of New Offices, and sent hither swarms of Officers to harrass our people, and eat out their substance.

He has kept among us, in times of peace, Standing Armies without the Consent of our legislatures.

He has affected to render the Military independent of and superior to the Civil power.

He has combined with others to subject us to a jurisdiction foreign to our constitution, and unacknowledged by our laws; giving his Assent to their Acts of pretended Legislation:

For Quartering large bodies of armed troops among us:

For protecting them, by a mock Trial, from punishment for any Murders which they should commit on the Inhabitants of these States:

For cutting off our Trade with all parts of the world:

For imposing Taxes on us without our Consent:

For depriving us in many cases, of the benefits of Trial by Jury:

For transporting us beyond Seas to be tried for pretended offences:

For abolishing the free System of English Laws in a neighbouring Province, establishing therein an Arbitrary government, and enlarging its Boundaries so as to render it at once an example and fit instrument for introducing the same absolute rule into these Colonies:

For taking away our Charters, abolishing our most valuable Laws, and altering fundamentally the Forms of our Governments:

For suspending our own Legislatures, and declaring themselves invested with power to legislate for us in all cases whatsoever.

He has abdicated Government here, by declaring us out of his Protection and waging War against us.

He has plundered our seas, ravaged our Coasts, burnt our towns, and destroyed the lives of our people.

He is at this time transporting large Armies of foreign Mercenaries to compleat the works of death, desolation and tyranny, already begun with circumstances of Cruelty & perfidy scarcely paralleled in the most barbarous ages, and totally unworthy the Head of a civilized nation.

He has constrained our fellow Citizens taken Captive on the high Seas to bear Arms against their Country, to become the executioners of their friends and Brethren, or to fall themselves by their Hands.

He has excited domestic insurrections amongst us, and has endeavoured to bring on the inhabitants of our frontiers, the merciless Indian Savages, whose known rule of warfare, is an undistinguished destruction of all ages, sexes and conditions.

In every stage of these Oppressions We have Petitioned for Redress in the most humble terms: Our repeated Petitions have been answered only by repeated injury. A Prince whose character is thus marked by every act which may define a Tyrant, is unfit to be the ruler of a free people.

Nor have We been wanting in attentions to our British brethren. We have warned them from time to time of attempts by their legislature to extend an unwarrantable jurisdiction over us. We have reminded them of the circumstances of our emigration and settlement here. We have appealed to their native justice and magnanimity, and we have conjured them by the ties of our common kindred to disavow these usurpations, which would inevitably interrupt our connections and correspondence. They too have been deaf to the voice of justice and of consanguinity. We must, therefore, acquiesce in the necessity, which denounces our Separation, and hold them, as we hold the rest of mankind, Enemies in War, in Peace Friends.

We, therefore, the Representatives of the united States of America, in General Congress, Assembled, appealing to the Supreme Judge of the world for the rectitude of our intentions, do, in the Name, and by Authority of the good People of these Colonies, solemnly publish and declare, That these United Colonies are, and of Right ought to be Free and Independent States; that they are Absolved from all Allegiance to the British Crown, and that all political connection between them and the State of Great Britain, is and ought to be totally dissolved; and that as Free and Independent States, they have full Power to levy War, conclude Peace, contract Alliances, establish Commerce, and to do all other Acts and Things which Independent States may of right do. And for the support of this Declaration, with a firm reliance on the protection of divine Providence, we mutually pledge to each other our Lives, our Fortunes and our sacred Honor.

Questions about the Passage

1. Outline the passage. What are the major sections into which you would divide it? What principles of classification have you used to make your divisions?
2. Jefferson includes a long, undivided list of grievances. Into what subcategories might they be divided? Look at the verbs he uses; consider the types of grievances he lists. Defend your decision.
3. What principles articulated by Jefferson might support civil disobedience?

Questions about the Argument

1. Do you think the truths that Jefferson enunciates in his second paragraph are indeed "self-evident"? Might his immediate audience have seen them differently?

2. Throughout the *Declaration*, identify words that carry emotional weight. To which emotions do they appeal?
3. The *Declaration* is often used as an example of effective argument. Make a case for its efficacy. How does Jefferson use appeals to ethos, audience, logos, and pathos to defend his position?
4. Why does this document belong in a casebook on civil disobedience?

William Lloyd Garrison, "Declaration of the National Anti-Slavery Convention"

One of the most powerful and influential voices for the abolition of slavery, William Lloyd Garrison (1805–1879) worked tirelessly his entire life for the end of slavery, the equal treatment of freed slaves, and the emancipation and full rights of women. As a young man, Garrison became convinced that slavery was a sin and that it must end immediately. He refused to consider any gradual elimination of slavery or compensation to slaveholders, and he rejected the prevailing notion of recolonization of the slaves to Africa. Garrison argued forcefully for his beliefs, which placed him on the radical fringe of abolitionism in the late 1820s and 1830s. On January 1, 1831, he began publication in Boston of *The Liberator*, which did not cease publication until the passage of the Thirteenth Amendment outlawing slavery in 1865. In his opening editorial, Garrison declared, "I *will be* as harsh as truth, and as uncompromising as justice. On this subject, I do not wish to think, or speak, or write, with moderation." For Garrison, abolition was a religious and moral crusade but not a political one; the Constitution, he believed, had betrayed the principles of the Bible and the *Declaration of Independence* and in fact condoned slavery.

The American Anti-Slavery Society was founded in December 1833 in Philadelphia with sixty-two white male delegates, four white women, and two black men at the convention. Garrison wrote the manifesto below for the convention. In 1840, the abolitionist movement split over the use of political means—Garrison and his followers continued to promote the methods of moral suasion proclaimed in the declaration of the AAAS, but others supported political action to change government policies on slavery. Garrisonians also refused to divide abolitionism from women's rights as the founders of the rival American and Foreign Anti-Slavery Society preferred. As you read the document, consider Garrison's attitudes toward law and toward the example of the American Revolution.

The Convention, assembled in the City of Philadelphia to organize a National Anti-Slavery Society, promptly seize the opportunity to promulgate the following DECLARATION OF SENTIMENTS, as cherished by them in relation to the enslavement of one-sixth portion of the American people.

More than fifty-seven years have elapsed since a band of patriots convened in this place, to devise measures for the deliverance of this country from a foreign yoke. The corner-stone upon which they founded the TEMPLE OF FREEDOM was broadly this—"that all men are created equal; that they are endowed by their Creator with certain inalienable rights; that among these are life, LIBERTY, and the pursuit of happiness." At the sound of their trumpet-call, three millions of people rose up as from the sleep of death, and rushed to the strife of blood; deeming it more glorious to die instantly as freemen, than desirable to live one hour as slaves.—They were few in number—poor in resources; but the honest conviction that TRUTH, JUSTICE, and RIGHT were on their side, made them invincible.

We have met together for the achievement of an enterprise, without which, that of our fathers is incomplete, and which, for its magnitude, solemnity, and probable results upon the destiny of the world, as far transcends theirs, as moral truth does physical force.

In purity of motive, in earnestness of zeal, in decision of purpose, in intrepidity of action, in steadfastness of faith, in sincerity of spirit, we would not be inferior to them.

Their principles led them to wage war against their oppressors, and to spill human blood like water, in order to be free. *Ours* forbid the doing of evil that good may come, and lead us to reject, and to entreat the oppressed to reject, the use of all carnal weapons for deliverance from bondage—relying solely upon those which are spiritual, and mighty through God to the pulling down of strong holds.

Their measures were physical resistance—the marshalling in arms—the hostile array—the mortal encounter. *Ours* shall be such only as the opposition of moral purity to moral corruption—the destruction of error by the potency of truth—the overthrow of prejudice by the power of love—and the abolition of slavery by the spirit of repentance.

5

Their grievances, great as they were, were trifling in comparison with the wrongs and sufferings of those for whom we plead. Our fathers were never slaves—never bought and sold like cattle—never shut out from the light of knowledge and religion—never subjected to the lash of brutal taskmasters.

But those, for whose emancipation we are striving,—constituting at the present time at least one-sixth part of our countrymen,—are recognised by the laws, and treated by their fellow beings, as marketable commodities—as goods and chattels—as brute beasts;—are plundered daily of the fruits of their toil without redress;—really enjoy no constitutional nor legal protection from licentious and murderous outrages upon their persons;—are ruthlessly torn asunder—the tender babe from the arms of its frantic mother—the heart-broken wife from her weeping husband—at the caprice or pleasure of irresponsible tyrants;—and, for the crime of having a dark complexion, suffer the pangs of hunger, the infliction of stripes, and the ignominy of brutal servitude. They are kept in heathenish darkness by laws expressly enacted to make their instruction a criminal offence.

These are the prominent circumstances in the condition of more than TWO MILLIONS of our people, the proof of which may be found in thousands of indisputable facts, and in the laws of the slaveholding States.

Hence we maintain—   10

That in view of the civil and religious privileges of this nation, the guilt of its oppression is unequalled by any other on the face of the earth;—and, therefore,

That it is bound to repent instantly, to undo the heavy burden, to break every yoke, and to let the oppressed go free.

We further maintain—

That no man has a right to enslave or imbrute his brother—to hold or acknowledge him, for one moment, as a piece of merchandise—to keep back his hire by fraud—or to brutalize his mind by denying him the means of intellectual, social and moral improvement.

The right to enjoy liberty is inalienable. To invade it, is to usurp   15
the prerogative of Jehovah. Every man has a right to his own body—to the products of his own labor—to the protection of

law—and to the common advantages of society. It is piracy to buy or steal a native African, and subject him to servitude. Surely the sin is as great to enslave an AMERICAN as an AFRICAN.

Therefore we believe and affirm—

That there is no difference, *in principle,* between the African slave trade and American slavery;

That every American citizen, who retains a human being in involuntary bondage, is [according to Scripture] a MAN-STEALER;

That the slaves ought instantly to be set free, and brought under the protection of law;

That if they had lived from the time of Pharaoh down to   20 the present period, and had been entailed through successive generations, their right to be free could never have been alienated, but their claims would have constantly risen in solemnity;

That all those laws which are now in force, admitting the right of slavery, are therefore before God utterly null and void; being an audacious usurpation of the Divine prerogative, a daring infringement on the law of nature, a base overthrow of the very foundations of the social compact, a complete extinction of all the relations, endearments and obligations of mankind, and a presumptuous transgression of all the holy commandments— and that therefore they ought to be instantly abrogated.

We further believe and affirm—

That all persons of color who possess the qualifications which are demanded of others, ought to be admitted forthwith to the enjoyment of the same privileges, and the exercise of the same prerogatives, as others; and that the paths of preferment, of wealth, and of intelligence, should be opened as widely to them as to persons of a white complexion.

We maintain that no compensation should be given to the   25 planters emancipating their slaves—

Because it would be a surrender of the great fundamental principle that man cannot hold property in man;

Because SLAVERY IS A CRIME, AND THEREFORE IT IS NOT AN ARTICLE TO BE SOLD:

Because the holders of slaves are not the just proprietors of what they claim:—freeing the slaves is not depriving them of property, but restoring it to the right owner;—it is not wronging the master, but righting the slave—restoring him to himself;

Because immediate and general emancipation would only destroy nominal, not real property: it would not amputate a limb or break a bone of the slaves, but by infusing motives into their breasts, would make them doubly valuable to the masters as free laborers; and

Because if compensation is to be given at all, it should be given to the outraged and guiltless slaves, and not to those who have plundered and abused them.

We regard, as delusive, cruel and dangerous, any scheme of   30
expatriation which pretends to aid, either directly or indirectly, in the emancipation of the slaves, or to be a substitute for the immediate and total abolition of slavery.

We fully and unanimously recognise the sovereignty of each State, to legislate exclusively on the subject of the slavery which is tolerated within its limits. We concede that Congress, *under the present national compact,* has no right to interfere with any of the slave States, in relation to this momentous subject.

But we maintain that Congress has a right, and is solemnly bound, to suppress the domestic slave trade between the several States, and to abolish slavery in those portions of our territory which the Constitution has placed under its exclusive jurisdiction.

We also maintain that there are, at the present time, the highest obligations resting upon the people of the free States, to remove slavery by moral and political action, as prescribed in the Constitution of the United States. They are now living under a pledge of their tremendous physical force to fasten the galling fetters of tyranny upon the limbs of millions in the southern States;—they are liable to be called at any moment to suppress a general insurrection of the slaves;—they authorise the slave owner to vote for three-fifths of his slaves as property, and thus enable him to perpetuate his oppression;—they support a standing army at the south for its protection;—and they seize the slave who has escaped into their territories, and send him back to be tortured by an enraged master or a brutal driver.

This relation to slavery is criminal and full of danger; IT MUST BE BROKEN UP.

These are our views and principles—these, our designs and   35
measures. With entire confidence in the overruling justice of

God, we plant ourselves upon the Declaration of our Independence, and upon the truths of Divine Revelation, as upon the EVERLASTING ROCK.

We shall organize Anti-Slavery Societies, if possible, in every city, town and village of our land.

We shall send forth Agents to lift up the voice of remonstrance, of warning, of entreaty and rebuke.

We shall circulate, unsparingly and extensively, anti-slavery tracts and periodicals.

We shall enlist the PULPIT and PRESS in the cause of the suffering and the dumb.

We shall aim at a purification of the churches from all   40 participation in the guilt of slavery.

We shall encourage the labor of freemen over that of the slaves, by giving a preference to their productions;—and

We shall spare no exertions nor means to bring the whole nation to speedy repentance.

Our trust for victory is solely in GOD. *We* may be personally defeated, bur our principles never. TRUTH, JUSTICE, REASON, HUMANITY, must and will gloriously triumph. Already a host is coming up to the help of the Lord against the mighty, and the prospect before us is full of encouragement.

Submitting this DECLARATION to the candid examination of the people of this country, and of the friends of liberty all over the world, we hereby affix our signatures to it;—pledging ourselves that, under the guidance and by the help of Almighty God, we will do all that in us lies, consistently with this Declaration of our principles, to overthrow the most execrable system of slavery that has ever been witnessed upon earth—to deliver our land from its deadliest curse—to wipe out the foulest stain which rests upon our national escutcheon—and to secure to the colored population of the United States all the rights and privileges which belong to them as men and as Americans—come what may to our persons, our interests, or our reputations—whether we live to witness the triumph of JUSTICE, LIBERTY and HUMANITY, or perish untimely as martyrs in this great, benevolent and holy cause.

Questions about the Passage

1. In what ways, according to Garrison, is the "enterprise" of abolitionism superior or equal to the American Revolution?
2. What is the goal of the American Anti-slavery Society (AAAS)?
3. What means will the AAAS use to fight slavery? What are the "carnal weapons" (paragraph 5) they reject?
4. What view of American law does the declaration express?
5. Why does the declaration reject compensation being paid to slaveholders when slavery is abolished?
6. Can you tell how Garrison and his associates at the convention intend to overthrow legal slavery?

Questions about the Argument

1. What audiences might Garrison's declaration be addressing?
2. What is the significance of the declaration's insistence that the slaves are a part of "our" people, of "our countrymen"?
3. Why do you think Garrison begins by citing the *Declaration of Independence*? Compare and contrast the final paragraph of this manifesto to the *Declaration of Independence*. How might echoing the *Declaration of Independence* further the goals of the AAAS? Jefferson sets up principles underlying his first premise. What principles does Garrison set forth? Jefferson supplies a list of grievances. Does Garrison do the same? If so, where, and what are they? Jefferson reasons from his premises to a conclusion. Does Garrison follow this model? If so, how?
4. Do you think there is a conflict between the AAAS declaration's use of the American Revolution and its renunciation of violence in favor of moral suasion? Make a case for your answer by citing passages from the text.
5. Does Garrison call for civil disobedience? Defend your answer with evidence from the text.

Frederick Douglass, "The Evolution of an Abolitionist"

Within three years of his 1838 escape from slavery in his native Maryland, Frederick Douglass (1817–1895) had become an abolitionist lecturer well known for his stirring accounts of his life as a slave. Douglass was deeply influenced by William Lloyd Garrison's paper *The Liberator* and became a strong proponent of Garrison's brand of immediate abolitionism. After the publication of Douglass's autobiographical accounts as the *Narrative of the Life of Frederick Douglass, An American Slave* in 1845, he and Garrison lectured together in both Great Britain (where Douglass fled after his book made him a celebrity fugitive slave) and in the United States. British friends bought his freedom in 1846, allowing him to return to the United States a free man. In 1846, he moved his family from New Bedford, Massachusetts, to Rochester, New York, where he cofounded a newspaper, The *North Star* (later *Frederick Douglass's Paper*), and a magazine, *Douglass' Monthly*, to argue for the abolition of slavery. In Rochester, he became a conductor on the Underground Railroad that had once helped him to escape slavery.

Douglass came to disagree profoundly with his mentor Garrison on the important issue of political action to end slavery. Especially after the passage of the Fugitive Slave Law of 1850, Douglass repudiated Garrison's idea that the American Constitution was proslavery and came to argue that the abolitionist cause needed more than moral suasion. Their break was bitter and long lasting. After the Civil War, Douglass turned to politics, campaigning for the Republican Party, serving on the Council of the District of Columbia and as marshall at the White House, and representing the United States as minister to Haiti.

The selections below demonstrate Douglass's powerful speaking style as well as his evolving position on how to bring about the end of American slavery. The first piece is the report of Douglass's speech to the tenth anniversary meeting of the AAAS, held in New York City in 1843. Some fourteen years later, Douglass spoke to a group celebrating the anniversary, commonly commemorated by U.S. abolitionists, of the emancipation of slaves in the West Indies. The third selection reprinted here is Douglass's description of his time as a conductor on the Underground Railroad in Rochester in the late 1840s and 1850s; he aided more than 100 slaves to escape to freedom.

The Anti-Slavery Movement, the Slave's Only Earthly Hope, 1843

Frederic[k] Douglas[s], was next introduced to the meeting.   1
He said:—"I have myself been a slave, and I do not expect to
awaken such an interest in the minds of this intelligent assembly, as those have done who spoke before me. For I have never

had the advantage of a single day's schooling, in all my life; and such have been my habits of life, as to instil into my heart a disposition I never can quite shake off, to cower before white men. But one thing I can do. I can represent here the slave,—the human chattel, the despised and oppressed, for whom you, my friends, are laboring in a good and holy cause. As such a representative, I do not fear that I shall not be welcome to all true-hearted abolitionists. (Applause.)

"I offer you, Mr. President, continued Douglas[s], the following resolution, and desire to say a few words in its support:

2. "Resolved, That the anti-slavery movement is the only earthly hope of the American slave.

"There is a truth, sir, asserted in this resolution that is almost every where, and by almost every body, denied. Instead of being regarded as a powerful aid to abolition, it is far too generally viewed as retarding that event. But this is a grievous error. I know, for I speak from experience. It has been imagined that the slaves of the South are not aware of the movements made on their behalf, and in behalf of human freedom, every where, throughout the northern and western States. This is not true. They do know it. They knew it from the moment that the spark was first kindled in the land. They knew it as soon as you knew it, sir, in your own New England. Did not petitions by thousands, immediately go forth for the abolition of slavery in the District of Columbia, and in the territories, and for the overthrow of the internal slave trade? Heard we not that? And in the curses of our masters against the abolitionists, did we not feel instinctively that these same abolitionists were our friends? And in every form of opposition to the great cause, did we not hear it?

"Prior this moment, sir, the slave in chains had no hope of   5 deliverance—no hope of any peace or happiness within this vale of tears. Darkness and despair rested gloomily upon his prospect, and not a ray of light was thrown across. But when he heard of this movement, hope sprang up in my mind, and in the minds of many more. I knew, I felt, that truth was above error, that right was above wrong, that principle was superior to policy: and under the peaceful and beneficent operation of abolitionism. I felt that I should one day be free." (Loud and protracted applause.)

The speaker went on to say that there was no hope for the slave in Church, or State, or in the working of society, framed as it now is; nothing whatever in any of the institutions of the day. But in the American Anti-Slavery Society, the slave sees an exposition of his true position in the scale of being. He finds that he is, indeed, a Man,—admitted, recognized as such, as he is by them, and he goes on, calmly and quietly, hoping in his chains that the day may come, when by their aid, he shall be relieved from his thraldom! (Applause.) For this society, sir, is above either Church or State; *it is moving both,* daily, more and more. What do we see? Massachusetts has closed her gaols, and her court-rooms, against the slave-hunters, and has bidden them to look for no aid at the hands of her people, in this unholy work.[1] Thus is the great work going on!

And, sir, the slave sees that God has raised up a mighty work in his behalf, among the people of the North, when he observes the reluctance with which the slave owner now makes his tours to the North. The slave is now not taken as a part of the retinue of his master, on the boot of the stage, as before. He soon finds his "property" among the missing, if he does: and then he comes back, and curses the abolitionists of the North; and, in answer to the question, where is Sam, or Dick, or Bill? slaves who have remained behind, hear him say, the infernal abolitionists have got hold of him, they begin to feel that they have friends, and that the time will come, when the exertions of such will be used for their liberation, as well as that of their brethren. This it is which teaches the poor slave where his hope is,—that it is in the "anti-slavery society,"—and in the growing feeling at the North, in favor of the oppressed, and against oppression. (Vociferous applause.)

And Mr. Douglas[s] wound up this extraordinary speech, with a feeling exhortation to abolitionists to go on, in the confi-

---

1.   In March 1843 the Massachusetts legislature, in response to a campaign launched by *Garrisonian* and "new organization" abolitionists to protest the arrest of fugitive slave George Latimer in Boston, prohibited the cooperation of state officials in the seizure and detention of fugitive slaves. This was the first personal liberty law passed after the U.S. Supreme Court invalidated such laws in *Prigg v. Pennsylvania* (1842). Stanley W. Campbell, *The Slave Catchers: Enforcement of the Fugitive Slave Law. 1850–1860* (New York, 1972), 13–14; Martin B. Duberman, *Charles Francis Adams, 1807–1886* (Boston, 1961), 80–84; Henry Wilson, *History of the Rise and Fall of the Slave Power in America.* 3 vols. (Boston, 1872–77), 1: 477–87.

dence of a good cause, to the breaking of bonds, the unloosing of shackles, and the liberation of the enchained, the enthralled, and the oppressed. He sat down amidst very warm and enthusiastic applause.

Questions about the Passage

1. According to Douglass, how does the abolitionist movement work to help slaves?
2. Why might people believe that the anti-slavery movement is "retarding" the abolition of slavery? How does Douglass refute this idea?

Questions about the Argument

1. What sense of Douglass's ethos do you get from this short passage? How does he use ethos to strengthen his argument?
2. How does he use pathos in his argument? Do you find it effective? Why or why not?

Power Concedes Nothing without a Demand, 1857

Let me give you a word of the philosophy of reform. The whole history of the progress of human liberty shows that all concessions yet made to her august claims, have been born of earnest struggle. The conflict has been exciting, agitating, all-absorbing, and for the time being, putting all other tumults to silence. It must do this or it does nothing. If there is no struggle there is no progress. Those who profess to favor freedom and yet depreciate agitation, are men who want crops without plowing up the ground, they want rain without thunder and lightning. They want the ocean without the awful roar of its many waters.

This struggle may be a moral one, or it may be a physical one, and it may be both moral and physical, but it must be a struggle. Power concedes nothing without a demand. It never did and it never will. Find out just what any people will quietly submit to and you have found out the exact measure of injustice and wrong which will be imposed upon them, and these will continue till they are resisted with either words or blows, or with both. The limits of tyrants are prescribed by the endurance of those whom they oppress. In the light of these ideas, Negroes will be hunted at the North, and held and flogged at the South so long as they submit to those devilish outrages, and make no resistance, either moral or physical. Men may not get all they pay for in this world, but they must certainly pay for all they get. If we ever get free from the oppressions and wrongs heaped upon us, we must pay for their removal. We must do this by labor, by suffering, by sacrifice, and if needs be, by our lives and the lives of others.

Hence, my friends, every mother who, like Margaret Garner, plunges a knife into the bosom of her infant to save it from the hell of our Christian Slavery, should be held and honored as a benefactress. Every fugitive from slavery who like the noble William Thomas at Wilkesbarre, prefers to perish in a river made red by his own blood, to submission to the hell hounds who were hunting and shooting him, should be esteemed as a glorious martyr, worthy to be held in grateful memory by our people.[1]

The fugitive Horace, at Mechanicsburgh, Ohio, the other day, who taught the slave catchers from Kentucky that it was safer to arrest white men than to arrest him, did a most excellent service to our cause.[2] Parker and his noble band of fifteen

1. On 3 September 1853, three U.S. deputy marshals attempted to arrest William Thomas, a fugitive slave employed as a waiter at the Phoenix Hotel in Wilkes-Barre, Pennsylvania. Thomas broke away from the officers but was wounded while trying to flee. Unable to run, Thomas plunged into the nearby Susquehanna River and refused to come out, declaring, "I will be drowned rather than be taken alive." Fearing that he might drown them as well, the deputies remained on the shore and alternated between taking additional shots at Thomas and trying to convince him to surrender. After about an hour of this grim standoff, the citizens of Wilkes-Barre drove away the officers. Aided by black friends, Thomas was helped from the river and made good his escape. New York *Daily Tribune.* 7 September 1853; *Lib.*, 16 September 1853; Campbell, *Slave Catchers*, 139–41.
2. Douglass probably refers to the attempted capture on 21 May 1857 of Addison White, a fugitive slave hiding in Mechanicsburg, Ohio. A party of five Kentuckians and two U.S. deputy marshals tried to arrest White at the farm of Udney H. Hyde, where he had found refuge. White shot one of the marshals and escaped. The case drew national attention when federal officers arrested Hyde for harboring an escaped slave. Hyde's friends, however, convinced a local court to issue a writ of habeas corpus against the marshals. A sheriff's posse overtook the marshals, freed Hyde, and jailed the federal officers. A series of suits and countersuits between the state of Ohio and the federal government followed. All charges eventually were dropped after a private subscription raised a thousand dollars to compensate Addison White's owner. New York *Daily Tribune*, 6 June, 9 July 1857; *ASB*, 6 June, 4, 18 July 1857; *Lib.*, 19 June, 24 July 1857; *The History of Champaign County, Ohio* (Chicago, 1881), 605–10; Campbell, *Slave Catchers*, 161–64.

at Christiana, who defended themselves from the kidnappers with prayers and pistols, are entitled to the honor of making the first successful resistance to the Fugitive Slave Bill.[3] But for that resistance, and the rescue of Jerry, and Shadrack,[4] the man-hunters would have hunted our hills and valleys here with the same freedom with which they now hunt their own dismal swamps.

There was an important lesson in the conduct of that noble Krooman in New York, the other day, who, supposing that the American Christians were about to enslave him, betook himself to the mast head, and with knife in hand, said he would cut his throat before he would be made a slave.[5] Joseph Cinque

3.   On 11 September 1851 Maryland planter Edward Gorsuch, accompanied by a party of neighbors, attempted to recover two of his runaway slaves in Christiana, Pennsylvania. The fugitives had found refuge in the home of William Parker (1823–?) who himself had escaped slavery in 1839. Parker refused to turn over the fugitives to Gorsuch, and the predominantly black community rallied against the slave catchers. A fight broke out during which Gorsuch was killed and the other whites driven off. Parker and several other black participants in the affair fled to Canada, where they settled permanently. Douglass himself assisted Parker during his secret passage through Rochester. Thirty-six blacks and five whites were eventually indicted for treason, but none was successfully prosecuted. William Parker, "The Freedman's Story," *Atlantic Monthly*, 17: 152–66 (February 1866), 17: 276–95 (March 1866); Jonathan Katz, *Resistance at Christiana: The Fugitive Slave Rebellion, Christiana, Pennsylvania, September 11, 1851* (New York, 1974), 18–21, 27, 74–80, 92–103, 169–70, 234–35, 260–61, 279; Campbell, *Slave Catchers*, 99–101, 151–54.

4.   One of the most famous of all fugitive slave "rescues" was the case of Frederick Wilkins, popularly called Shadrach. An escaped slave from Virginia, Shadrach was working as a waiter in a Boston restaurant when arrested by a U.S. deputy marshal on 15 February 1851. The captive was taken directly to a hearing before Slave Law Commissioner George Ticknor Curtis. While Shadrach's lawyers motioned for a delay to prepare a defense, a crowd of blacks gathered in the courthouse. Without warning, the crowd broke into the hearing room and spirited Shadrach away before the court officers could react. Shadrach successfully reached Canada and none of his rescuers ever was punished. Campbell, *Slave Catchers*, 148–51; Quarles, *Black Abolitionists*, 205–6; McDougall, *fugitive Slaves*, 47–48.

5.   On 14 July 1857 a native African caused great excitement in Brooklyn harbor by climbing naked up the rigging of the brig *Flora* on which he had just arrived in America. The African, reportedly a member of the Krooman tribe, had become frightened by stories that upon landing he would be kidnapped and sold as a slave. The Krooman eventually felt or jumped overboard and was rescued. Two days later the New York *Daily Times* reported that the African still was aboard his ship and "avows his intention to kill himself before he will be taken." New York *Daily Times*, 15, 17 July 1857; *Lib.*, 24 July 1857.

on the deck of the *Amistad*, did that which should make his
name dear to us.[6] He bore nature's burning protest against
slavery. Madison Washington who struck down his oppressor
on the deck of the *Creole*, is more worthy to be remembered
than the colored man who shot Pitcaren at Bunker Hill.[7]

Questions about the Passage

1. What point is Douglass making with his series of metaphors at
   the end of paragraph 1?
2. What does Douglass mean by a "physical" struggle?

6.   In 1839 a group of recently enslaved Africans successfully revolted while being
     shipped along the Cuban coast on the *Amistad*. Unfortunately, these self-emancipated
     members of the Mendi tribe blundered into United States waters and were arrested
     for piracy. After a highly publicized legal battle, the Supreme Court freed the
     Africans in March 1841. Lewis Tappan, a wealthy New York merchant and aboli-
     tionist, had befriended the jailed Africans and conceived a plan to send them home
     as Christian missionaries. Cinque (c. 1817–79) was the leader of the *Amistad* uprising
     and generally spoke for the Mendis while in America. Cooperating with Tappan, he
     even gave public addresses to attract contributions for the missionary project. When
     the group was returned to Africa in 1842, Cinque soon went back to his own people
     and apparently became a chief among them. In 1879 Cinque returned to the Mendi
     mission station about a week before his death. His Christian name, Joseph, was
     given him by the Cuban slave traders. Blassingame, *Slave Testimony*, 30–46; Mary
     Cable, *Black Odyssey: The Case of the Slave Ship Amistad* (New York, 1971), 12–13,
     52–55, 110, 113–14, 118–23, 139–40, 149–50; Wyatt-Brown, *Lewis Tappan*, 205–20;
     William A. Owens, *Slave Mutiny: The Revolt on the Schooner Amistad* (New York, 1953),
     50, 287; *DANB*, 111–12.
7.   Although the story is difficult to substantiate, tradition holds that emancipated slave
     Peter Salem (1750–1816), alias Salem Middleux, fired the shot that killed British
     marine major John Pitcairn (1722–75) during the Battle of Bunker Hill on 17 June 1775.
     Salem had been freed by his Framingham, Massachusetts, owners so that he could
     enlist as a minuteman. Salem fought in the battles of Concord, Saratoga, and Stony
     Point as well as Bunker Hill. The death of Pitcairn, the officer who had commanded
     the British troops at Lexington, attracted general approval from Americans. A contri-
     bution was taken up for Salem and he was congratulated personally by General
     Washington. After the war, Salem returned to Massachusetts and worked as a cane
     weaver near Leicester. He died in the Framingham poorhouse. William C. Nell, *The
     Colored Patriots of the American Revolution* (Boston, 1855), 394–96; Benjamin Quarles,
     The Negro in the American Revolution (Chapel Hill, 1961), 10–11; Sidney Kaplan, *The
     Black Presence in the Era of the American Revolution, 1770–1800* (Washington, D.C.,
     1973), 17–19; Robert M. Ketchum, *Decisive Day: The Battle for Bunker Hill* (Garden City,
     N.Y., 1974), 174–75, 180; *DANB*, 539–40.

3. What does Douglass expect American slaves to do? How does this contrast with his message in the previous selection?

Questions about the Argument

1. What does Douglass assume about his audience?
2. How does Douglass's use of example affect the persuasiveness of his argument?
3. Compare the ethos and pathos in this selection to their use in the previous selection. Has Douglass's persona changed? Have his ideas?

Stationmaster and Conductor on the Underground Railroad, 1892

One important branch of my anti-slavery work in Rochester, in addition to that of speaking and writing against slavery, must not be forgotten or omitted. My position gave me the chance of hitting that old enemy some telling blows, in another direction than these. I was on the southern border of Lake Ontario, and the Queen's dominions were right over the way—and my prominence as an abolitionist, and as the editor of an anti-slavery paper, naturally made me the station-master and conductor of the underground railroad passing through this goodly city. Secrecy and concealment were necessary conditions to the successful operation of this railroad, and hence its prefix "underground." My agency was all the more exciting and interesting, because not altogether free from danger. I could take no step in it without exposing myself to fine and imprisonment, for these were the penalties imposed by the fugitive-slave law for feeding, harboring, or otherwise assisting a slave to escape from his master; but, in face of this fact, I can say I never did more congenial, attractive, fascinating, and satisfactory work. True, as a means of destroying slavery, it was like an attempt to bail out the ocean with a teaspoon, but the thought that there was *one* less slave, and one more freeman—having myself been a slave, and a fugitive slave— brought to my heart unspeakable joy. On one occasion I had eleven fugitives at the same time under my roof, and it was necessary for them to remain with me until I could collect sufficient money to get them on to Canada. It was the largest number I ever had at any one time, and I had some difficulty in providing so many with food and shelter, but, as may well be imagined, they were not very fastidious in either direction, and were well content with very plain food, and a strip of carpet on the floor for a bed, or a place on the straw in the barn-loft.

The underground railroad had many branches; but that one with which I was connected had its main stations in Baltimore, Wilmington, Philadelphia, New York, Albany, Syracuse, Rochester, and St. Catharines (Canada). It is not necessary to tell who were the principal agents in Baltimore; Thomas Garrett was the agent in Wilmington; Melloe McKim, William Still, Robert Purvis, Edward M. Davis, and others did the work in Philadelphia; David Ruggles, Issac T. Hopper, Napolian, and others, in New York City; the Misses Mott and Stephen Myers were forwarders from Albany; Revs. Samuel J. May and J. W. Loguen were the agents in Syracuse; and J. P. Morris and myself received and dispatched passengers from Rochester to Canada, where they were received by Rev. Hiram Wilson. When a party arrived in Rochester it was the business of Mr. Morris and myself to raise funds with which to pay their passage to St. Catharines, and it is due to truth to state that we seldom called in vain upon whig or democrat for help. Men were better than their theology, and truer to humanity than to their politics, or their offices.

On one occasion while a slave master was in the office of a United States commissioner, procuring the papers necessary for the arrest and rendition of three young men who had escaped from Maryland (one of whom was under my roof at the time, another at Farmington, and the other at work on the farm of Asa Anthony, just a little outside the city limits), the law partner of the commissioner, then a distinguished democrat, sought me out, and told me what was going on in his office, and urged me by all means to get these young men out of the way of their pursuers and claimants. Of course no time was to be lost. A swift horseman was dispatched to Farmington, eighteen miles distant, another to Asa Anthony's farm, about three miles, and another to my house on the south side of the city, and before the papers could be served all three of the young men were on the free waves of Lake Ontario, bound to Canada. In writing to their old master, they had dated their letter at Rochester, though they had taken the precaution to send it to Canada to be mailed, but this blunder in the date had betrayed their whereabouts, so that the hunters were at once on their tracks.

So numerous were the fugitives passing through Rochester that I was obliged at last to appeal to my British friends for the means of sending them on their way, and when Mr. and Mrs. Carpenter and Mrs. Croffts took the matter in hand, I had never any further trouble in that respect. When slavery was abolished I wrote to Mrs. Carpenter, congratulating her that she was relieved of the work of raising funds for such purposes, and the characteristic reply of that lady was that she had been very glad to do what she had done, and had no wish for relief.

Questions about the Passage

1. Why did Douglass participate in the Underground Railroad? Do you find his reasons understandable?
2. Does Douglass convey the danger and anxiety of the whole enterprise? If so, how?

Questions about the Argument

1. What audience is Douglass addressing? Is this the same audience he addressed in either of his earlier selections?
2. What seems to be Douglass's attitude toward his actions in the past? How can you tell?
3. Assisting escaping slaves entailed breaking federal law. Can you infer Douglass's view of his law-breaking?

William Still, "The Underground Railroad"

William Still (1821–1902) was an abolitionist, writer, and successful businessman. His parents had been slaves—his father had bought his freedom, and his mother escaped—and after leaving the farm in New Jersey where he had been born, he moved to Philadelphia. There, in 1847, Still found a job as a janitor and clerk with the Pennsylvania Society for the Abolition of Slavery. He soon became involved with aiding escaping slaves. After the passage of the 1850 Fugitive Slave Act, Still became the chairman of the Philadelphia Vigilance Committee, the activist arm of the abolition society that secretly transported slaves fleeing the South. While an active member of the Underground Railroad resisting the Fugitive Slave Act, Still kept a journal and collected accounts from the slaves who escaped; he also kept newspaper articles, letters from abolitionists and former slaves, and legal documents. He published this material in his book, *The Underground Railroad,* in 1873. It is one of the few accounts by an African American author of the anti-slavery movement. The excerpt below, in which Still describes the experiences of one "passenger" on the Underground Railroad, demonstrates the real dangers in violating the Fugitive Slave Act.

Mary Epps, alias Emma Brown

A Slave Mother Loses her Speech at the Sale of her Child—
Mary fled from Petersburg and the Robinsons from Richmond.
A fugitive slave law-breaking captain by the name of B., who owned a schooner, and would bring any kind of freight that would pay the most, was the conductor in this instance. Quite a number of passengers at different times availed themselves of his accommodations and thus succeeded in reaching Canada.

His risk was very great. On this account he claimed, as did certain others, that it was no more than fair to charge for his services—indeed he did not profess to bring persons for nothing, except in rare instances. In this matter the Committee did not feel disposed to interfere directly in any way, further than to suggest that whatever understanding was agreed upon by the parties themselves should be faithfully adhered to.

Many slaves in cities could raise, "by hook or by crook," fifty or one hundred dollars to pay for a passage, providing they could find one who was willing to risk aiding them. Thus, while the Vigilance Committee of Philadelphia especially neither charged nor accepted anything for their services, it was not to be expected that any of the Southern agents could afford to do likewise.

The husband of Mary had for a long time wanted his own freedom, but did not feel that he could go without his wife; in fact, he resolved to get her off first, then to try and escape himself, if possible. The first essential step towards success, he considered, was to save his money and make it an object to the captain to help him. So when he had managed to lay by one hundred dollars, he willingly offered this sum to Captain B., if he would engage to deliver his wife into the hands of the Vigilance Committee of Philadelphia. The captain agreed to the terms and fulfilled his engagement to the letter. About the 1st of March, 1855, Mary was presented to the Vigilance Committee. She was of agreeable manners, about forty-five years of age, dark complexion, round built, and intelligent. She had been the mother of fifteen children, four of whom had been sold away from her; one was still held in slavery in Petersburg; the others were all dead.

At the sale of one of her children she was so affected with   5 grief that she was thrown into violent convulsions, which caused the loss of her speech for one entire month. But this little episode was not a matter to excite sympathy in the breasts of the highly refined and tender-hearted Christian mothers of Petersburg. In the mercy of Providence, however, her reason and strength returned.

She had formerly belonged to the late Littleton Reeves, whom she represented as having been "kind" to her, much more so than her mistress (Mrs. Reeves). Said Mary, "She being of a jealous disposition, caused me to be hired out with a hard family, where I was much abused, frequently flogged, and stinted for food," etc.

But the sweets of freedom in the care of the Vigilance Committee now delighted her mind, and the hope that her husband would soon follow her to Canada, inspired her with expectations that she would one day "sit under her own vine and fig tree where none dared to molest or make her afraid."

The Committee rendered her the usual assistance, and in due time, forwarded her on to Queen Victoria's free land in Canada. On her arrival she wrote back as follows—

TORONTO, March 14th, 1855.

DEAR MR. STILL:—I take this opportunity of addressing you with these few lines to inform you that I arrived here to day, and hope that this may find yourself and Mrs. Still well, as this leaves me at the present. I will also say to you, that I had no difficulty in getting along, the two young men that was with me left me at Suspension Bridge. They went another way.

I cannot say much about the place as I have been here but a short time but so far as I have seen I like very well. you will give my Respect to your lady, & Mr & Mrs Brown. If you have not written to Petersburg you will please to write as soon as can I have nothing More to Write at present but yours Respectfully

EMMA BROWN (old name MARY EPPS).

Questions about the Passage

1. What laws were broken in order for Mary Epps to escape?
2. What evidence does Still provide to justify this lawbreaking?
3. What does Still think of Captain B? What do you think of him?

Questions about the Argument

1. What is the impact of including the actual letter by Mary Epps, the escaped slave? What does Still accomplish by allowing her to speak for herself?
2. How does this account use both ethos and pathos?

John P. Parker, "True to My Word"

Like Frederick Douglass, John Parker (1827–1900) was the son of a white man and black slave. Born in Norfolk, Virginia, at the age of 8 Parker was taken from his mother and sold. He was chained to an old man, who was kind to him, in a long walk from Norfolk to Richmond. The man was beaten to death in front of the boy. He was filled with rage and bitterness that he perhaps drew upon the rest of his life. After purchasing his freedom for $1800 at the age of 18, he moved to Indiana and then to southern Ohio, where he became a talented iron molder and inventor. His first work on the Underground Railroad, "my own little personal war on slavery," as he called it, was in 1845 in Ripley, Ohio, a town on the Ohio River, across from the slave state of Kentucky. By 1850, Parker and his family moved to Ripley, where he established a small foundry and continued his Underground Railroad activities. Parker is believed to have aided over 1,000 slaves to reach freedom. During the Civil War, Parker was a recruiter for black units of the Union Army. The reminiscence reprinted here was obtained in an extensive interview by a white reporter and historian who had grown up in Ripley and who admired Parker.

By this time I had become proprietor of an iron foundry. I had married and purchased a home next to my place of business, both of which were located on the bank of the river. There was working for me a man [named Srofe] who lived across the river in Kentucky [and] whose father owned several people.

This man kept chiding me about my habits of prowling around at night, taking charge of fugitives. I stoutly denied such proclivities, but from time to time he would come back to the subject, until one day he said to me, "You are such a brave fellow, why don't you run away some of the old man's people?" I promptly disclaimed any such purpose, but at the same time I secretly vowed I would take him at his word. . . .

It was the third night before my chance came. . . . The two men came down the road and passed me. I hurried to a cornfield near the highway, where, hiding in the fence corner, I could get a good view of anyone passing by before I spoke.

In a little while I saw a figure coming back. I lay with both eyes peering through the cracks of the rail fence, anxiously waiting for a good look at the man's face. This time I saw plainly it was the one I wanted. As he came opposite me, without moving, I called to him softly. . . .

He walked on for a short distance, then turned and came   5
back. In the meantime I hurried as fast as I could to the woods, keeping within the shadow of the fence.

Once within the protection of the forest I came out on the highway, and waited for my man to return. He came back leisurely so as not to excite suspicion. You may imagine he was curious to know who I was and what was wanted. He knew me by reputation, so when I gave him my name he desired no further credentials.

When I told him I wanted to run him away, he said he had a wife and a little baby, and would not go and leave them. Being determined to execute my plan, I asked him to be ready to go the following night. I would take them all. He fell in with my scheme, and before we parted it was all arranged. He was to meet me at the same place a week later, claiming he could not be ready in a day. . . .

True to my word, a week later I was at the appointed place to meet my party of runaways. . . . I concealed my boat carefully, for I wanted no miscarrying of my plans, and after lying in the bushes for a while, my man not showing up, I decided to go after him. It was ticklish work, but I felt it to be necessary if I expected to carry out my plan. . . .

Things had gone wrong, just as I supposed. The man was so scared he could hardly talk to me. He said since the night of the interview, he had been under watch. The folks in the big house had a suspicion he and his wife were planning to run away, and as a precaution compelled him to bring the baby to them every night. The little one was placed at the foot of the bed in which the owner and his wife slept. The old man had placed a chair at his side, on which was a lighted candle and a pistol, and threatened to shoot the first person he found in the room after dark. Besides, a close watch had been kept on all of the cabins to see that none of their occupants were abroad at night. While he was talking he was looking around constantly, as if he expected someone to swoop down on us. . . .

Without wasting time, I proposed that the two of them go   10
with me, leaving the baby behind. This the woman would not listen to; her mother love prompted her to select bondage with her little one rather than freedom without it. When I endeavored to open the subject again she became hysterical for fear I was going to compel her to go against her will. Seeing my efforts were unavailing, I dropped the discussion.

I then proposed to the man that he enter the sleeping room of the big house and rescue the baby from the foot of the bed. This he refused to do, as he was afraid of the big pistol at his owner's head. I attempted to bolster up his courage by holding up to him the hopes of freedom, but he was not to be moved.

As I did not feel it was my duty to endanger my life as well as my liberty on their behalf, I pressed the woman to go to the rescue of the baby. I think she would have made the effort, but for her husband, who was thoroughly cowed by the fear of the man of the house.

When I urged her again she hesitated, and as she faltered the man broke in, saying that they were not anxious to leave and thought they better not try. From the tenor of the talk I knew that nothing could be expected from them, and any effort of rescue must come from myself. To press them further meant that they would abandon the trip, and I would return home empty-handed.

Having gone this far I decided to go all the way, enter the forbidden room, and rescue the child from the bed. Coming to this decision, I made them get their possessions in readiness to move. The woman, who was a servant in the house, described its interior, which was very simple indeed. From the small porch at the rear of the house, she said a door opened into a large living room. From this a door led into the sleeping apartment where the child was to be found. There were no locks on any of the doors, [they] being held by wooden latches. . . .

Standing on the threshold of this strange house, I am frank to   15
say I felt the graveness of my position. For a moment my nerve left me, and I am positive I would have run at the least noise.

As my eyes became used to the darkness of the place, my courage came back to me. The floor of the kitchen was of rough boards, so that my footing was uncertain. As I picked my way across the room it seemed to me I struck every loose board in the place. The large crack at the bottom of the door of the sleeping room, through which the rays of the candle showed, guided me surely to my destination.

At the door I hesitated, for I felt I was taking my life in my hand in opening it. If I only knew whether the man was a sound or a light sleeper, it would have eased my mind just then. The wife too was an unknown quantity. These and a multitude [of] other things came to my mind as I stood with my hand on the latch of the sleeping room, ready to open it, to an unknown fate. Twice I put pressure on the latch and twice my heart failed me. The third time my thumb pushed down on the fastening, and it gave way. It was the last point at which I hesitated, for as the latch noiselessly left its place, I felt I was given over to the execution of the task, whatever might be the results; to retreat now was impossible. . . .

While I was standing there, the man turned over restlessly, with his face away from the chair and the pistols. I reasoned it out that the child would be on the woman's side, because she was the one who would take care of it during the night. With this in mind, I stooped down, and under the shadow of the bedstead made my way on my hands and knees across the floor to the woman's side of the bed. . . .

Peeping around the foot of the bed, I saw a bundle lying close to the edge. Without waiting to see what it was, I dragged it toward me, and getting a firm hold pulled it off the bed. As I did there was a creak of the [bed]springs and the next moment the room was in darkness. There was no cause for secrecy now, so I jumped to my feet and rushed to the door. I heard the stool upset and the pistols fall. I heard the quick breathing of the man as he sprung out of bed and began feeling around on the floor in the dark for his weapons. Opening the door with a jerk, I ran across the kitchen out into the yard, with the bundle still in my arms. From their position in the room the man and woman saw me hurry out of the house, toward the road.

Confident of my success, they [my two adult fugitives] started toward the river. When I was within a few rods of them, I heard the crack of a pistol and a bullet went singing over my head. . . .

There was a skiff at the landing, which I made the man turn   20
loose, so that we could not be pursued. My own little craft was soon made ready, and I made the man lie down in the bottom of the boat, so that only two persons could be seen from the shore. Instead of going directly across, which would land me in front of my own house, I rowed up the river. I could see the other boat float down with the current, so that I felt there was no danger from that quarter.

We were about a third of the way across the river when we saw lights down at the landing which we had just left. We were still in plain sight, and I heard the voice of my employee shouting the name of the man in the bottom of the boat, warning him to come back. His threats fell on deaf ears, as I only increased my efforts to get across the river. . . .

Securing my skiff, we hurried up the bank to the home of my friend the attorney. I only took time to tell him he must look after the fugitives, and then hastened home to prepare for the visit I expected would follow. Without striking a light I undressed and got into bed. It was not time to sleep, so I lay awake arranging my plans.

Soon I heard voices outside, then a loud knocking at the door. I was out of bed at the first sound, and throwing up the window I demanded who was making such a row. There were three men below, and the man who worked for me was spokesman. He was evidently surprised to find me, as he suspicioned me the first one, and expected I was away with the fugitives. In spite of finding me at home he began accusing me of running away his father's people. I protested.

"But you run them away," he cried. "No one but you would   25
steal that baby."

"What baby?" was my response.

"You know all about that baby, and it is in your house."

Ordinarily I never permitted anyone to search my premises.
This time I did not care, so I told them to wait while I put on
my clothes, and I would come down and take the party
through the house myself. This seemed to take them back completely, but I knew the longer I kept them busy with me the less
likely they were to find their people. After consuming considerable time in dressing I went down.

The old man had his horse pistols in his hand, and he was
mad clear through. I am sure if the old man had found his people in the house, he would have shot me down in cold blood.
We went through the place room by room. They were completely crestfallen when the last corner was searched, and they
failed to find their runaways. As the young fellow went out he
turned and said, "I believe you were over the river just the
same, and know where my people are." . . .

Srofe hung around my shop the rest of the [next] day, but he   30
never came back to work for me. If he had only kept still, I
would never have thought to run his people off. But he put me
on my mettle, so I rather felt called upon to carry out the enterprise, to his own discomfiture.

Questions about the Passages

1. Why does Parker decide to assist the slaves of his employee's
   father to escape?
2. What do we learn about the personalities of the escaping slaves?
   What do you think of them?

Questions about the Arguments

1. The interviewer to whom Parker spoke was white. Can you see
   any sign that Parker shaped his recollections for a white audience? If so, what evidence do you see?
2. Does Parker appeal to our emotions? How?
3. What kind of man is Parker? What is Parker's attitude toward
   breaking the law? How did he judge his own actions? As his readers, what is our judgment?

Writing Assignments

Conversations

1. Imagine a conversation between Garrison, the older Douglass (after he broke with Garrison), several slaves, and some people undecided about the cause of abolition. What do the two abolitionists say to someone who is still in slavery? What do they say to the fence sitters?

2. The writers in Chapters 5 and 6 have, for the most part, made the case for nonviolence as a necessary component of civil disobedience. Choose three or four advocates who would make a counterclaim that violence is sometimes called for. For example, you might select Antigone, Socrates, Jefferson, Magnes, or the older Douglass. What arguments would they make against those who always oppose the use of violence?

Writing Sequence One: The Conductors' Actions

1. Assume you are writing brief newspaper profiles in the 1850s of each of the Underground Railroad conductors we have read. Decide what questions you would ask in an interview of each one. Sketch out the conductors' answers.

2. Building on the interviews in the previous question, construct a theory of the conductors' beliefs, philosophy, and types of action. Support your theory with evidence from the texts.

3. Take a position on the theory you have constructed about what the Underground Railroad conductors were doing and why they took the actions they did. Are they right or wrong to break the law to help slaves escape? In order to write a persuasive essay, in addition to your own position, you must consider the audience of the time. How will you persuade them? What characteristics and knowledge (or lack of knowledge) must you consider when making your case?

Writing Sequence Two: Declarations

1. Explore the two declarations in this chapter. What structural and rhetorical characteristics do they share? Given these two examples, how would you define and describe a declaration?

2. Compare and contrast the audiences of the two declarations. Who were the intended audiences? Were they friendly, neutral, or hostile? Consider the purposes of the declarations. Are they meant to persuade or to inspire those already committed to the cause?

3. Analyze how Garrison builds on Jefferson's work. Now that you have examined the structure, audience, and rhetorical strategies of both declarations, explain how Garrison makes *The Declaration of Independence* serve his own purposes in the AAAS declaration.

7

Civil Rights Movement

The United States in the 1940s and 1950s was a very different place for blacks and whites than it is today. Segregation of the races, most especially in the South, was enshrined in custom and in law. Segregation, and its attendant inequalities for blacks in schooling, housing, travel, work, and political representation, was the target of protest throughout its existence; however, the modern civil rights movement can be dated from the late 1950s. Several important legal decisions, culminating with the Supreme Court's 1954 decision in *Brown v. Board of Education*, which declared so-called separate but equal schools to be unconstitutional, stimulated blacks and whites to end segregation and unequal treatment of African Americans.

"Nonviolent direct action," which can include civil disobedience, was a term apparently first used by the pacifist organization Congress of Racial Equality (CORE) in the early 1940s, although blacks had practiced such protest going back 100 years. In the early 1940s, CORE began protesting segregated public transportation, as Bayard Rustin describes in his memoir. When Rosa Parks refused to sit at the back of the bus in Montgomery in 1955, she was not the first black to do so; but her action led to blacks launching a one-day local boycott of the bus system, which was transformed by a local minister, Martin Luther King, Jr., into a much larger resistance movement. The Montgomery bus company was forced by the protracted boycott and protest to desegregate its facilities. Other communities began to use the nonviolent weapons of the boycott, the picket, and the sit-in to protest the inequalities of American society.

Participants in the sit-ins of 1960 and the "freedom rides" of 1961 share their memories of their beliefs and actions in this chapter. John

Lewis and Diane Nash were young black students who put their lives in danger to practice nonviolent direct action in the way Gandhi had in India. It is striking how very young people, often not out of their teens, were empowered by their study of Gandhi's ideas to change their world. Merrill Proudfoot, an older white clergyman and professor, also risked his safety to act on his beliefs in support of his black students. Rustin, Lewis, and Proudfoot also acted out of their deep commitment to their Christian faith, as did many of the leaders of the civil rights movement—quite a few of them also clergymen. There is no doubt that the civil rights movement transformed American public and political opinion. In 1964, Congress passed the Civil Rights Act, which forbade discrimination in public accommodations and withheld federal funds from segregated school districts. The Voting Rights Act of 1965 eliminated many of the tactics used in the South to prevent blacks from voting.

By 1966, the civil rights movement began to split apart as more militant voices in the black community became impatient with the slow rate of change and with nonviolent means of protest. The wave of riots in the black ghettos of several major cities in 1965 and 1966 also weakened the unity of the movement. After King's assassination in April 1968, rioting intensified. The violence confirmed the worst fears of critics of the civil rights movement: To break the law was to step down a dangerous path. But from this point on in American political life, many other activists, such as those who opposed the Vietnam War, nuclear weapons, environmental degradation, or legalized abortion, embraced the tactics of nonviolent civil disobedience.

Bayard Rustin, "Nonviolence vs. Jim Crow"

Committed to ending injustice nonviolently and to equal rights for all human beings, Bayard Rustin (1910–1987) is too little known for his brilliant organizing and committed activism for civil rights, freedom, and peace. Born and raised in the historic—but segregated—Underground Railroad stop of West Chester, Pennsylvania, Rustin was a gifted student, athlete, and singer. His grandmother was a Quaker, and her teachings of the equality of all before God and the path of nonviolence shaped the young man's beliefs. As early as high school, he refused to sit in the balcony with other blacks and was arrested for sitting in the white section. This was the first of over twenty-five arrests during his career of social protest. After studying at several colleges, Rustin moved to New York City where he supported himself singing with famed folk singers Josh White and Leadbelly. He also worked as a youth organizer for the Young Communist League, which he joined in the mid-1930s because of its support for desegregation in the South. He became disillusioned with the Communist Party and resigned in 1941. He then started working for the Fellowship of Reconciliation (FOR), an international pacifist organization based on Christian principles. Rustin was a cofounder in 1942 of the Congress of Racial Equality (CORE) under FOR's sponsorship. CORE was founded on an American version of *satyagraha,* the Gandhian principle of nonviolent direct action. In 1943, Rustin went to prison for twenty-eight months as a conscientious objector, even though he could have chosen alternative service as a longtime Quaker; he chose prison because he believed that draft boards treated religious and nonreligious objectors unequally. After his release, he continued to work for CORE and FOR, he traveled to India to work for Gandhi's Congress party and to Africa, and he also headed the pacifist War Resisters League.

Rustin will be best remembered for his vital contributions to the civil rights movement. When the Montgomery bus boycott began in late 1955, Rustin offered his services as an organizer and theoretician to Martin Luther King, Jr. Rustin is credited by historians for practical guidance and for bringing King and his associates to endorse Gandhian nonviolent direct action. Rustin stayed in the background in the 1950s because black leaders feared that his homosexuality and past Communist connection could be used to harm the civil rights cause. He was a key adviser to King, even drafting early letters and speeches for him, as well as an important fundraiser and tactician. He is widely acknowledged as the architect of the massive 1963 March on Washington, where King delivered his "I Have a Dream" speech before a crowd of nearly a quarter of a million people. The next year, Rustin organized a boycott of 400,000 New York Public School students to protest the school board's reluctance to integrate the schools. In the mid-1960s, he came to oppose the violence advocated by the more radical black activists, even as he came to support more political action after the first phase of the civil rights movement.

The passage below, about a 1942 bus trip from Louisville to Nashville, comes from early in Rustin's CORE career and demonstrates his use of nonviolent direct action to promote racial equality.

> Recently I was planning to go from Louisville to Nashville by bus. I bought my ticket, boarded the bus, and, instead of going to the back, sat down in the second seat. The driver saw me, got up, and came toward me.

"Hey, you. You're supposed to sit in the back seat."

"Why?"

"Because that's the law. Niggers ride in back."

I said, "My friend, I believe that is an unjust law. If I were to   5
sit in back I would be condoning injustice."

Angry, but not knowing what to do, he got out and went into
the station. He soon came out again, got into his seat, and
started off.

This routine was gone through at each stop, but each time
nothing came of it. Finally the driver, in desperation, must
have phoned ahead, for about thirteen miles north of Nashville
I heard sirens approaching. The bus came to an abrupt stop,
and a police car and two motorcycles drew up beside us with
a flourish. Four policemen got into the bus, consulted shortly
with the driver, and came to my seat.

"Get up, you———nigger!"

"Why?" I asked.

"Get up, you black———!"   10

"I believe that I have a right to sit here," I said quietly. "If I
sit in the back of the bus I am depriving that child—" I pointed
to a little white child of five or six—"of the knowledge that
there is injustice here, which I believe it is his right to know.
It is my sincere conviction that the power of love in the world
is the greatest power existing. If you have a greater power, my
friend, you may move me."

How much they understood of what I was trying to tell them
I do not know. By this time they were impatient and angry.
As I would not move, they began to beat me about the head
and shoulders, and I shortly found myself knocked to the floor.
Then they dragged me out of the bus and continued to kick
and beat me.

Knowing that if I tried to get up or protect myself in the
first heat of their anger they would construe it as an attempt
to resist and beat me down again, I forced myself to be still
and wait for their kicks, one after another. Then I stood up,
spreading out my arms parallel to the ground, and said, "There
is no need to beat me. I am not resisting you."

At this three white men, obviously Southerners by their
speech, got out of the bus and remonstrated with the police.
Indeed, as one of the policemen raised his club to strike me,

one of them, a little fellow, caught hold of it and said, "Don't you do that!" A second policeman raised his club to strike the little man, and I stepped between them, facing the man, and said, "Thank you, but there is no need to do that. I do not wish to fight. I am protected well."

An elderly gentleman, well dressed and also a Southerner,   15 asked the police where they were taking me.

They said, "Nashville."

"Don't worry, son," he said to me. "I'll be there to see that you get justice."

I was put into the back seat of the police car, between two policemen. Two others sat in front. During the thirteen-mile ride to town they called me every conceivable name and said anything they could think of to incite me to violence. I found that I was shaking with nervous strain, and to give myself something to do, I took out a piece of paper and a pencil, and began to write from memory a chapter from one of Paul's letters.

When I had written a few sentences, the man on my right said, "What're you writing?" and snatched the paper from my hand. He read it, then crumpled it into a ball and pushed it in my face. The man on the other side gave me a kick.

A moment later I happened to catch the eye of the young   20 policeman in the front seat. He looked away quickly, and I took renewed courage from the realization that he could not meet my eyes because he was aware of the injustice being done. I began to write again, and after a moment I leaned forward and touched him on the shoulder. "My friend," I said, "how do you spell 'difference'?"

He spelled it for me—incorrectly—and I wrote it correctly and went on.

When we reached Nashville, a number of policemen were lined up on both sides of the hallway down which I had to pass on my way to the captain's office. They tossed me from one to another like a volleyball. By the time I reached the office, the lining of my best coat was torn, and I was considerably rumpled. I straightened myself as best I could and went in. They had my bag, and went through it and my papers, finding much of interest, especially in the *Christian Century* and *Fellowship*.

Finally the captain said, "Come here, nigger."

I walked directly to him. "What can I do for you?" I asked.

"Nigger," he said menacingly, "you're supposed to be scared   25
when you come in here!"

"I am fortified by truth, justice, and Christ," I said. "There's
no need for me to fear."

He was flabbergasted and, for a time, completely at a loss
for words. Finally he said to another officer, "I believe the
nigger's crazy!"

They sent me into another room and went into consultation.
The wait was long, but after an hour and a half they came
for me and I was taken for another ride, across town. At the
courthouse, I was taken down the hall to the office of the
assistant district attorney, Mr. Ben West. As I got to the door I
heard a voice, "Say, you colored fellow, hey!" I looked around
and saw the elderly gentleman who had been on the bus.

"I'm here to see that you get justice," he said.

The assistant district attorney questioned me about my life,   30
the *Christian Century*, pacifism, and the war for half an hour.
Then he asked the police to tell their side of what had
happened. They did, stretching the truth a good deal in spots
and including several lies for seasoning. Mr. West then asked
me to tell my side.

"Gladly," I said, "and I want *you*," turning to the young
policeman who had sat in the front seat, "to follow what I say
and stop me if I deviate from the truth in the least."

Holding his eyes with mine, I told the story exactly as it had
happened, stopping often to say "Is that right?" or "Isn't that
what happened?" to the young policeman. During the whole
time he never once interrupted me, and when I was through
I said, "Did I tell the truth just as it happened?" and he said,
"Well . . ."

Then Mr. West dismissed me, and I was sent to wait alone in
a dark room. After an hour, Mr. West came in and said, very
kindly, "You may go, *Mister* Rustin."

I left the courthouse, believing all the more strongly in the
nonviolent approach. I am certain that I was addressed as
"Mister" (as no Negro is ever addressed in the South), that I
was assisted by those three men, and that the elderly gentleman
interested himself in my predicament because I had, without

fear, faced the four policemen and said, "There is no need to beat me. I offer you no resistance."

Questions about the Passage

1. What reason does Rustin give the bus driver for sitting in the white-only section of the bus? What reason does he give the policemen?
2. Why do you think the three white men try to help Rustin?
3. Why does Rustin give the assistant district attorney's name but no others?
4. Do Rustin's experiences support his conclusion in his final paragraph?

Questions about the Argument

1. Rustin does not begin his very straightforward account with any philosophical or political statements. Do you find learning his reasons along with the driver and the policemen effective? How might the impact on you differ if Rustin had prefaced the piece with theory?
2. This piece was originally published in *Fellowship: The Journal of the Fellowship of Reconciliation*. What assumptions does Rustin make about his audience?
3. What strategies does Rustin use to establish his ethos?
4. Is there an argument in this account? See if you can outline one.

John Lewis, "A Young Man Joins the Civil Rights Movement"

John Lewis (1940–) is the son of Alabama sharecroppers. The first member of his family to graduate from high school, Lewis attended the American Baptist Theological Seminary in Nashville, Tennessee, as he describes in the passage below. The following year he enrolled concurrently in Fisk University and received a B.A. from the seminary in 1961 and a B.A. in religion and philosophy in 1967 from Fisk. After his beginnings in the civil rights movement described here, Lewis went on to found the Student Nonviolent Coordinating Committee (SNCC) with several other college students in April 1960. He was a Freedom Rider in the protest of segregated interstate bus terminals organized by CORE in the spring of 1961; during the ride, a bigot knocked him unconscious in Montgomery, Alabama, one of many beatings and injuries he suffered in the civil rights movement. In September 1961, the Interstate Commerce Commission outlawed racial segregation in interstate bus depots. SNCC, under Lewis's chairmanship from 1963 to 1966, became one of the most important civil rights organizations. He was one of the planners of the 1963 March on Washington and was a keynote speaker there. In 1965, he became a conscientious objector, and in 1966, he cofounded the Southern Coordinating Committee to End the War in Vietnam. That year, he left SNCC, which had elected the militant Stokely Carmichael.

After completing his degree at Fisk, Lewis worked for the Southern Regional Council in various capacities, including as director of its Voter Education Project, which registered nearly 4 million new voters (including Lewis's mother). In 1977, President Jimmy Carter appointed Lewis the director of U.S. operations for ACTION, a federal agency for community-level economic recovery programs. Lewis was elected to the Atlanta City Council in 1981 and to the U.S. House of Representatives in 1986, where he still represents Georgia's Fifth Congressional District. In 1998, Lewis published his autobiography, *Walking with the Wind: A Memoir of the Movement*. The passage below comes from William R. Beardslee's 1977 oral history of participants in the civil rights movement, *The Way Out Must Lead In*.

> In 1955 there was the Montgomery bus boycott. Montgomery was only fifty miles away. I was fifteen years old, in the tenth grade, at an all-black county high school. The black high schools were considered training schools, while the white high schools were considered high schools. Being in the training school, passing the white high school, and then seeing Martin Luther King, Jr., and the black people of Montgomery organize themselves in such a way that fifty thousand people, for more than a year, walked rather than rode segregated buses had a tremendous impact on me. We didn't get a television until very late, but we followed the boycott on radio. We didn't have a subscription to the newspapers at home, but the high school did, so I would go to the library and read the Montgomery paper. I'd read all of the black papers, and I got very excited about what was going on. In a sense, I think that particular event probably changed the direction of my life more than anything else.

I had never met Martin Luther King, Jr., but I admired him greatly. I'd seen pictures of him, and I heard him on some Sunday mornings preaching on the radio. I'll never forget a sermon that he preached once, in Montgomery. It was something like Paul's letter to the American Christians. He took his sermon from Paul's letter to the church at Corinth. It was this whole thing about love. And it was really . . . very social . . . it had great emphasis on the aspect of this life and this world. He was saying to the black people in Montgomery, Alabama, and to his church in particular, that it was not enough for people to be concerned with streets that are paved with gold, and the gates to the Kingdom of God, but they had to be concerned with the streets of Montgomery, and the gates and doors of certain stores that discriminated against people, and places that refused to hire people in Montgomery.

In 1956 I told my minister that I had the call to preach, and I preached my trial sermon in February of that year. After that, I conducted the devotion, or the convocation at school on special occasions. I graduated from high school in 1957, and I wanted to come to Atlanta to college. My greatest desire was to come to Morehouse College, but it was impossible; I didn't have the resources. I just happened to be reading an old Southern Baptist newspaper, and it mentioned a seminary in Nashville, American Baptist Theological Seminary. Somehow it struck me because it said, in effect, that there was no tuition, and that a student could work and provide room and board. I applied there and was accepted.

I had followed the Montgomery bus boycott and what Dr. King had done. On campus the first thing I tried to do was organize a local chapter of the NAACP. The college president objected to that because the school was jointly supported by both black and white church organizations.

At the seminary they paid me $42.50 for washing pots and   5
pans three times a day and serving the food. Out of that I paid about $37 for room and board. I had a few dollars left. I had grown up on a farm, and I knew something about manual work and labor. but these pots and pans were some of the biggest and heaviest I'd ever seen. They were for cooking in the larger kitchens, and if they were full of water, they were almost impossible to lift. I did it for the first two years of school

and I enjoyed it for I felt that it was necessary. It was a way of seeing myself through those few years of college.

The Nashville Christian Leadership Council started conducting a series of nonviolent workshops in the city during the school year '58–'59. I started attending some of these workshops, along with some of the other students from the schools in town. The workshops were primarily discussions about the philosophy and the discipline of nonviolence. Discussions were based on the New Testament, Gandhi, Israel, India, Africa, Thoreau, and the whole question of civil disobedience and passive resistance. We met almost the entire school year.

The following year we started discussing nonviolence more or less as a social action, as a method of bringing about social change. In November, 1959, a group of students met with someone who was deeply involved in the whole Movement. He had been teaching and leading these workshops. We decided to test some of the large department stores downtown. We went in two different groups to restaurants and lunch counters. That was the first time that I could say that I was literally refused, that I had been denied, that someone told me, "No, you cannot be served." When I was growing up, people just knew better than to challenge. Your parents or somebody had said to you that you're black, you're supposed to go to that water fountain, you're not supposed to go to that lunch counter, you're not supposed to go downstairs to the theater. So you knew. You were conscious about it. You never really violated the customs or traditions. This was a deliberate attempt to violate it. It was the first time in my life that it was ever said to me, "No, you cannot eat here. We won't serve you." It was never said until 1959. In a sense, we expected it, but we wanted to establish the fact that the places of public accommodation did not serve mixed groups or did not serve blacks.

From that particular day in November when we had test sit-ins, we started regrouping, looking forward to more actions. We continued to meet in Nashville and continued to prepare for massive nonviolent sit-in efforts. In the meantime, on February 1, 1960, the students in Greensboro, North Carolina, had the first well-publicized sit-in. Then students throughout North Carolina started sitting in. We received a telephone call from one of the students saying, "What are the students in Nashville going to do?" Then, "What can you do to support the students in North Carolina?" We began sitting in downtown.

I'll never forget that series of days when we went down and sat there . . . I don't know . . . it was like a holy crusade, in a sense. Something told you just to stay there . . . the simplicity, the spirit, the sense of community that existed among the students. For the most part, during those early sit-in demonstrations in February, 1960, it was primarily black students, but there were some white students. We wanted to project the best image for the Movement. When some of the young whites would come up and put lighted cigarettes down our backs, or beat us, or spit on us, we never retaliated. We sat there. There was this great sense of feeling on the part of all the participants that it was necessary to do. Even some of the people who felt that they couldn't be nonviolent, that they couldn't adhere to the philosophy and the discipline of nonviolence, would say, "Well, I will not come down and participate in the sit-in; but I will drive my car, or drive my father's car." They'd transport people.

That went on for several weeks until the last day in   10
February. We all got arrested. A minister in the city, very active in civil rights efforts, had come to us early that morning and said that he understood from the merchants that we would be arrested. The minister said, "If you go down, you probably will be beaten. There are a lot of young hoodlums on the streets, and you will probably be arrested." That day a small group of us showed up. A few went in first and sat at the lunch counter. People came up and literally started beating the students or putting cigarettes out down their backs. They knocked people off the counter. The police came in and arrested all of the people sitting at the counter. They didn't arrest the people doing the beating, but they arrested all of the nonviolent students. Some of us that were at another variety store, only a door or so away, were asked to come down there and sit because the people had been arrested. We came, and we all were arrested. At the end of the day, 98 of us went to jail.

When the students on the campuses heard about it, about 500 of them came to continue the sit-in demonstration. More people got arrested. We went to jail. I didn't want to go to jail, but nonetheless it was a tremendous feeling to know that we had been able to dramatize the fact that segregation did exist and that there was something wrong about it. I guess many of us, most young black people, particularly in the South, grow up with a tremendous amount of fear of going to jail. Where I was brought up there was a street named Love Street. My mother used to warn us when we went to town, "Don't go down on Love Street." It was a bad place. Love Street is what Auburn Avenue is to Atlanta, or what Hunter Street is to Atlanta, what 125th Street is to Harlem. My mother would warn us that if we went to Love Street we would go to jail, the law would get us. We were told going to jail was the worst thing a person could do. It was a disgrace to go. First, it was bad for the person involved, then it was bad for the family, and it was bad for the family name.

I'll never forget the night in jail. It was just like a victory. For the most part, I don't think any of these people had been in jail before. In jail we became, in a sense, a bond, a circle of trust. Even in Nashville there had been rivalry between the different colleges and universities, but going to jail and getting involved in the sit-in movement helped to cut across schisms. In my estimation, the people there literally grew up overnight in that sit-in. We organized ourselves. We elected a spokesman. We had an organization right there in the jail cell. During the period that we stayed in, we had committees for clean up, for exercise, and for people who needed to study or do their homework. It was a strong group of people.

My mother, after hearing that I had been arrested and jailed, said in effect, "You should get out of this Movement and get out of that mess." I remember writing my mother in jail and saying something about acting according to my Christian faith and my conviction, and that I must go through to do what I'm doing. From that time on, because of going to jail, I guess a schism did occur for a period of time between myself and my family. They really did not understand. I never tried to widen the breach. I kept trying to get them to understand. It was not until 1963 that my family began to understand me. The period 1960 to 1963 was difficult.

During that period the real family, in a sense, was not my family. The family was not my mother, my father, my sisters, my brothers, my first cousins, and my grandparents but the people in the Movement, a sort of inner circle. We were a circle of trust, a sort of band of brothers. Those people, the people that I struggled with, and went to jail with, and went to lunch counters and on the freedom rides with, these folks really became my family. I think Martin Luther King, Jr., himself, sort of being the symbolic leader, gave all of us . . . not just the participants in the Movement but to many more blacks and whites also, a sort of sense of somebodyness. Being involved tended to free you. You saw segregation, you saw discrimination, and you had to solve the problem, but you saw yourself also as the free man, as the free agent, able to act.

After what Martin Luther King, Jr., had to say, what he did,   15 as an individual you couldn't feel alone again. You sort of destroyed a sense of being alone or a sense of alienation, the sense that you're just out there some place. I think the Movement itself, not just Dr. King, but this whole Movement, sort of integrated, brought different people together, and said, "You're not just so and so, here, or you're not just a student, but you're a part of something." It gave a sense of pride and it was a new sense of identity, really. You felt that you had some sense of control over what was happening and was going to happen.

The community was tremendously important. There was a kind of togetherness which was one of the underlying, strong ingredients in nonviolence. If something happened to one person, it happened to all of us. If one person would go to jail, we all would go; and if one person would suffer, we all shared in that suffering.

Even before the sit-ins, I guess, I started giving serious consideration to becoming a conscientious objector. Later I got classified and had to say no to the draft. Nonviolence for many people was not just a method, not just a technique, but a way of life. It was so for me.

After the sit-ins I continued in school. In 1961 the Congress of Racial Equality initiated a program to test a Supreme Court ruling outlawing segregation in areas of interstate travel. They started recruiting people to go on the Freedom Ride in the spring of 1961, and I applied to go.

I was accepted, and all those who were going to start the Ride were supposed to be in Washington. We were supposed to get there a few days early to go through a period of orientation. There were seven whites and six blacks going on the Ride. This was my first time in Washington, the week of May 4, 1961.

[After orientation,] we left the next day for Richmond, 20 Virginia. We didn't have any problems in Virginia. Through North Carolina there were a very few minor problems. Two days later, we arrived in Rock Hill, South Carolina. We got off the bus, started walking toward the waiting room, opened the door, and three young white guys just came at us, really fist-fighting, and they literally knocked us down. That was the first violence on the Freedom Ride, and it was the first real violence for me. I had been arrested and hit here and there; but that was the first time I was really hurt, and it left a scar. We got up and stood there. In a matter of minutes the state police arrived and asked us if we wanted to press charges. We said no. I had to leave the Freedom Ride briefly, but I was supposed to rejoin on Monday in Montgomery. In the meantime, the bus continued through South Carolina, Georgia, and Alabama. At Anniston, Alabama, people burned one bus; on the other bus, people were beaten at the bus station in Birmingham. I was waiting in Nashville to rejoin the Ride. In Nashville we heard that CORE had cancelled the Ride. Some of us felt that the Ride should continue. A group of us—students in Nashville that were part of the student movement—started calling together different community people and ministers, saying that we must go. We had a meeting around nine or ten o'clock that night. We talked until six o'clock in the morning. We finally convinced the adult community to make the necessary money available for us to go on the Freedom Ride. We left that Wednesday morning, May 17, 1961. There were ten of us, two white students and eight black students. We started toward Birmingham. Right outside the city a policeman stopped the bus. He got on and said, "Where are the Freedom Riders? I understand you have Freedom Riders on this bus." He arrested two of the people. When we got to Birmingham, other members of the police department got on the bus and said, "We're taking you in to the city jail, and we're placing you in protective custody of the Birmingham Police Department."

Early the next morning the sheriff came to the jail and said he was taking us back to Nashville. We said that we were on a trip, that we were on our way to Montgomery, and on to Mississippi and New Orleans. They put all of us and our baggage in two station wagons and a big limousine and took us to the Alabama/Tennessee state line. They left us there on the highway, saying that if a train or bus came by, maybe we could find our way back to Nashville.

We didn't know anybody. We walked across the railroad tracks and located a black family—they must have been in their seventies—and they were literally frightened to death. They didn't know what to do. They were staying on a white man's farm. They had heard about the Freedom Riders. They put us all in a back room in their house. When daylight came, the old lady sent her husband to two or three different grocery stores in the community to buy food for us. They didn't tell anyone we were there. We got on the telephone, called Nashville, and told them what had happened. We told them we wanted to continue, so they sent down a car. We rode by car to Birmingham. When we got to the bus station, we tried to get on, but we couldn't; they wouldn't let us board any of the buses.

There were delays; there was a mob threatening us at one time. I think Robert Kennedy was in touch with the Greyhound Company. We got a bus the next morning. We were given police protection from Birmingham to Montgomery. There was an arrangement that two officials of Greyhound would be on the bus, that a state patrol car would go with us, and that a small plane would fly above us. So we started out.

I was glad that the Ride was going to go on, but I just had an eerie feeling because I didn't know what to expect on the other end. It had been arranged that there would be transportation the moment we arrived in Montgomery to pick us up and take us to Reverend Abernathy's church. It was a strange feeling to travel down the highway on public transportation with that type of protection.

Before we got to the Montgomery city line, the state patrol   25
car and plane disappeared. When we drove up to the bus
station, there was no sign of life. I had never seen it like that
before, and I had gone to that station for four continuous years,
going home for the Christmas holidays, Thanksgiving
holidays, and returning sometimes in the summer. Nothing
was around that station.

The moment the bus stopped, all the reporters and television
people just sort of swarmed out there. Then out of the clear
blue . . . I'm talking about just like a flash, and I don't know . . .
to this day, I do not understand where the people came from,
but there was a mob of about two thousand people that just
came out there and literally just took the press people apart.
They started beating one reporter and blood started gushing
from his head. There was an NBC camera man who was
working with Frank McGee at the time. They took his camera,
one of these huge things, and just busted it across him. People
were trying to get up trees or on top of the buildings to get
away. We couldn't go anyplace.

When the mob had beaten the reporters down, they turned
on us and they started beating us. I remember saying to the
group, "Do not run. Let's stand here together." Our baggage
was taken from us and burned right there on the street. I was
hit and left unconscious there in the street for about forty-five
minutes, according to the Montgomery paper. But I remember
as I was lying there on the street and just bleeding, the Attorney
General of Alabama came up and served an injunction on me
for traveling through the State of Alabama as part of an
interracial group. I thought that was the end. It was one of the
most frightening experiences in my life. I was also quite
concerned about some of the other people.

Before we were beaten we did make it a point to get the girls
away. We got all the young ladies in a cab except two white
students. This black cab driver refused to let the two white
girls get in and said, "This is the law." One of the black girls
challenged him and said she would drive the cab because they
were trying to get away. The cab driver wouldn't let them. He
just took the black girls. President Kennedy had sent down a
newspaper editor as his personal representative. This man saw

the mob trying to get to the young ladies. After the cab left with the black girls, and the mob started behind the two young white girls, he got between them and the two young girls ran toward a church. A church official let them in and that's the only thing that saved them. The editor was beaten in the street so badly that he had a concussion. A post office official hid some of the black students, and some of the white fellows, in the basement of the post office. This was the white postmaster in Montgomery, in 1961, hiding people in the basement of the post office.

Questions about the Passage

1. Why do you think that Lewis and his fellow students needed a year of study of civil disobedience and nonviolent resistance before taking the first step of being refused service in a Nashville restaurant? Recall what King said about the preparation necessary for civil disobedience.
2. What does Lewis mean when he says the Nashville sit-in was "like a holy crusade" (paragraph 9)? How do you understand his statement in paragraph 14 that "being involved tended to free you"?
3. Why does Lewis think that a sense of community is vital to the success of nonviolent direct action (see paragraph 16)? Do you think he is right?

Questions about the Argument

1. What sort of person was John Lewis in the years he describes? What details included here influence our knowledge and view of Lewis's character?
2. Like Rustin's account, Lewis's reminiscences are not organized as an argument. Nevertheless, his position and the conclusions he drew from his experiences are clear. What are the ingredients for successful civil disobedience according to Lewis? Why is nonviolent resistance the best form for protesting the injustice of segregation?

Merrill Proudfoot, from *Diary of a Sit-In*

Charles Merrill Proudfoot (1923–1998) was a Presbyterian clergyman, scholar, teacher, and social justice activist. He received a B.A. from Austin College, his M. Div. from Austin Presbyterian Theological Seminary, and an M.A. and Ph.D. in Religion from Yale University. Later in life, he earned another M.A. and Ph.D. in philosophy from the University of Kansas and an M.A. in counseling from the University of Missouri, Kansas City. Ordained in Texas in 1950, Proudfoot worked for three years as a pastor there before beginning his long teaching career. He taught philosophy and religion at the predominantly black Knoxville College from 1957 to 1965, when the events recorded in his diary took place. Proudfoot then taught at Park College, in Parkville, Missouri, for thirty-two years, retiring in 1994. His publications include *Diary of a Sit-In* (1962), *Suffering: A Christian Understanding* (1964), and a number of essays on race relations and South Africa. Proudfoot was also one of the authors of the Presbyterian Church's policy statement on conscientious objectors and, after he accepted his homosexuality at the age of 54, a contributor of an autobiographical essay to *Called Out: The Voices and Gifts of Lesbian, Gay, Bisexual and Transgendered Presbyterians* (1995). In addition, Proudfoot visited prisoners and advocated for their welfare, making monthly visits for seventeen years to the U.S. Disciplinary Barracks at Ft. Leavenworth. He also served on the board of the Western Missouri Coalition for the Abolition of the Death Penalty.

The lunch counter sit-ins began in Greensboro, North Carolina, in February 1960. Sit-ins spread quickly among young people across the South. John Lewis and other college students started similar sit-ins in Nashville, and the students in Knoxville, Tennessee, including some at Proudfoot's college, were moved to sit in to protest segregation. Few professors, and even fewer white professors, participated in these sit-ins, but Proudfoot was one of them; he had promised Robert Booker, the president of Knoxville College's student body, he would. On the first day of the sit-in, June 9, 1960, Proudfoot wrote, "I found myself—a white, bespectacled college professor at the usually conservative age of thirty-six—advancing to my baptism by fire as a sit-in demonstrator!" His diary covers about six weeks, until the downtown merchants of Knoxville agreed to desegregate their counters. The passage below came midway through the protest. It is followed by a brief reflection on civil disobedience from the book's original Afterword.

Today our movement is in crisis and all of us know it. Open violence flared again, and one store has made a countermove we didn't expect.

Spurred by the rising excitement, between sixty and seventy came to sit-in today, enough to hit nearly all the stores whose counters remain open. Miller's was excluded because we hear they have at last completely closed theirs. I chose to go to Walgreen's because I hadn't yet experienced what it is like there. (I found out!) A tall brawny young Negro man named Logan was our leader. I asked him what his work was. He said, "I was working for a cab company until last week, but when I heard about the sit-ins I quit my job so I could help with them. I was only making fifteen or twenty dollars a week, and by working in the sit-ins maybe I can do some real good." What a spirit! Logan is not very well educated, but has a deep sense of justice and seems to know Christian love as more than a theory. He kept tight control of the group. One boy of twelve was with us; Logan called him "Junior" and kept reminding him sharply to sit back on his stool until I pointed out that when Junior sat back, his feet didn't touch the floor! The kids want to do their part, but we shouldn't involve them in some of the things that may happen.

Walgreen's is the only place we go that has booths; Logan and I occupy one together. A man in a white jacket who seems to be in charge of the counter manifests his hostility from the beginning. As he passes by our booth, he conspicuously spits on the floor. The next time he tosses a lighted cigarette on me; it rests in a fold of my coat. I would prefer to ignore it, but must pluck it off before it burns a hole in my good suit. I want to examine the coat to see if it is damaged, but I must not do anything here that will indicate anxiety. A young white fellow stops at our booth, inquires about Robert Booker, whom he says he knows. Now I see him bring coffee which he has ordered to one of our Negro boys and a coke to another. I wish he had not done that. The demonstrators do not touch the drinks. Logan suggests that the drinks may be drugged; I had not thought of that! The man in the white coat comes to pick up the drinks. He deliberately spills the coke over the demonstrator, and now the coffee, exclaiming with mock apology, "Oh, excuse me!"

A woman customer brushes close to our booth and mutters to me, "Take your niggers and get out of here!"

A group of white boys who appear to be high school age   5 come up to our booth and begin to tantalize me. I do not recognize the fellow who heckled me before; these boys have a younger appearance, but their line is the same: "Come on with us, fellow; we're going to show you where you belong!" I am apprehensive, but somehow actual danger is never so fearful as dreaded danger.

As they continue their heckling, I look straight ahead at Logan. Suddenly I feel myself drenched with what seems a terrific lot of liquid. My glasses are filmed over; I take them off and hold them in my clenched hands. My eyes smart— what was the stuff? The liquid has gone down all over my "preachin' suit." I notice crushed ice too, and realize it must have been a coke—a tall coke, not poured or spilled, but the contents thrown over me by one of these boys from a distance of two feet. Logan utters quiet words of encouragement; he is a great strength to me. I can sense as though I had eyes all over my head that everyone in the establishment is looking at me; I feel I have the sympathy of most of them. Nevertheless, it is a mortifying experience to be attacked in public by another person and not be able to do anything in your own defense.

I breathe a bit easier, for the boys have left us now, but I see one go into the kitchen and speak to some employee—the man in the white coat?—and I fear he is up to no good. Now they are back, heckling me again. I look straight forward, pretending to pay no attention. Suddenly I am jolted by a severe blow on the left side of my face. My first thought is of being hit by a batted tennis ball when I was six years old—it stings like that. It did not feel like the blow of a clenched fist; it must have been done with the open hand.

Logan reminds me I am not to strike back, but I hardly need that advice. I do not feel like striking back physically, but does one just sit here and let a young punk use him for a punching bag? Suddenly the blow comes again, again hard. Failing to get any response, one or two of the boys grab me and start pulling me from the booth. I slide my glasses to Logan as we have prearranged, and hold on.

At precisely this moment a young white man who has been eating in a booth near ours rises and takes the situation in hand. He is impressively large and young enough to be damaging. Sternly he says to the boys, "You fellows have gone far enough and now you'd better get out of here! Look, I'm neutral in this, but this fellow was just sitting here. You could be arrested for what you've done. You'd better get out of here before you get into real trouble!"

I wish I could see the boys' faces! They meekly leave and the   10 man leaves too. I will never know his identity and therefore can never thank him, but I have a feeling he would not wish to be thanked by me. What he did, he did not do for me, but for his sense of decency and order. What a travesty of both it is that a *customer* should have to restore order! I cannot imagine why any hard-headed business man would allow his store to become a scene of riot.

Nevertheless, here is a clear example of the effectiveness of the non-violent approach. It has caused this "neutral" to declare himself for decency and order. A more crucial test will be what he now says about serving Negroes in Walgreen's, and this I will never know. About the effect of non-violence on the agitators themselves, I have some reservations. I believe now that if I had at any time risen from my seat and said "Boo!" to those boys, they would have left me alone. Declared non-resistance brings out the bully in those who are inclined to be bullies.

Logan asks me, "What did the man mean when he said 'impure?'" It takes me some time to realize Logan means the word "neutral." I explain to him what a "neutral" is and am even more impressed with the boy's educated heart. I suppose any one of the white gang could have defined "neutral," but their knowledge hasn't made them good citizens or given them a fair attitude toward their fellow-man.

Half an hour has passed. At exactly 1:00 P.M., the counter lights are turned off. The man who I assume to be the counter manager comes to our booth and says in a decent way, "We've closed now; wouldn't you like to leave?" Logan asks me for advice (since this is his first day as a leader), and I tell him, "I think we could leave as soon as all the others are gone," meaning the customers. This seems to satisfy the manager.

Shortly after this, a man stops at our booth and says, "Hey, preacher." I turn, thinking he has a serious purpose. The man is of medium stocky build, black hair slicked back, and appears to be about thirty. He jeers, "Was your mother one?" Surprised, I treat it as a joke and turn forward again. The man proceeds to sit down in a booth along the rear wall with another man; a waitress comes, seems to be conversing with them. Suddenly the man rises from the booth, winds up like a baseball pitcher, and throws something with power down the row of booths at some target behind and to the right of me, I see a white object whiz by in the air.

A woman behind me screams, "Who threw that salt shaker? You've hit my baby! If I had hold of the dirty sonofabitch that hit my baby, I'd tear him in pieces!" The whole place is thrown into turmoil. A crowd collects, some coming in off the street. I can only think of one thing—supposing they charge that one of the Negroes did it! I get the impression the baby is badly injured.

A man who seems to be the manager of the entire store   15
comes to our booth and advises, "You'd better go now." We are definitely ready, but the question now is, "Will we be allowed to go?" For by now the police have arrived and are talking to the woman. Logan goes over to ask the police if it is all right for us to leave. The police are not getting anywhere; nobody is admitting that he knows who threw the shaker. I keep an eye on the culprit who sits innocently in his booth. I am determined not to leave the store until I have told what I know; even if it were not for honesty's sake, it would be to protect our group. Perhaps the police will get around to questioning us. At last the manager comes to me and asks if I know who did the throwing. I tell him without pointing to where the man is sitting. "The waitress must have seen it, because she was standing right beside his booth," I add.

"The waitress says she didn't see anything." That figures; I thought she was flirting with them.

A siren wails, a man in a white uniform enters the store— apparently a police officer on ambulance duty. They talk with the woman some more. Logan finally gets through to the police and they give us permission to leave. The policemen now move back to the booth where the guilty party is sitting.

The eight or nine Negroes encircle me to give me protection as we move through the crowd, but I tell them I will have to stay because I witnessed the offense; I ask for one Negro youth to stay with me. Just at this point the police officers escort the culprit and his companion from the store. They have apparently made an arrest. Greatly relieved that no one has accused us—for the opportunity must have made it a temptation—I give my name and address to the store manager and leave with our whole crew.

A crowd which includes a great many white youths is gathered on the sidewalk outside the store. Our danger is so real we can almost smell it, like dogs whiffing the wind. My only safety is in my Negro friends. How topsy-turvy my world has become, when I feel apprehensive among white strangers and perfectly safe only when Negroes are around! I have learned a lot since I came to the college three years ago; my attitude then was not unlike that of the department head at the University who avows that he always rolls up his car windows and locks his doors when he drives through a Negro neighborhood! The white South has always depended on the Negro population for its security and comfort, but in subtle ways that are easy to overlook. It would be good for every white person to have this experience I am having of knowing that my physical safety is completely in the hands of Negro friends.

A few steps from Walgreen's I run across a friend from Norris, Tennessee, who, not knowing our danger, expects me to stop and chat with him for a moment. I ask him to walk along with us, quietly explaining why I cannot stop. The Negro youths stay with me all the way to the parking garage and, despite my protests, wait outside until I drive off.

As I drive home, I am in a state of agitation. In my mind   20 the pieces of evidence become exaggerated into a certainty that the baby is dead or dying. I suffer an agony of conscience: "If we had left immediately when we were first asked, none of this would have happened—Does this not make me a murderer? During those first calm days, it seemed impossible that it could ever come to this! How thin is the line between peace and violence, between life and death, between hope and desperation."

Because in my emotional excitement I do not wish to be alone, I stop at the Reese's and share my experiences with them. From there I call Crutcher, who gives as his opinion, "The papers ought to know about this!" Hardly any time elapses before reporters from both the *News-Sentinel* and United Press International call. I am almost afraid to ask about the baby, but one of the reporters mercifully tells me that he doesn't think there has been any serious injury. The salt shaker hit the mother and fell down against the baby. But the baby was only fourteen days old! The object was thrown with great force and obviously went far wide of its intended mark, whatever that may have been. Supposing it had hit just a few inches lower against the infant's head! The *News-Sentinel* reporter rings back, saying that his boss wants to know what kind of doctor I am—a medical doctor? "No, a doctor of philosophy—from Yale University." I sense his disappointment. I can appreciate that if he could tie in the American Medical Association with the sit-ins, it would make quite a sensational story! The word has spread quickly and friends are beginning to call to express their concern. I am basking in the glow of attention, to the point that I am almost hurt that the Associated Press has not yet called!

Questions about the Passage

1. What are the rules that Proudfoot and Logan must follow in their sit-in at the segregated store's lunch counter?
2. What case for civil disobedience does Proudfoot make?

Questions about the Argument

1. Does Proudfoot create sympathy for the difficulty of his task? If so, how? How does the first-person narration shape our attitude to him?
2. What sense of Proudfoot's ethos do you have? How does the fact that this is a day-by-day diary affect his readers' perception of him?
3. Who is Proudfoot's audience? What clues do you have to who his intended audience is?
4. Compare Proudfoot's case for disobeying unjust laws to King's. Do they agree?

Diane Nash, "The Philosophy of the 'Beloved Community'"

Diane Nash (1938–) was raised in Chicago in an African American, middle-class Catholic family. She attended Howard University but transferred to Fisk University in Nashville, where she studied English. In Nashville, she encountered segregation personally for the first time, and she was profoundly disturbed by it. Like her fellow Fisk student John Lewis, she attended student workshops on Gandhi's teachings that were led by James Lawson, a black divinity student at Vanderbilt University who had studied in India. The 1960 sit-ins that began in Greensboro reached Nashville as they had reached Merrill Proudfoot's Knoxville. In February of that year, Nash, Lewis, and other students began sit-ins protesting segregated Nashville lunch counters. As she explains below, Nash was initially skeptical of the nonviolent resistance method she had studied, but she was impressed by the courage of its practitioners and its effectiveness in the struggle against racism. Attractive and articulate, Nash became the unofficial spokesperson of the sitting-in students. She became a founding member of SNCC in April 1960. She and three other students were arrested for attending a CORE meeting in Rock Hill, South Carolina, and, following the SNCC policy of "jail, no bail," they spent thirty-seven days in jail, enduring hard labor and racial taunts. SNCC rejected bail in order to pack the jails, highlight the injustice of Jim Crow segregation, and reduce the demonstrators' dependency on families and friends. Diane Nash also participated in and coordinated some of the Freedom Rides of 1961, pushing to continue even when CORE and Attorney General Robert Kennedy's special assistant urged the SNCC students to stop in Alabama. She married James Bevel, another civil rights worker, and was four months pregnant when she was jailed in Jackson, Mississippi, for teaching nonviolent techniques to black children. She insisted on remaining in jail to condemn the court system; although sentenced to two years in prison, she only served a short time. Nash worked for both SNCC and King's organization, the Southern Christian Leadership Conference (SCLC), devising the strategy for its 1965 voting rights campaign in Selma, Alabama. After 1965, when SNCC became a more militant organization, Diane Nash Bevel left it as well as SCLC. She has continued her work against racism, and for peace, and works as an educator in Chicago. She remains committed to nonviolent resistance, as she suggests in the piece below, part of an oral history done in 1988 at a SNCC reunion.

I think history's most important function is to help us better cope with the present and the future. So I'd like to talk about the philosophy behind the civil rights movement that drove it in its very early stages. We aspired in the sixties to the redeemed community or, as we frequently called it, the beloved community. A community recovered or fulfilled, a community that could become more of what its potential was. We defined the beloved community as a community that gave to its citizens all that it could give and allowed its members to then give back to the community all that they could. Our goal was to reconcile, to heal and to rehabilitate, to solve problems rather than to simply gain power over the opposition, and it really comes to the question of do you believe that human beings can be healed, can be rehabilitated. It's very interesting to me that so many of the struggles for liberation in the world seek to create a beloved society, a society where human beings get along, where democracy is practiced, but those struggling for liberation try to achieve these ends by killing people. And in spite of the fact that efforts toward liberation had been going on for thousands of years and in each generation, it's surprising to note with all that effort for so long, that there are still relatively few places on earth where the level of social, economic, and political liberation is very high. So it pays, I think, to go back and look at our methods and see if it isn't possible to become more efficient in terms of how we struggle for liberation. I think that the philosophy behind the movement of the sixties was very special, unique in terms of my own life in the late sixties. In the early sixties I had been very much dedicated to what we called nonviolence; in the late sixties I decided that it was an impotent, probably ineffective way to struggle for liberation. And I felt that way for a few years until I noticed that I hadn't killed anybody, I hadn't been to the rifle range, I hadn't blown up anything and truly, I had done very little during that period of time where I had decided that violence was the way to go, and I also noticed that the movement had not attracted large numbers of people in the kind of meaningful social action that it had attracted while we were using the philosophy of nonviolence.

Now, there is a connectedness with other historical periods and also a connectedness worldwide. We really used the philosophy that Mohandas Gandhi developed In India. He called it *satyagraha*, which is the Hindi word for holding onto truth. A young minister by the name of James Lawson had been to India, had spent some time in prison in this country because he was a conscientious objector. He refused to go into the Korean War, but he had studied Gandhi's philosophy in India and brought that philosophy to Nashville. Many of us who were students there at the time attended workshops regularly and became educated in the philosophy and the techniques that Gandhi used toward the independence of India from Great Britain.

I would like to mention a few of the basic tenets underlying the philosophy. First, we took truth and love very seriously. We felt that in order to create a community where there was more love and more humaneness, it was necessary to use humaneness and love to try to get to that point. Ends do not justify means. As Gandhi said, everything is really a series of means. We took truth very seriously; in fact, I'm sure I've lived an entirely different kind of life as a result of having been exposed to the philosophy in those early years. Truth now for me has very little to do with being good or doing what's right. It's more relevant to me in terms of providing oneself and people around one with accurate information upon which to base our behavior and base our decisions.

That principle has been very well understood I think in the natural sciences. It's quite clear that when scientists are calculating their mathematical problems or conducting experiments, they try to be as accurate and as truthful as possible. I think that that might be one reason why the natural sciences are in the space age and the social sciences are in primitive stages. Lying is institutionalized in our social relations. Countries lie to countries. The whole purpose of the CIA is to spy and to lie, and the FBI also. Governments of countries lie to the citizens. Boyfriends lie to girlfriends, girlfriends to boyfriends, husbands and wives to each other. In our personal relationships or governmental, economic, and business relationships we come to expect a great deal of untruth.

I think another fundamental quality of the movement is that   5
we used nonviolence as an expression of love and respect of the opposition while noting that a person is never the enemy.

The enemy is always attitudes, such as racism or sexism, political systems that are unjust, economic systems that are unjust, some kind of system or attitude that oppresses, not the person himself or herself. We had some illustrations of that in that one of the managers in particular of a lunch counter in Nashville who was the opposition the first year that we had sit-ins, 1960, became an ally the second year and he was talking to managers of the restaurants that we were trying to desegregate the second year and saying, "Well, I know how it is, it sounds really difficult but it's not so bad," and was actually encouraging the managers to desegregate.

Another important tenet, I think, of the philosophy was recognizing that oppression always requires the participation of the oppressed. So that rather than doing harm to the oppressor, another way to go is to identify your part in your own oppression and then withdraw your cooperation from the system of oppression. Guaranteed if the oppressed withdraw their cooperation from their own oppression, the system of oppression cannot work. An example of that would be the Montgomery bus boycott in 1955–56. For many years, Montgomery blacks assumed that Alabama whites were segregating them on buses. But in order to have segregated buses, it was necessary for the blacks to get on the bus, pay their fare, and walk to the back of the bus. When Montgomery blacks decided that there weren't going to be segregated buses anymore, there were segregated buses no more. It didn't take any change on the part of whites; when the blacks decided, then there were no longer segregated buses. So then, you have to ask yourself the question, well, who was segregating the buses all this time?

I think there's a thin line between what's known as blaming the victim and identifying appropriate responsibility, and I think that when you do identify your own responsibility in an oppressive situation, it then puts you in a position of power, because then you are able to withdraw your participation and therefore end the system.

There is so much about the philosophy that people as a whole never knew, because what was reported in the newspapers was just the fact that the demonstrators were not hitting back or not creating violence. But there were five steps in the process that we took a community through. The first step was investigation, where we did all the necessary research and analysis to totally understand the problem. The second phase was education, where we educated our own constituency to what we had found out in our research. The third stage was negotiation, where you approach the opposition, let them know your position, and try to come to a solution. The fourth stage was demonstration, where the purpose was to focus the attention of the community on the issue and on the injustice. And the last stage was resistance, where you withdraw your support from the oppressive system, and during this stage would take place things such as boycotts, work stoppages, and nonsupport of the system.

I think that the philosophy that started in Nashville, that was borrowed from India, the philosophy of the Student Nonviolent Coordinating Committee in its early days, has a great deal of merit. Everything considered, there was a considerable amount of social change achieved. There were some deaths, a number of injuries. But in looking at the efficiency of that struggle and comparing the number of casualties, I think that the philosophy that Gandhi developed works, and appears to me to be more efficient than many violent struggles. I would really urge you to do some studying of the history of nonviolence and some reading of how it works. I think it's got great potential for today and I think that we need to really get past the idea that going to the polls and voting is enough. I think we'd better take this country and its economics and politics into our own hands. We, the people. If we don't, we're going to lose more and more control of it. Nonviolence is certainly an approach that we should look into.

Some people think it was the influx of northerners, of whites, that made the redemptive community idea dissipate. I don't agree; I think it's possible for even a large-scale movement to operate as a band of brothers and sisters, a circle of trust. The reason wasn't that new people came in, I think we did not devote enough time and energy into the education of the people coming in. In Nashville, we started the teaching process before the sit-ins began in Greensboro on February 1, 1960. So there was quite a bit of time for them to become well versed. But what happened was that we got involved in going to jail and organizing and what have you and I think did not devote enough time and energy into training new people. When I first got exposed to the philosophy. I really didn't think it would work. And I had had a lot of training in it. But it was the only thing that was going on in Nashville that was trying to do something to combat the problem. And so I said well, I'll go along with it, but I really didn't think it would work. It was only in the process of using it that I finally became convinced. I always had the feeling that many of the people from throughout the South, including a number of people who were in SNCC, probably did not understand it to the level that many of us did in Nashville. And so I think education was the key.

It's true that one of the things that worked for us was that people like Bull Connor played into our hands by attacking us and getting it all onto the news. Now it seems that the system has learned to play the game, and people have wondered if a nonviolent movement can still succeed when those in power understand how to defuse it. Well, I do believe it can. One of the problems that we had was with the term "nonviolence" because it means absence of violence. And that term does not really describe the process. Absence of violence is really just one aspect of it. This is a whole, very active program, a process that a community is taken through. I think that the many demonstrations or efforts that are called "nonviolent" are only in terms of there being an absence of violence. They are not using the whole spectrum of activities in preparation and withdrawal of support. You really have to analyze what supports the system, what's financial, what's political, what's PR, and how the people as a whole are participating. So I think we haven't really been using the entire process of nonviolence. So even if the opposition understands this and we understand it, I think we can prevail.

Another thing. I think it's important to understand that today we are past the point of protests and attempting to show the government or show the powers that be that we don't like X, Y, or Z. I think we have to begin thinking of how we are going to solve it and make the ends of any demonstrations or efforts along that line what it is that we are going to do. For instance, if we object to the way the media is covering something, then we know that the media is controlled by the powers that be. It has very limited use to let the media or the government or whomever know that we don't like it. They know that we don't like it already. The idea is, decide what you need and do it yourself. Take matters into your own hands and do it yourself.

I sometimes think that there is kind of a mass masochism that we're all suffering from right now. Our water is poisoned. Our air is being poisoned. The soil, the toxic waste. We're eating food with cancer-causing chemicals. All kinds of gross things that go on and we read about them in the newspapers and maybe make a comment or two to each other, "Isn't that awful that they are doing this to us?" and then we turn the page of the newspaper and go on off to work the next morning or to school the next morning, tra la. As though our life isn't being threatened. If you were about to eat and I told you that the cook who was about to bring your food was in the next room poisoning your food and you just proceeded to go on and eat it, it would be clear that you were crazy. With all the social problems that we have right now, it's clear to me that we're not acting in a psychologically healthy manner. I think one thing that we need to do is stop lying to ourselves and realize that our life is being threatened.

Questions about the Passage

1. Why does Nash believe it is important to discuss the history of the civil rights movement?
2. How are truth and love the bases of the movement, according to Nash?
3. What role does Nash say the oppressed play in fighting oppression?
4. What is the weakness, according to Nash, of the term "nonviolence" (paragraph 8)?

Questions about the Argument

1. Nash combines personal recollection with laying out the history and principles of the movement. How successful is this combination?
2. Nash spoke at a Student Nonviolent Coordinating Committee (SNCC) reunion but knew her words would be part of a book

about SNCC. How does her audience affect her presentation? Is she attempting to persuade her audience?

3. Compare Nash's articulation (paragraph 8) of the steps in nonviolent resistance to King's. Do they agree completely? What might account for their differences, if any?

Photographs and Cartoons, "Recording and Interpreting: Images of the Civil Rights Movement"

Visual images, not just written texts, can also be arguments, especially about current issues being debated. Photographs capture a specific image in time. But a photo can convey a viewpoint or tell a story. The photographer omits some of what he or she sees in order to create a particular view of the events. The photographer might compose the photo as an artist composes a painting, perhaps shooting many frames but choosing only a single image to send a message.

Editorial cartoons are also time-bound. They are very much of the moment. They rely on visual associations, jokes, and allusions. They convey a message economically by careful selection of ideas but with few words. They rely heavily on the use of pathos.

Questions about the Photograph (Fig. 7-1)

This photo, by Shel Hershorn, was taken in 1958 at Brown's Basement Luncheonette in Oklahoma.

1. Describe what seems to be happening in the photo.
2. What are the roles of the various groups of people in that photo?
3. What physical aspects of the luncheonette does the photo emphasize? Be sure to consider lighting and atmosphere.

Questions about the Argument

1. What does the stance of the police officer suggest?
2. What message does the divider that runs horizontally convey? Why might Hershorn have chosen the viewpoint behind the onlookers to take the photo? Where do we, the viewers of the photograph, seem to be standing? What effect does our location have on our reading of the photo?

Figure 7-1

Questions about the Photograph (Fig. 7-2)

Bruce Davidson took this photo in Birmingham in 1963.

1. Describe what seems to be happening in the photo.
2. Read the expressions on all three faces.
3. What are the focal (central) points of the photo? Why is the movie marquee in focus?

Questions about the Argument

1. What does holding hands normally suggest? How does the photo undermine our expectations about holding hands?
2. What argumentative use does Davidson make of the movie marquee?
3. Formulate a claim that the photo supports.

Figure 7-2

Questions about the Cartoon (Fig. 7-3)

This cartoon, by the well-known cartoonist Herb Block ("Herblock"), appeared in the *Washington Post* on September 6, 1963.

1. Look at the setting and the figures, as well as the caption, of the Herblock cartoon. What story does the cartoon tell?
2. Who are the figures meant to represent? Who, beside the man in the cartoon, would make the statement in the caption?

Questions about the Argument

1. What claim does the cartoonist seem to be asserting about the statement in the caption? How do the setting and figures in conjunction with the caption work to support this claim?
2. Are you persuaded by the claim and its proof? Be prepared to support your answer.
3. Look back to the Davidson photo (Fig. 7-2). What connections do you see between the two images?

Figure 7-3

Questions about the Cartoon (Fig. 7-4)

This cartoon by Clifford H. Baldowski ("Baldy") was published in the *Atlanta Constitution* on July 28, 1963.

1. What issues does the cartoon raise about civil rights demonstrations?
2. Why are there conflicting messages on the signs?
3. What impact do the demonstrators have on the restaurant and its patrons?
4. Look carefully at the people in the cartoon. What can you infer about them? Which characters do you think the audience is meant to identify with?

Figure 7-4

Questions about the Argument

1. State the claim the cartoonist is making in the cartoon. Connect the caption to his claim.
2. Compare the Baldy cartoon to the Hershorn photo (Fig. 7.1). In which is the viewer closer to the action? What emotions does each image evoke? Which makes the more effective use of pathos?
3. How effective do you find the appeal to emotion as support for the claim in both the cartoon and the photo?

Writing Assignments

Conversations

1. Imagine that you are an interviewer on a serious talk show (for example, Charlie Rose or Jim Lehrer). You have invited Rustin,

Proudfoot, Lewis, and Nash for a discussion of the civil rights movement. As a good interviewer, be sure to ask your guests to address the following issues: Why did they become civil rights activists and nonviolent resisters? What do they see as the main strength of the movement? What do they see as their own contribution to the theory or practice of nonviolent direct action? Do not structure your show merely as a question-and-answer session but encourage the guests to engage in a discussion with each other. Try to differentiate the voice of each speaker.

2. Imagine a conversation between the conductors on the Underground Railroad from the previous chapter and the civil rights workers we have read in this chapter. What common ground do they share? On what issues might they disagree? Are their actions similar or not—is breaking the Fugitive Slave Law like breaking Jim Crow segregation laws?

3. Working on your own, title each cartoon and each photograph (four titles). In class, divide into four groups, assigning each group a cartoon or a photo to consider. Agree on the best title in your group, and defend your group's choice to the rest of the class in a well-developed paragraph.

Writing Sequence One: To Sit In or Not to Sit In

1. Brainstorm a list of the issues, problems, or questions that the practice of civil disobedience in the civil rights movement raises for you. Identify and explore informally the one or two questions or issues that most interest you. You might consider the different categories of laws that are broken, the risks involved in practicing civil disobedience, and the responses of others to your actions. Try to put yourself in the position of the participants in the protests, of the whites reading about the protests and watching them on television, of the blacks who were opposed or too frightened to participate, and of those charged with enforcing the law.

2. Write a brief for an argument that takes a position on a civil rights movement issue you explored in the preceding assignment (see Chapter 3 for an example of a brief). Be sure to identify the audience you are addressing. What will your audience need to know? What assumptions about the issue do you need to make explicit? List the sources (minimum of three) you expect to use to support your position.

3. Write a short argumentative essay (4–5 pages) from your argument in brief. Your position should be stated in a clear thesis. Support for the thesis should come from your reading in this section. Use a minimum of three sources.

Writing Sequence Two: The Civil Rights Movement in Perspective

1. Choose one civil disobedience theorist, such as Antigone, Thoreau, Tolstoy, or Gandhi (do not choose King). For example, what would Gandhi say about Nash and Rustin, or how might Thoreau view Lewis and Proudfoot? What would your theorist think of the work of the practitioners in the civil rights movement? How much would the theorist approve of? Where might he or she disagree with the ideas or actions of the civil rights workers?

2. Write a short argumentative essay that makes the case that one or more of the civil rights activists we have read were acting in accord (or not in accord) with the theorist you wrote about in question 1. For example, if you look at John Lewis as your activist, do his actions accord with Thoreau's theories? Use evidence from the texts to support your thesis.

3. Now consider your own view of the civil rights movement after thinking about it from another thinker's viewpoint. Did the movement adhere to the principles of civil disobedience as you understand them? Be sure to use evidence from both the earlier writers on civil disobedience we have read as well as from the writers in this chapter.

8

Peace Movements

Civil disobedience in protest of war has a long history in the United States. Today's activists against war who practice civil disobedience may look back to their ideological ancestors such as John Woolman and Henry David Thoreau. A century before Thoreau spent his celebrated night in Concord Jail for not paying the poll tax, Woolman, an eighteenth-century Quaker, refused to pay taxes to support either war or slavery. Two centuries after Woolman, Presbyterian minister Maurice McCrackin examined his faith and conscience much as Woolman had and came to a similar conclusion. He could not pay the portion of his federal taxes that supported war. Today, Kathy Kelly has deliberately earned too little to pay income taxes for over twenty years in order not to support American wars.

In the twentieth century, civil disobedience to both world wars also included draft resistance and the refusal to serve in the military. The War Resisters League was founded in 1923 to oppose war through civil disobedience. Bayard Rustin was one of its members, and he refused to serve in World War II. The development of nuclear weapons and the horrors of Hiroshima and Nagasaki motivated antiwar groups to use and build upon the civil disobedience tradition they inherited and to learn from Gandhi's ideas in action in the struggle for Indian independence. Dorothy Day and others in the Catholic Workers movement were arrested rather than obey New York City's civil defense drills. They refused to partake in any way in making nuclear war a reality. Kathy Kelly is a follower of the Catholic Workers in her sit-ins and demonstrations against U.S. support for Central American violence, the School of the Americas, nuclear weapons, and the Iraqi wars.

Civil disobedience in opposition to war reached a peak during the Vietnam War. Protesters and draft resisters built their actions on both American traditions of peace activism and on the recent civil disobedience successes in the civil rights movement. The *Declaration of Conscience Against the War in Vietnam* looks back to *The Declaration of Independence* and Garrison's Anti-Slavery Society declaration. Vietnam War draft resister James Rowland saw himself as a radical like Thoreau, willing to go to jail for his actions.

The two-and-a-half centuries of American civil disobedience in opposition to war also demonstrate the deep and long-standing influence of Christianity on the thinking of those involved in civil disobedience against war. Woolman, McCrackin, Day, and Kelly all acted out of religious convictions that led them to break the law deliberately. As McCrackin wrote, "Disobedience to a civil law is an act against government, but obedience to a civil law that is evil is an act against God."

John Woolman, "On Paying Taxes"

John Woolman (1720–1772) was an American Quaker minister who opposed slavery, mistreatment of Indians, and war. His influence has extended beyond his own day through his *Journal*, a record of his spiritual inner life. Born in New Jersey of Quaker parents, Woolman was a successful storekeeper who also taught and drew up wills and conveyances. Very committed to his religious beliefs, in his early 20s he was recognized as a minister by his home congregation (the Society of Friends has no ordained or paid clergy). With the moral support of his New Jersey church, he went on missionary travels up and down the Atlantic coast. He preached eloquently against slavery, war, and cruelty to Indians. He taught himself tailoring as a simpler form of earning a living, and he attempted to live a strictly simple life according to his beliefs. He traveled on foot whenever possible, he wore undyed clothes because slaves made the dyes and were harmed in their manufacture, and he did not eat sugar because of its connection to the slave trade. In 1754, the Yearly Meeting of Society of Friends in Philadelphia published Woolman's pamphlet, *Some Considerations on the Keeping of Negroes*, and in 1776 the Meeting prohibited Friends from owning slaves.

The 1757 section of Woolman's *Journal* below questions the paying of taxes to a government making war. The French and Indian War

(1754–1763) made his questions more than merely academic. As a Quaker, Woolman was a pacifist, and here in answering his own questions he examines his conscience and examples of Christian lives.

1757

A few years past, money being made current in our province for carrying on wars, and to be sunk by Taxes laid on the Inhabitants, my mind was often affected with the thoughts of paying such Taxes, and I believe it right for me to preserve a memorandum concerning it.

I was told that Friends in England frequently paid Taxes when the money was applied to such purposes. I had [conference] with several Noted Friends on the subject, who all favoured the payment of such taxes, Some of whom I preferred before myself, and this made me easier for a time: yet there was in the deeps of my mind, a scruple which I never could get over; and, at certain times, I was greatly distressed on that account.

I all along believed that there were some upright-hearted men who paid such taxes, but could not see that their Example was a Sufficient Reason for me to do so, while I believed that the Spirit of Truth required of me as an individual to suffer patiently the distress of goods, rather than pay actively.

I have been informed that Thomas à Kempis lived & died in the profession of the Roman Catholick Religion, and in reading his writings, I have believed him to be a man of a true Christian spirit, as fully so as many who died Martyrs because they could not join with some superstitions in that Church.

All true Christians are of [one and] the same spirit, but their   5
gifts are diverse; [Jesus] Christ appointing to each one their peculiar Office, agreeable to his Infinite Wisdom.

John Huss Contended against the Errors crept into the Church, in opposition to the Council of Constance, which the historian reports to have consisted of many thousand persons. He modestly vindicated the cause which he believed was right, and though his language and Conduct toward his Judges appear to have been respectful, yet he never could be moved from the principles settled in his mind. To use his own words: "This I most humbly require and desire of you all, even for His sake who is the God of us all, that I be not compelled to the thing which my Conscience doth repugn or strive against." And again in his answer to the emperor "I refuse nothing, most noble Emperor whatsoever the council shall decree or determine upon me, this only one thing I except, that I do not offend God and my Conscience."[1] At length rather than act contrary to that which he believed the Lord required of Him, he chose to Suffer death by fire. Thomas à Kempis, without disputing against the Articles then generally agreed to, appears to have laboured, by a Pious Example as well as by Preaching & writing to promote Virtue and the Inward Spiritual Religion, and I believe they were both sincere-hearted followers of Christ. [To me it looks likely that they were both in their proper places.][2]

True Charity is an excellent Virtue, and to sincerely Labour for their good, whose belief in all points, doth not agree with ours, is a happy case. To refuse the active payment of a Tax which our Society generally paid, was exceeding disagreeable; but to do a thing contrary to my Conscience appeared yet more dreadfull. When this exercise came upon me I knew of none under the like difficulty, and in my distress I besought the Lord to enable me to give up all, that so I might follow him wheresoever he was pleased to lead me, and under this Exercise I went to our Yearly Meeting at Philad[a], in 1755, at which a Committee was appointed, some from each Quarter to Correspond with the meeting for Sufferings in London, and another to Visit our Monthly and Quarterly meetings, and after their appointment before the last Adjournment of the meeting, it was agreed on in the meeting that these two Committees should meet together in Friends School House[3] in the Citty, at a time [when the Meeting stood adjourned] to consider some [cases] in which the cause of Truth was concerned: and these Committees meeting together had a weighty conference in the

---

1. Note by Woolman. Fox's "Acts and Monuments," p. 233.
2. MSS. A and B. Both include the last sentence of this paragraph, omitted by Committee of 1774 in first edition, p. 82.
3. "Friends' School House"; No. 119 South 4th St., Philadelphia, on the site of the present Forrest Building.

fear of the Lord, at which time I perceived there were many Friends under a Scruple like that before mentioned.[4]

As Scrupling to pay a tax on account of the application[5] hath seldom been heard of heretofore, even amongst men of Integrity, who have Steadily born their testimony against outward wars in their time, I may here note some things which have opened on my mind, as I have been inwardly Exercised on that account.

From the Steady oposition which Faithfull Friends in early times made to wrong things then approved of, they were hated and persecuted by men living in the Spirit of this world, & Suffering with firmness, they were made a Blessing to the Church, & the work prospered. It equally concerns men in every age to take heed to their own Spirit: & in comparing their Situation with ours, it looks to me there was less danger of their being infected with the Spirit of this world in paying their taxes, than there is of us now. They had little or no Share in Civil Government, neither Legislative nor Executive & many of them declared they were through the power of God separated from the Spirit in which wars were, and being Afflicted by the Rulers on account of their Testimony, there was less likelyhood of uniting in Spirit with them in things inconsistent with the purity of Truth. We, from the first settlement of this Land have known little or no troubles of that sort. The profession, which for a time was accounted reproachfull, at length the uprightness of our predecessors being understood by the Rulers, & their Innocent

4.   MS. A. P. 709. Here follow two Extracts from the *Journal* of John Churchman—1st Edit. 1779, pp. 68 ff, 169 ff, John Woolman writes, "Since I had finished my Narrative of this Affair, having been favoured by my Beloved Friend John Churchman with the perusal of some notes which he made concerning some Exercise he went through on Account of our Testimony against Wars, as they contain some things relative to Facts, hereafter Spoken of, I thought good by his permission to copy the Substance of them in this place." A note in margin directs, "If this Journal be printed, let all the Quotn from J. Churchman's Notes be left out." J. Churchman's *Journal* was printed in 1779: he died 2, 7 mo. 1775, and the "extracts" are there given entire. They describe his visits to the assembly, then sitting in the State House [now Independence Hall], Phila. in 1748, and again in 1755. On the first occasion he went alone. Seven years later, twenty Friends presented the address.

5.   Note by John Woolman—"Christians refused to pay taxes to support Heathen Temples. See Cave's Primitive Christianity, part iii. page 327."

Sufferings moving them, our way of Worship was tolerated, and many of our members in these colonies became active in Civil Government. Being thus tryed with favour and prosperity, this world hath appeared inviteing; our minds have been turned to the Improvement of our Country, to Merchandize and Sciences, amongst which are many things useful, being followed in pure wisdom, but in our present condition that a Carnal mind is gaining upon us I believe will not be denied.

Some of our members who are Officers in Civil Government   10 are in one case or other called upon in their respective Stations to Assist in things relative to the wars, Such being in doubt whether to act or crave to be excused from their Office, Seeing their Brethren united in the payment of a Tax to carry on the said wars, might think their case [nearly like theirs, &] so quench the tender movings of the Holy Spirit in their minds, and thus by small degrees there might be an approach toward that of Fighting, till we came so near it, as that the distinction would be little else but the name of a peaceible people.

It requires great self-denial and Resignation of ourselves to God to attain that state wherein we can freely cease from fighting when wrongfully Invaded, if by our Fighting there were a probability of overcoming the invaders. Whoever rightly attains to it, does in some degree feel that Spirit in which our Redeemer gave his life for us, and, through Divine goodness many of our predecessors, and many now living, have learned this blessed lesson, but many others having their Religion chiefly by Education, & not being enough acquainted with that Cross which Crucifies to the world, do manifest a Temper distinguishable from that of an Entire trust in God.

In calmly considering these things it hath not appeared strange to me, that an exercise hath now fallen upon some, which as to the outward means of it is different from what was known to many of those who went before us.

Questions about the Passage

1. What is Woolman's issue or problem that he describes in the first three paragraphs?
2. What does Woolman find in the teachings and lives of Thomas à Kempis and John Huss (Jan Hus) to help him think through his own position?

3. According to Woolman, what is the difference in the contemporary situation of the Friends (Quakers) in colonial America in comparison to their position in England? Why is that different role in
American civil society and government important to Woolman?
4. What is Woolman concerned might happen to the Friends if they
continue to pay their taxes and serve in government (paragraph 10)?
5. In paragraph 11, Woolman clearly states the greatest difficulty
facing pacifists. What is it? In his view, how can believers become
and remain truly pacifist?

Questions about the Argument

1. Woolman's writings were a vehicle for his own spiritual explo-
rations. How does the journal form contribute to his ethos? Do
you find him credible? Does the form add to his persuasiveness?
2. Examine Woolman's argument in paragraph 10. Is it valid? Or
would you consider it a slippery slope fallacy? Be prepared to
support your position.

Maurice McCrackin, "Pilgrimage of a Conscience"

Maurice McCrackin (1905–1997) was a man committed to peace and justice throughout his long life. He was born in Ohio and raised in Illinois,
where he became an ordained Presbyterian minister and served several
churches; in 1945, he came to Cincinnati, his home for the rest of his life.
There McCrackin became increasingly active in protesting injustice and
war. He led pickets against prominent segregated institutions such as
the Conservatory of Music and Coney Island, an amusement park. In
1948, he was a founding member of the Peacemakers, a group that practiced and promoted war-tax refusal and also encouraged the refusal of
draft registration. Like Thoreau and Woolman before him, McCrackin
publicly announced his intention in 1949 of not paying taxes to support
war, withholding 80 percent of his income tax. He was arrested in 1958
for nonpayment of income tax. This form of civil disobedience seemed
so unusual that the federal judge ordered McCrackin to undergo psy-
chiatric tests before sentencing him to a six months' sentence, of which
the minister served forty-two days. As a war-tax protester, he was part
of a tiny but dedicated group, which grew during the Vietnam War; their
numbers reached an estimated 20,000 in the early 1970s. In 1961, the
Cincinnati Presbytery suspended McCrackin's ordination, but he started
a nondenominational church in Cincinnati, taking many of his former

congregants with him. The Presbytery reversed its decision in 1987, admitting it had made an error. Arrested more than twenty times for his acts of civil disobedience, McCrackin was still active into his late 80s, describing his work as "coming to the people with your body." He was arrested in 1988 at a protest at the U.S. Department of Energy's uranium-processing center in Cincinnati, and was arrested again in 1990, at the age of 85, when he climbed the White House fence and poured red dye into a fountain to symbolize the bloodshed of the Gulf War. His last arrest came in 1993, as he protested a loss of housing for the poor. In the passage below, he articulates some of the principles that guided him through his many years of activism.

I decided that I would never again register for the draft nor would I consent to being conscripted by the government in any capacity. Nevertheless each year around March 15 without protest I sent my tax payments to the government. By giving my money I was helping the government do what I so vigorously declared was wrong. I would never give my money to support a house of prostitution or the liquor industry, a gambling house or for the purchase and distribution of pornographic literature. Yet year after year I had unquestionably been giving my money to an evil infinitely greater than all of these put together since it is from war's aftermath that nearly all social ills stem.

Income tax paid by the individual is essential to the continuance of the war machine. Over 50% of the military budget is paid for by individuals through their income tax payments and 75% to 80% of every dollar he pays via income tax goes for war purposes.

Again I examined what the principle of personal commitment to Jesus meant to me. Through the years I have tried to achieve a personal relationship with Jesus. This is the burden of the Christian gospel, that Jesus can be known personally and that he can bring a saving power into a man's life. For us as Christians to know Jesus personally has reality only as we try earnestly to grow more like him "unto the measure of the stature of His fullness." If we follow Jesus afar off, if we praise his life and teachings but conclude that neither apply to our daily living, what are we doing but denying and rejecting him? Jesus speaks with authority and with love to every individual, "Follow me. Take up your cross. Love one another as I have loved you."

What would Jesus *want* me to do in relation to war? What *must* I do if I am his disciple? This was the conclusion I reached: If I can honestly say that Jesus would support conscription, throw a hand grenade, or with a flame thrower drive men out of caves, to become living torches—if I believe he would release the bomb over Hiroshima or Nagasaki, then I not only have the right to do these things as a Christian, I am even obligated to do them. But if, as a committed follower, I believe that Jesus would do none of these things, I have no choice but to refuse at whatever personal cost to support war. This means that I will not serve in the armed forces nor will I voluntarily give my money to help make war possible.

Having had this awakening, I could no longer in good conscience continue full payment of my federal taxes. At the same time I did not want to withdraw my support from the civilian services which the government offers. For that reason I continued to pay the small percentage now allocated for civilian use. The amount which I had formerly given for war I now hoped to give to such causes as the American Friends Service Committee's program and to other works of mercy and reconciliation which help to remove the roots of war.

As time went on I realized, however, that this was not accomplishing its purpose because year after year the government ordered my bank to release money from my account to pay the tax I had held back. I then closed my checking account and by some method better known to the Internal Revenue Service than to me, it was discovered that I had money in a savings and loan company. Orders were given to this firm, under threat of prosecution, to surrender from my account the amount the government said I owed. I then realized suddenly how far government is now invading individual rights and privileges: money is given in trust to a firm to be kept in safety and the government coerces this firm's trustees into a violation of that trust. But even more evil than this invasion of rights is the violence done to the individual conscience in forcing him to give financial support to a thing he feels so deeply is wrong. I agree wholeheartedly with the affirmation of Presbytery made in February of 1958, that, "A Christian citizen is obligated to God to obey the law but when in conscience he finds the requirements of law to be in direct conflict with his obedience to God, he must obey God rather than man."

Disobedience to a civil law is an act against government, but obedience to a civil law that is evil is an act against God.

At this point it came to me with complete clarity that by so much as filing tax returns I was giving to the Revenue Department assistance in the violation of my own conscience, because the very information I had been giving on my tax forms was being used in finally making the collection. So from this point on, or until there is a radical change for the better in government spending, I shall file no returns.

Questions about the Passage

1. What role does Jesus' example play in McCrackin's thinking about tax resistance?
2. What role does individual conscience play in his thinking?
3. What religious principle does McCrackin cite to support his decision?

Questions about the Argument

1. Evaluate the argument by analogy McCrackin makes in his first paragraph.
2. What is the rhetorical purpose of this piece? How does the author's ethos contribute to that purpose?
3. What authorities does McCrackin use to support his position?
4. What assumptions underlie McCrackin's argument? Do you agree with them? If you disagree with his assumptions, do you accept the validity of his reasoning? Do you accept the truth of his conclusion?

Dorothy Day, "On Pilgrimage"

Dorothy Day (1897–1980) is best known as the founder of the Catholic Worker movement, an important social reform group. As a young woman, Day became a socialist while attending the University of Illinois for two years. She became a journalist and worked for a socialist and a Communist newspaper; she also joined the Industrial Workers of the World (IWW) in 1916. A supporter of women's suffrage and a pacifist,

Day was arrested in November 1917 for picketing the White House during a women's suffrage demonstration. After working for a few years as a nurse during the World War I influenza epidemic, Day returned to journalism in the 1920s. She was married for a few years, and she had one daughter, after which she explored Roman Catholicism, finally joining the church in 1927. In 1932, Day met Peter Maurin, a French Catholic social reformer, and the following year they began to publish *The Catholic Worker,* a monthly newspaper. The paper was the voice of a movement that combined Day's radical social beliefs with the church's teachings. The movement embraces pacifism, voluntary poverty, and caring for the destitute with free housing, food, and clothing; Catholic Workers apply Jesus' words, "Go, sell what you have, and give to the poor" (Matt 19:21), to themselves quite literally. Within three years, the paper's circulation was 150,000, and the group's St. Joseph's House of Hospitality for the poor and unemployed in New York City became the model for such houses in other cities. The Catholic Workers' opposition to all war led Day and others in the movement to support Catholic conscientious objectors during World War II and to refuse both to pay income tax and to participate in air-raid drills during the Cold War. She continued her work until the end of her life. In 1973, at the age of 76, she was arrested at a California demonstration in support of Cesar Chavez and the United Farm Workers. Her supporters went to the Vatican to start the canonization process for Day in the late 1990s.

Dorothy Day also published a number of books, including an autobiography in 1952, *The Long Loneliness,* in addition to her regular columns for *The Catholic Worker,* one of which appears below. In this piece published in the July–August 1957 issue, she discusses the Catholic Workers' nonviolent resistance to atomic bomb testing and their civil disobedience actions in refusing to participate in civil defense drills.

> The feast of St. Cyril and Methodius, July 7. Sunday, at the office. It is as hot as blazes, real dog days, and most of the office is out, at meetings or at the beach. The soup line is finished, two hundred or so fed, and Roy Duke is out in the courtyard, in the shade of the tenement next door, slicing tomatoes. There is a basket of celery and one of green peppers on either side of him, a colorful setting. I would like to say that these came from our garden farm in Staten Island, but there the crops have not come in yet, and a drought has not helped matters. . . .
>
> There is the usual complaint of some of the older readers who also drop in to call, that the paper is not what it used to

be. Too much stuff about war and preparation for war, and the duty of building up resistance. But I repeat, in Peter Maurin's day, the problem was unemployment. It was the time of depression. We still need to build up the vision of a new social order wherein justice dwells, and try to work for it here and now. We still need to perform the works of mercy because in spite of full employment there is still sin, sickness and death, and the hunger and homelessness and destitution that go with so much sickness, and our industrial system.

But the work of non-violent resistance to our militarist state must go on. Some readers, and old friends too, ask us why we do not protest Russian tests as well as English and American. We can only say that we have—over and over. In the two talks I gave on May Day before left wing groups, I stressed the numbers of unannounced nuclear tests made in Russia. Why don't we picket the Russian embassy, another wants to know. For one thing, we have only one chronic picketer, Ammon Hennacy, and for another, we believe in taking the beam out of our own eye, we believe in loving our enemy, and not contributing to the sum total of hatred and fear of him already in the world.

Of course we know that the Communists also come with arms, with the use of force, with the threat of liquidation to all who do not conform. It is that very use of force that is the heart of the problem today. The means become the ends. We cannot force people to be good, to be just, to share with their brothers. But Peter Maurin said, We must make the kind of society in which it is easier to be good. We must make it, and we can only begin with the works of mercy, with sharing what we have, with voluntary poverty.

We must do more. We cannot keep silent in the face of the bomb tests, we cannot ignore what we have done in the past to Hiroshima and Nagasaki. Each year on that anniversary, beginning August 6, Ammon Hennacy fasts for as many days as there are years since the bomb was dropped. This year he will fast. He has already fasted twelve days last month in front of the Atomic Energy Commission offices in Las Vegas, Nevada.

In addition to this demonstration of dissent, there will be our third annual protest during the civil defense drill in which the public is supposed to participate by taking shelter, next Friday, July 12. This will be before we go to press for our July–August issue, and is one of the reasons why I wish to write this column now. If we again refuse to take shelter, but go out into the streets, in our refusal to play war games as Ammon Hennacy puts it, we are liable again to a jail sentence. The first year we were only in prison a day or two days awaiting bail,—the second year we were sentenced to five days, and it is hard to tell what will happen this year. We may be ignored as crackpots, but we have to reconcile ourselves to being a "spectacle to the world, to angels and to men,"—"to being fools for Christ."

Why Do We Do It

It is not because we can say with St. Peter that we are obeying God rather than man, that we do this. There is nothing in this command of the civil defense authorities in itself that is against the law of God. But is generally acknowledged, that *there is no defense*. So it is a farce to pretend there is. There is no defense but decentralization, a return of those in the city to the land, or to the small town. One young physicist instructor from Purdue demonstrated at the same time we did,—allowed himself to be arrested, and sentenced, just so that he could protest the foolishness of these games last year. He paid his $25 fine and left the court, always careful not to associate himself with us pacifists and crack pots.

The main reason we make our protest, those of us from *The Catholic Worker*, is to do penance publicly for our sin as Americans for having been the first to make and use the atom bomb. As the priest editor of the *Boston Pilot* said, "This is an unconfessed sin, and as such not forgiven." We publicly confess our share in the guilt of our country, and are willing to give up our freedom by this act of civil disobedience. It is not an easy thing to do, physically speaking. As I woke up this morning I thought of that hard narrow iron bed which was suspended from the wall, in the tiny cell at the Woman's House of Detention. I thought of the crowded conditions, how Deane's bed was moved into my single cell to make room for another prisoner. I thought of the gray ugliness of the surroundings that the girls tried to alleviate in little ways as they served out their long sentences, by scrubbing, draping, decorating in whatever way they could through the long months. The sooty few feet of recreation space on the roof, the capacious floors for medicinal services, and the scanty space for recreation and occupational therapy. The work is all done by the inmates and there is not enough of that to go around. There are long periods to lie in your bunk and contemplate the four narrow walls, the tiny sink, the toilet in the corner which is also a chair with a metal table in front which comes down from the wall—your dining cubicle in case you are confined to your cell. You find nothing there you want to satisfy but the most elementary instinct of mind or body or soul. And yet the strange and tragic thing is that so many women have found temporary content and safety there from their drab and sin-filled lives while their health was built up and with it the craving to go out and continue the only life they knew.

We know what we are in for, the risk we run in openly setting ourselves against this most powerful country in the world. It is a tiny Christian gesture, the gesture of a David against a Goliath in an infinitesimal way.

We do not wish to be defiant, we do not wish to antagonize. We love our country and are only saddened to see its great virtues matched by equally great faults. We are a part of it, we are responsible too.

We do not wish to be defiant, we atone in some way, with this small gesture, for what we did in Hiroshima, and what we are still doing by the manufacture and testing of such weapons.

Questions about the Passage

1. According to Day, why do the Catholic Workers not picket the Russian embassy? Why do you think her readers wanted them to picket there?
2. What reasons does Day give for protesting atomic bomb tests and civil defense drills? Are the Catholic workers willing to be arrested and go to jail? Why or why not?
3. In what ways are their acts atonement, as Day calls it in her last paragraph?

Questions about the Argument

1. How does Day establish authority in this piece?

2. What is the impact of beginning with a description of the office? Why do you think Day chose to begin with the heat and quiet of a summer day?
3. Carefully consider Day's use of the first person in this piece. Who is her audience? Who is "we"? Why might supporters still need encouragement and teaching?

"Declaration of Conscience against the War in Vietnam"

Protest against the Vietnam War began as a movement distinct from pacifist opposition to all war in early 1965, when the bombing of North Vietnam began. The protests included civil disobedience from the beginning. Among the protesters were longtime peace movement activists and veterans of the civil rights movement. Both groups brought their ideas, strategies, and techniques. As early as April 1965, some 25,000 people, mostly dressed in skirts, ties, and jackets, marched against the war in Washington, D.C. That summer, draft resisters began to burn draft cards publicly, and in northern California, members of the Vietnam Day Committee tried to halt troop trains by lying on the tracks. Also in 1965, three Americans burned themselves to death to protest the war in Vietnam, including an 82-year-old woman. As protest to the war mounted, marches and actions grew larger and louder; of the half-million people who marched in Washington in May 1971, about 14,000 were arrested.

The drafters of the "Declaration of Conscience Against the War in Vietnam" created it at the end of 1964. They were influenced by a 1960 French manifesto supporting civil disobedience against the French government's suppression of the Algerian independence movement. There were eventually about 4,000 signers of the "Declaration of Conscience," and they included many well-known names in nonviolent resistance. Peace activists such as Dorothy Day and Ammon Hennacy signed; civil rights leaders including John Lewis and Bayard Rustin signed; prominent intellectuals and academics such as Erich Fromm, Linus Pauling, Paul Goodman, and Staughton Lynd signed as well. The declaration was delivered to the White House in August 1965 and was published jointly by the Catholic Worker, the Committee for Nonviolent Action, the Student Peace Union, and the War Resisters League.

> **Because** the use of the military resources of the United States in Vietnam and elsewhere suppresses the aspirations of the people for political independence and economic freedom;

Because inhuman torture and senseless killing are being carried out by forces armed, uniformed, trained and financed by the United States;

Because we believe that all peoples of the earth, including both Americans and non-Americans, have an inalienable right to life, liberty, and the peaceful pursuit of happiness in their own way; and

Because we think that positive steps must be taken to put an end to the threat of nuclear catastrophe and death by chemical or biological warfare, whether these result from accident or escalation—

We hereby declare our conscientious refusal to cooperate with the United States government in the prosecution of the war in Vietnam.

We encourage those who can conscientiously do so to refuse to serve in the armed forces and to ask for discharge if they are already in.

Those of us who are subject to the draft ourselves declare our own intention to refuse to serve.

We urge others to refuse and refuse ourselves to take part in the manufacture or transportation of military equipment, or to work in the fields of military research and weapons development.

We shall encourage the development of other nonviolent acts, including acts which involve civil disobedience, in order to stop the flow of American soldiers and munitions to Vietnam.

NOTE: *Signing or distributing this Declaration of Conscience might be construed as a violation of the Universal Military Training and Service Act, which prohibits advising persons facing the draft to refuse service. Penalties of up to 5 years imprisonment, and/or a fine of $5,000 are provided. While prosecutions under this provision of the law almost never occur, persons signing or distributing this declaration should face the possibility of serious consequences.*

Questions about the Passage

1. What exactly do the signers oppose?
2. What actions do the signers endorse?
3. What do the signers state they will do? What do they urge others to do?

Questions about the Argument

1. Who are the different audiences of this declaration? Explain your answer with evidence from the text. (*Hint:* Look at the signers listed in the introduction and look carefully at who is addressed.)
2. Identify the premises and conclusions of the argument. Which is the main conclusion? How do the other conclusions relate to the main one? Are the conclusions supported by the premises?
3. If you take the main conclusion plus a premise, you will have an enthymeme. Work out the unstated premise of the enthymeme in one or more of the "because" statements.
4. What impact might the final italicized statement have had on the original audience? What impact does it have on you decades later?
5. Does this declaration have anything in common with the previous declarations in this casebook? If so, what? If not, how does it differ?

James Taylor Rowland, "Against the System"

James Taylor Rowland was one of many thousands of young men who confronted being drafted to serve in the military in Vietnam in the 1960s and early 1970s. His letters to a friend about his decision to refuse the draft, written between February 1965 and July 1967, were included in *We Won't Go: Personal Accounts of War Objectors* (1968). In this collection, draft counselor Alice Lynd gathered over two dozen accounts of draft resisters as well as aids for those who wished to refuse, such as a copy of the Selective Service application for conscientious objector status. Lynd and her husband Staughton Lynd are Quakers and have been key participants in the civil rights, antiwar, labor, and anti–death penalty movements for forty years. Alice Lynd is best known today as a lawyer and advocate for prisoners; she and her husband have written or edited six books together. Jim Rowland's thoughts and reasons for refusing to be drafted are particular to him in his time and place, but they also raise larger issues about civil disobedience for today's careful reader.

> I FIRST became acquainted with draft refusal through my cousin, Robert Anderson. Rob's dad mentioned that Rob had refused to be inducted, and was waiting for the U.S. to take the next step. (Rob eventually spent thirteen months on a two-year sentence here at Lompoc.) Thus, Rob showed me that people actually *did* just refuse.

Naturally, it took a long time for me to evaluate and analyze all of the positions possible concerning the draft. The decision to refuse to take the physical, and to be inducted, was a hard decision to make. I was under a lot of pressure to change my position, so I was constantly evaluating my stand—in fact, I did my hardest thinking during the last two months before I was imprisoned. I would suspect my actions here were typical of the actions of other draft refusers; after all, one would have to have an overdeveloped martyr complex to go to prison unaffected by the tremendous contradictions such action entails.

I refused the draft on two grounds, moral and political. Politically: The United States' policies in Latin America, in the Congo and of course, Vietnam, are the result of imperialism— American imperialism. Such policies must be protested and organized against, and must be confronted directly. Draft refusal is a political act with great potential, and deserves to be given much wider support. As a political act, its effect is all out of proportion to the deed: that of one man going to jail. Morally: quite simply, taking part in the bestiality that is Vietnam would be unthinkable. Can the refusal to cooperate, in any way, with the butchery, the strafing, the napalming, ever be questioned? To be a man with honor, means to say "no!" to the ugly, gnawing creature that is the U.S. foreign policy.

February 23, 1965: . . . Rob is a noncooperator with the draft. He won't acknowledge the government's right to ask, or rather to order him into the army. The judge said that Rob was in open rebellion with the government, and to sentence him to less than two years would be a disservice to all of the "boys" who are giving two years of their lives to the army. Rob considers the whole U.S. government to be immoral, and that is why he won't cooperate with it. When you look at what the sovereign government of the land of the Yahoos did in the Congo, in Guatemala, Syria, Cuba, and is doing now in South Vietnam, it becomes increasingly difficult to disagree with him. . . .

May 17, 1965: Many times I have wondered whether it might 5 not be better to die now, rather than continue to live. But I have a curiosity about my fellowman; were I to die now, it would be like leaving one hell of a good play in the middle of the first act. The hero, mankind, may end by having all his hopes ruined, but I still want to see the end, even if the play makes me morose.

Mankind has made some progress, and barring the destruction of it all, I think it just might make something of itself someday. We are now witnessing the key to the betterment of all the peoples of the world: the destruction of capitalism, and the rise of socialism. So long as one class exploits another, as long as profit is more important than the human being toiling to earn that profit, as long as governments continue to function for the benefit of the wealthy and/or privileged, then mankind cannot attain a true civilization, wherein no one need worry about the rent, food, medical bills, or old age. Yes, I think I'll stick around to see this little play. There's an interesting world outside our door—let's go and watch. . . .

You asked if I were motivated by anything. Yes, by a desire to know and learn, to experience new knowledge, to evaluate, to participate, to create and change, to better, and hopefully never worsen. That's it.

July 20, 1966: Well, it looks like things are going to be moving right along here. I awoke this morning to find that I had been reclassified I-A, and am to report to a San Francisco draft board on Monday, presumably to be drafted. I, as you know, intend to refuse to be drafted by this son-of-a-bitchin' system, so I guess before long I will be in prison for my independence. Frankly, I had no idea that it would come so soon, but I am rather glad it did, because it's pretty nerve-racking, having this hanging over my head. I have known that it would come someday for a long time, and now that it has come, I no longer have this dread.

. . . I frankly don't feel like writing much. I'm going to walk in the city for a while, until I regain my equilibrium.

July 26: . . . I probably didn't make myself clear in the last letter, as to the exact situation here, so I will now explain the exact process of draft refusing. First of all, what I had just received was a form to fill out, asking all sorts of questions, and also an order to report for my physical, which comes a couple of weeks before you are actually drafted. Since I am protesting the whole capitalistic, imperialistic setup, I naturally refused to fill out any of their goddamn forms, and I also refused to report for the pre-draft physical. This means I will be declared "delinquent" by my draft board, and they will send me a notice to report for immediate induction, which I of course will ignore—or at most, send them a letter back, explaining why I cannot be a part of the draft, and why I must protest against the U.S. government.

The only way to stop the aggressor is to physically confront 10 him. To accept a conscientious objector status in the hope of registering some protest against the government is to engage in spurious reasoning. To become a CO is no protest at all, for one is neatly pigeonholed by the government, no confrontation having actually taken place; and without a confrontation, all propaganda value is lost. Therefore I find no alternative but to register an effective protest against the U.S. government by refusing to report for military service.

. . . It seems to me that if one categorically makes the assertion that there is free will, then one is an ass. It doesn't take the omnipotence and omniscience of a god to limit one's choice of action. For instance, I have a desire to go to school right now, to work a little, and to generally hang loose. But, that choice has been precluded. So, I can exercise my free will in one of several ways: I can allow myself to be inducted into the army; I can go to jail for my beliefs; or I can get the hell out of the country. Those are the only choices open to me. I was not able to use my will to pick the choices. I can exercise my will only after the preliminary selection of choices has been made for me. And, in my psychological background, I imagine one could discern the reason for my being unable to get out of the country, hence the choice is further limited by forces beyond my conscious control. Only two choices were left to me, and I chose the one which to me seemed most ethical. The puzzle is, did I really have free will regarding those last two choices, or did my ethical training and belief preclude even that? Hmmm. . . .

August 12, 1966: About this draft thing. Yes, I have looked at the pragmatic side of it. I, of course, have thought about getting a job in the future, but I don't really think that that matters. I intend to go back to school, if that is at all possible. If it turns out that an M.D. is out of the question, then I will go for a Ph.D. If I can't go back to school, because of my record, then tough shit, I just won't be able to go. I cannot let a thing like that hinder me at this time. The important thing is for a protest to be made against the criminal policies of our government. Whenever a person undertakes the task of *really* protesting his government, not just marching around with a goddamn picket sign, but really protesting, he has to be mature enough to realize just what the consequences are likely to be. When [murdered civil rights workers] Goodman, Chaney, and Schwerner were working in Mississippi in 1964, they realized what they were up against, but they went ahead. As it turns out, they lost their lives in the bargain. And so it is with all people who see the choices, who are free to make the choices, whose histories are not yet determinate. But, for all that I have lost, there is one thing I have gained, which can now never be taken away from me, and that is my self-respect. Now that I have made this very important decision, in the future I need not worry whether or not I will do the right things according to my conscience—I know I shall. If I had failed here, the future would have been always in doubt, but now I have no fear. I think the worst kind of fear, of dread, is the fear that you yourself will fail to act according to your conscience. That fear is now gone. I am one of the freest men in this country. Can you understand that?

When Thoreau was jailed for refusing to pay his taxes for American imperialism, Emerson came along, looked at Thoreau in prison, and asked, "What are you doing in there?" Whereupon Thoreau answered, "What are *you* doing out *there?*" So, you see, I am not bothered by going to prison. What bothers me is that so many self-styled "radicals" are not going to prison. A radical should make of himself such a thorn in the side of the government that it has but one choice, and that is to imprison him.

August 20, 1966: Early in the week I received my "delinquency notice" from my draft board, and the day before yesterday, I received my order to report for induction. According to the order, I am to report to Local Board 33, at 106 East Roosevelt, the twenty-ninth of this month, at 8 A.M. Now, I'll have you know, I won't even be up at 8 A.M. I have already sent the board another letter telling it that I won't be there the twenty-ninth, or any other date. Now the waiting begins, and we shall see just what they intend to do. . . .

September 21, 1966: Still no word on when I am to be arrested.   15
You can never tell when the ax will fall, only that it will some day.

I feel like one of the Franks, [family of Anne Frank] that I ought to be living in hiding.

October 31, 1966: When I wrote the last letter I was so much in the dumps. . . . I haven't been that depressed in years. Depression is not for me. . . . When I was younger I had periods of depression, deep, pit-like depression. I thought I had grown out of this, but I see I haven't. The whole draft thing has made me depressed, I guess. I think you understand this. In fact, I know you do. Prison is a break in my life, I'm burning my bridges behind me. Those left on the other shore are going to have to build their own bridges over to me if they want me. I'm no longer making the effort. The people in my past who hate me, who don't understand me, who patronize me, who tolerate me, and become puzzled by me, are gone. Friends, some good, some not so good, are probably lost. Does it matter? Well, beneath my iconoclastic exterior, I do care; but sometimes it is more important to make a stand, though your friends turn against you. Whether you turn against me or not is not a worry. I know you see the logic of my actions. And, it's easier to be hated than tolerated.

. . . It is easily imaginable that I will get four or five years. I don't feel like a martyr, and I haven't a martyr's desire to be pilloried so he will be admired. That is scant compensation. Besides, most people who question me don't have any feelings but a wonder that crazymen such as myself are allowed to run loose. Well, you just do what you have to do. I feel lonely. But what is my loneliness compared with the crying of burned children in Vietnam?

[*Arraigned, December 19, 1966*]

December 21, 1966: . . . I did spend a night in the city jail. Jesus, what a jail! The worst in all creation, I am convinced. The feds don't accredit it for federal prisoners—they can be held only overnight. I was all set to be taken to Tucson (actually Florence), when my parents got me out on my own recognizance. . . . It's better than being in prison, generally.

[*Tried, February 6, 1967*]

Federal Prison, Lompoc, California, March 29, 1967: I got here   20
February 23rd, so I'll be moving out of here into another unit (cell block) this week. All new prisoners stay in A & O unit a

month or so for tests, exams, lectures, etc. But I won't be in the other unit long, because I am here on a sixty-day observation only. My number, YE-253, stands for Youth Evaluation, which means they doubt my sanity (or at least the judge feels he needs more information before sentencing me). So, I'll be back in Florence in late April, for holding until my court date. Then I get my final sentence, which will probably be the Youth Corrections Act, a splendid piece of misfortune which will keep me here up to four years. Cheers. They have to release me January 23rd, 1971, no matter what, though, and it looks like I will be here a while, as paroles for draft refusers are scarce now. To have a radical's conscience, one has to pay a radical's price, and it's worth it.

. . . Stay cool, and don't worry, I'm fine. I look ahead confidently. My convictions haven't changed—rather, I am positive, I am unshakable, in the belief that a better world can come about through radical socialism. We must remain radical, and live radically, without compromise.

Hopefully, more men will refuse. Thousands have gotten out of the draft through various means: II-S deferments, admitted drug addiction, feigned homosexuality, and the like. But the question is—is merely saving one's own self enough? Or does a stand, a moral and political stand, need to be made? Obviously, I feel men should refuse to cooperate, not in the pitifully small numbers of today, but by the hundreds. The way to point out the illegitimacy of the system is not by taking draft physicals, trying for deferments, etc., for every act of this type furthers the aims and control of the system, and lends it greater legitimacy. Only by standing up and saying, shouting, "We won't go!", is it possible to begin to build a cohesive movement in the struggle against the system.

Questions about the Passage

1. What does Rowland mean when he calls draft refusal "a political act" (paragraph 3)? What seems to be Rowland's opinion of the American government? Of the whole American economic and political system? Why does Rowland reject taking conscientious objector status?

2. What do you think Rowland means by *really* protesting his government" (paragraph 12)? What is wrong with marching with a picket sign, according to him?
3. How does Rowland feel about going to prison? Do his feelings undermine his commitment to draft refusal?
4. How does Rowland distinguish himself from men who escape the draft through various falsehoods and ploys? Why does he condemn them?

Questions about the Argument

1. Describe Rowland's ethos. What kind of person do you find him to be? Remember that his original audience was a single friend to whom he was writing.
2. Try to lay out Rowland's objections to American government and its policies. How does he see his act of civil disobedience in relation to these objections? What seems to be his political philosophy?
3. Make the best case you can for Rowland's actions (either individually or in a small group). Now try to refute his position. You might put together a class debate on the issue.
4. How might you use a personal narrative such as this one as part of an argument about the use of civil disobedience in protests against the Vietnam War?

Photographs, "The Faces of Protest"

Questions about the Photograph (Fig. 8-1)

Don Cravens took this photo at a Vietnam protest march in Berkeley, California, in 1965.

1. What do you notice first in the picture? What has the photographer done to bring this element to your immediate attention?
2. What can you infer about the woman holding the sign? Look at her expression and body language. What can you infer about the other people in the photo, particularly the man pushing the wheelchair and the woman next to him?

Figure 8-1

Questions about the Argument

1. Do you think the photographer's message is the same as the woman's sign? What interests Cravens more—the sign's message or the people at the march?
2. How does this photo use pathos?

Questions about the Photograph (Fig. 8-2)

This photo of Vietnam War draft resisters burning their draft cards was taken in 1968 in Union Square, New York City. The resisters are being sprayed with water by counterprotesters.

1. Examine the setting, the young men's clothing, and their facial expressions. What do the classical column and pediment suggest? Why do you think the draft resisters are dressed in suits and ties?
2. What can you infer about the men from their faces and postures?
3. As a viewer, how distant do you feel from the action of the photo?

Figure 8-2

Questions about the Argument

1. Do you think a claim can be derived from this photo? If so, what is it?
2. Is there any use of pathos in the photo? If so, what is it?
3. Compare this photo with Cravens's photo (Fig. 8-1). Which has the stronger claim? Which evokes stronger emotion in you? Explain your answer.
4. Imagine that you may only select one of these two photos to represent civil disobedience against the Vietnam War. Which would you select? Which would be more effective for a hostile audience? A neutral audience? A sympathetic audience? Justify your selection.

Kathy Kelly, "Civil Disobedience in My Life"

Kathy Kelly (1952–) has dedicated her life to nonviolent resistance to war. Born and raised in Chicago, she attended college at Loyola University there and earned a Masters in Religious Education from the Chicago Theological Seminary. She taught at a Jesuit high school for six years, during which time she became an active member of the Catholic Worker movement, a committed pacifist, and a tax resister. In our interview, she describes one of the ways she has avoided paying income tax—she has not paid federal income tax for over twenty years. As part of the Missouri Peace Planters, she tied ribbons to nuclear missile silo lids, put up banners such as "Farms Not Arms," and planted a few corn kernels and flower seeds in 1988. She was arrested at Whiteman Air Force Base for trespass and served nine months of her one-year sentence at a maximum-security federal prison. Since the 1980s, Kelly worked to stop U.S. support for Central American dictatorships, including demonstrating peacefully at the U.S. Army's School of the Americas (now called the Western Hemisphere Institute for Security Cooperation) at Fort Benning, Georgia, every year for the last fourteen years. Kelly also was an organizer and participant in peace observer teams in Nicaragua (1986), Iraq (the Gulf Peace Team, 1991), Sarajevo (1992), Bosnia (1992 and 1993), and Haiti (1994).

In 1995, Kathy Kelly and a small group of friends founded Voices in the Wilderness (VitW) in order to protest and confront the authorities responsible for what they believed were illegal and immoral sanctions against Iraq. The group has made many trips to Iraq to bring medicine, in direct violation of the U.S. and UN sanctions. Kelly has made twenty-one trips to Iraq since January 1996; in fact, she was leaving for Iraq a few days after this interview, in August 2003, despite having just learned that the Justice Department was suing VitW for $20,000 in fines for violating the sanctions. In addition to the trips to Iraq, Kelly and others fasted, marched, and demonstrated to protest the Iraq sanctions, always trying to publicize the terrible toll they were taking, especially on Iraqi children. (The British medical journal *The Lancet* published an estimate in December 1995 that over half a million children under the age of 5 had died as a direct result of the sanctions.)

Kathy Kelly is the author of many articles and contributed to two books about Iraq, *War and Peace in the Gulf* (2001) and *Iraq Under Siege* (2000). She speaks often to church, college, and peace groups in an effort to educate people about the injustices she resists. She has received many awards for her work, including three nominations for the Nobel Peace Prize in 2000, 2001, and 2003.

Interview with Kathy Kelly
August 19, 2003

Interviewers: Evelyn Asch and Sharon Walsh

How did you become aware of civil disobedience, and who influenced you to practice civil disobedience?

I regarded civil disobedience as a fairly exotic notion in my younger years. It was the kind of thing that I would read about when teachers in high school introduced us to the Reverend Dr. Martin Luther King or to Mohandas Gandhi. I think I was aware of the Berrigans, certainly during the Vietnam War in my high school and college years. But the idea that Kathy Kelly would ever get involved in being arrested and possibly going to prison would have been about the most remote suggestion for me.

But I did become more and more aware that there was a big disjointedness in my life, a lack of coherence, because I was studying for a master's degree down in Hyde Park in Chicago, taking many of my courses with Jesuit students and teachers, who certainly advocated scriptural injunctions to love the poor, to be identified with the poor. I was aware of liberation theology, but I never saw any poor people. And so I finally was—I think compelled—to head north and investigate, anyway, a soup kitchen that I knew of, in part because two Catholic Workers had come down to my neighborhood (I think they really wanted to visit the local bar), but they also wanted to trace the donor of checks. I did at least send some checks there—not very large ones maybe once in a while. . . . I felt I should go up to this soup kitchen that I knew about, and I was saying to myself I can't any longer just talk about meeting the needs of poor people. So I did that. I started to volunteer and immediately realized that my life could become much easier, and I just moved up to the neighborhood. And after I began to live there and rubbed shoulders with some of the finest and the kindest people in the world, I also began to realize that these were people who took the works of mercy very, very seriously and they were completely opposed to the works of war.

And I guess you could say I married into the heightened awareness of civil disobedience. I knew of people taking action, but it still seemed that that would be a distant step for me. But I married Karl Meyer, and he was a protégé of Dorothy Day. And when he was 17 years old, he was being arrested with Dorothy Day and Ammon Hennacy during the New York actions when a handful of people would sit out on a park bench during the nuclear air-raid drills and everyone else was supposed to go underground in the subway system. So I began to hear Karl's stories. He'd been in jail for two years in the course of the Vietnam War. He was a war-tax refuser, and that began to make an awful lot of sense to me. And many of Karl's friends or his mentors would come through Chicago, and I'd hear their stories. And it does happen that people have an affinity in having gone to jail at various times—sometimes together—and   5
talk about those old stories, so it didn't seem so remote.

I would say that I was to some extent converted by neighbors . . . who were desperately poor. I lived on a street called Kenmore, and, honestly, my building was the only one that was completely intact, that hadn't had a fire or some crumbling, which was to the advantage of landlords who then could claim insurance and move people out. And so a lot of the buildings were abandoned. Most of my neighbors didn't have any income, or else maybe they had a little bit of SSI [Supplemental Security Income, a federal income program for the aged and disabled] money that came in—a lot of disability, a great deal of mental illness, alcoholism, homelessness, despair.

And so it didn't make any sense at all for me to go off to my teaching job, at the time at St. Ignatius College Prep, and teach religion classes about social justice and ethics and peacemaking and disarmament, and then turn around and take a big chunk of my salary and put it toward exactly what I didn't believe in, the possible buildup of weapons during the height of the Cold War, and then have my neighbors abandoned and hungry and homeless and needy. So I began to practice war-tax refusal, which is, I think, an everyday matter of civil disobedience. And the Jesuits agreed that I could lower my salary beneath the taxable income, and they would take the money I didn't take and put it directly into what I wanted it spent on. And that was wonderful because I, and a handful of other teachers who were doing the same thing in various places in Chicago but all living in this neighborhood, were able to keep help keep funding flowing for many activities in the neighborhood . . . [including] the buildup of the Pledge of Resistance [groups who pledged to commit or support civil disobedience in the event the United States intervened in Central America] and nonviolent activity to try to help refugees from Central America by protesting any U.S. aid to some of the dictatorships and paramilitaries that were afflicting them.

Eventually, it seemed more and more necessary for us to confront U.S. military aid that was going directly to the governments, particularly of El Salvador and Guatemala and for the U.S.-funded *contras* making attacks in Nicaragua. And that occasioned a fairly regular series of activities, very creative actions—we struggled hard to make sure that they stayed nonviolent—in which we would go to the Federal Building and try to persuade elected officials to stop sending the money that aided these brutal dictatorships or paramilitary oppressions against civilians. We knew they were civilians because they were coming into our homes, literally living with us, and into our neighborhoods.

So there were arrests that maybe involved a slap on the wrist, you know; we would be released after maybe an overnight in jail. And we would go to court, and it was clear that the judges didn't want to punish us very much. Maybe we'd be given a penalty, and we all knew we weren't going to pay the penalty. But it did get our feet wet. I always think it is very, very important if people are going to risk imprisonment to try it out, see how it feels for one or two nights and not jump into a lengthy prison sentence. So I suppose that was my experience, more or less, getting my feet wet.

* * *

Could you tell us about your protest at the missile site?

It was a very amazing day of my life [August 15, 1988]. That was   10
a day that my heart was actually thudding. I was very worried about climbing over a barbed wire fence. . . . This was outside Kansas City. One hundred and fifty intercontinental ballistic missiles surround Kansas City, and there are 1,000 found throughout the Midwest. We called ourselves Missouri Peace

Planting. We wanted to communicate the idea we think is so true, that land is meant to grow corn and wheat and not to harbor weapons of mass destruction. . . . It was a good approach in as much as we did communicate to the farmers something about their land and how it was being used.

So when I landed on the missile silo site with my banners under my arm and nine little pieces of corn in my pocket, I hung the banners, which said, "Farms, not Arms. Disarm and Live," and I planted the corn, my first and only agricultural act. And then my heart started to calm down, and I sat down on the lid of this intercontinental ballistic missile. Pretty soon I could start to hear the birds chirping away and the crickets creaking, and it was a lovely morning. It was probably one of the calmest of mornings, and all of a sudden I heard a vehicle speeding down a country road, and it skittered to a halt, and there was a machine gun mounted on top of it. Four camouflaged soldiers climbed out with . . . helmets, and walkie-talkies, and weapons, and they surrounded the perimeter of the site, and they were crouched down. And one of them spoke into the walkie-talkie and said, "All personnel, please clear the site," and I was trying to do whatever they said because this was pretty new for me. And they told me to put my hands up in the air, and up went my hands. "Step to the left, step to the right, step to the left." And then I thought, ooh, they're going to want me to climb that fence, but they had the key, so I was quite relieved about that. And then they handcuffed me when I stepped outside of the weapon site, and they told me to kneel down. And then three of them got back into the vehicle, and I wondered if they were going to check the manual and see what they were supposed to do next.

I was kneeling in the tall grass. The soldier that they left behind had a gun aimed right at my head, a rifle; [he was] standing behind me. I certainly didn't think he was going to shoot me. I wasn't the least bit afraid of that. And it just seemed kind of artificial to both be there without any conversation. Now, I imagine he probably wasn't supposed to talk to me, but I did start to talk to him. . . . I started to tell him about why we had done this. I told him a little bit about the kids in my neighborhood. [I was] teaching in an alternative school. Three children—well, teenagers—were dead at the end of every year. There were only fifty kids in the school, and they died, I've always believed, primarily because of poverty. Even though the deaths could be marked in an official report to drive-by shootings or gang warfare. And I told him that we were very concerned for the children in his family or neighborhood as well as the kids we loved and the kids in the Soviet Union.

And then I asked him, "Do you think the corn will grow?"

And he said in a very thick southern accent, "I don't know, ma'am, but I sure hope so."

And then I said, "Would you like to say a prayer?"   15
"Yes, ma'am."

And we said the "Our Father" together, but before that I'd said the prayer of St. Francis: "Lord, make me a means of your peace. Where there is hatred, let me sow love. . . ." At the end of the "Our Father," he said, "Amen."

Then, he said to me, "Ma'am, would you like a drink of water?"

And I was very, very thirsty, and I said, "Oh, yes, please."

I never turned around to . . . check it out. . . . He said,   20
"Ma'am, would you tip your head back?"

I did that, and he poured water down my throat, and it dribbled down my chin. And I've always thought that he taught me so much that day. When things are very complex or sometimes overwhelming, there's a tendency to divide into the good guys and the bad guys, all black or all white— some kind of division. That's not really the way things work. This young man took a risk in order to perform an act of kindness for a perfect stranger. The other soldiers could have come back; and I can only guess that in order for him to pour the water down my throat, he had to put the gun down. They may have said in the manual, "Keep your prisoner fed and watered," but I greatly doubt that it said, "Put your gun down to do it." So I hope that I can keep that lesson in the forefront of my own mind. Certainly never to dehumanize somebody that is on the opposite side of a line that you tend—always to try to win people over but also not to draw boxes and put people in boxes and declare that one side is good and one side is bad. It's been very important for those who work in Iraq.

* * *

We kept doing the actions. We'd go out every day as soon as we were released from the county jails we were held in. We'd go right back out and do it again and again. . . . So by the time I went to court I could have served thirty months, but instead a judge ran some of the sentences concurrently, so I served nine months of a one-year sentence in a maximum-security prison in Lexington, Kentucky.

Can you explain how the work for peace you have been doing in Iraq came out of your earlier actions of civil disobedience? What are the connections?

Ammon Hennacy once said, "You can't be a vegetarian between meals, and you can't be a pacifist between wars." That was kind of hanging in my awareness.

And, then, there was Daniel Berrigan who said, "One of the   25 reasons we don't have peace is that the peacemakers aren't always ready to pay the same price required by the war makers." And that was kind of hanging there. I'd gotten out of my year in prison [for the missile protest]. Maximum security does make you feel as though you can put up with a good deal . . . you can tolerate quite a lot. . . . I'd also done a twenty-eight-day water-only fast under George Bush I at the School of the Americas, which wasn't civil disobedience but was sort of like a long retreat.

* * *

By 1995, we realized that we couldn't continue to look the other way [from the impact of sanctions on Iraq]. But because we knew something about organizing nonviolent civil disobedience, because there was such a huge need to dramatize the conflict and the challenge to these policies, we felt very, very responsible. So eight of us, who had been to Iraq before, during, or immediately after the First Gulf War, were sitting at the kitchen table back there. . . . We literally didn't leave that kitchen table until we had crafted a document in the form of a letter to U.S. Attorney General Janet Reno, saying that we would travel to Iraq and break the sanctions. It was really easy to figure out what to do. We have a law that says it's against U.S. code to bring medicines or anything into Iraq. We [Voices in the Wilderness] just decided to break that code. And that we did, seventy times we broke the prohibition. And we were present each time the United States did a bombing campaign in the "Desert Fox" bombing and again in this most recent offensive [2003].

And the Justice Department now says that we owe them $20,000 [in penalties]. . . . Initially, we were threatened with $250,000, but $12 million potential. Then it was $1 million in penalties and a $250,000 administrative penalty [for the first action only]. . . . We always acknowledged the penalties. Sometimes even without any penalty notice, we just knocked on the U.S. attorney's door downtown: We just want you to know we've broken the law. We don't want you to think we're sneaking around. . . . We wouldn't discontinue [our actions]. . . . In December 2002 here we received a $10,000 penalty on our campaign and $10,000 on me personally . . . and again we said we won't be paying any of these penalties. Money is entrusted to us—we're meant to either bring more relief or continue just speaking out to bring more attention to these issues.

* * *

I think that many, many people will say to themselves, those people wanted to bring medicine and some relief over to needy people. Arguably, the sanctions solidified Saddam Hussein's regime and punished children in the process, and maybe they [VitW] didn't do something criminal. And many will say, maybe the decision on the part of the United States to go to war without any evidence that would pass muster in a court of law that Iraq was tied up with al Qaieda, that Iraq had weapons of mass destruction—maybe that was violating international law. I think it was a war that was immoral, unjust, unauthorized, and counterproductive. I think we went to war against Iraq because we could, and now we're finding that it's not turning out as easy as we thought.

What you were just saying really connects to my last question. How do you see what you do affecting public opinion? How important is it to change the minds, not just of officials, but of the general public?

Changing the minds of the general public is so crucial. Realtors   30
say, "Location, location, location." And we have to say, "Education, education, education." I suppose I almost have to rein
myself in—I feel so strongly about things. I know rationally that
we have to become many more than we already are in order to
make a difference. And I know rationally that sometimes if we
seem too overwhelming we can scare people away, and I don't
want to do that. . . . We would be delusional if we think that
we can put our foot on the gas pedal, press down, and pick up
momentum . . . push harder, push harder. It's necessary
always to keep trying to further invent nonviolent movements,
and I'll . . . probably join another one, I'm sure. But what we
see, I think, in an underlying subtext of two ongoing wars, and
the first is the war of western culture against the biodiversity of
Mother Earth. The second is the war of U.S. culture against
weaker countries whose resources we want to control. The fundamental tie that binds those two wars is our culture.

And so the question becomes, "How do we change our
culture?" And I very much favor the tactics of Gandhi and
King in terms of civil disobedience. I think the wisdom of
Gandhi in being able to find the right symbols that inspired
huge numbers of people all across India to change their culture
pretty radically—that's what we're in need of.

* * *

**What would you say to people who are made uncomfortable
by deliberate lawbreaking, even though the actions are
nonviolent, because it seems to be an attack on the common
compact we make?**

I think the Constitution is very, very important, and I'm all for
the social fabric and, in a sense, the social contract. And the
Constitution says Congress shall make no law that prohibits
the assembly of people for the redress of grievance. There are
all kinds of prohibitions against that! Almost every time I've
been in some public demonstration, I have seen that as my
responsibility to gather with other people for a public
grievance because we've tried other outlets and have not
gotten anywhere. And there's a definite urgency, so that we

had to do something to dramatize the urgency of our claim. And I never want to be involved with people who want to do "hit and split," break a law and then run. You know I'm quite serious when I say, "Don't do the crime if you can't do the time." I think you have to first consult—what's the maximum amount of penalty? Argue your case in court, film the drama if there's educational merit to it, but then if you're sentenced to prison, go in there and try to be of service to other prisoners and learn from the whole experience. So I don't feel myself to be a scofflaw.

I also do claim my religious right to resist warfare. I was schooled in the tradition that counsels love of enemies, love of neighbor, never to kill, and that's a religious right. So I won't let anybody, ever, pull me in to kill. Count me out! I was kind of fond of a lot of the kids that were part of gangs in this neighborhood. They did bad things, and I wish they wouldn't have, but if any one of those kids had ever come up to me and said, "Kathy, would you give me the money to buy a gun? We're short," I would never, ever do it.

Why would I ever give a big group of people funding to buy nuclear weapons? I have a big responsibility to protest this, to interfere with this, to dramatize resistance to it. We are talking about a planet, and species that inhabit this planet, and children, who aren't responsible for what their elders have done if we don't get a grip on it—and we are now manufacturing precision low-yield nuclear weapon devices that can hit in a bathtub. These robust nuclear-bunker penetrators that are tiny enough that they can be detonated—there's a part that burrow underground. They irradiate the ground and the groundwater. And one of these days, every one of these newly created weapons is going to be used. There's never been a time in history that people created these things and did not use them. We're like a train hurtling to go over an abyss, and everybody— everybody that would be a detractor of me and say she is lessening the social fabric—they're all on that train. Some travel first class, some travel in the second-class cars, some are under the tracks, getting ground up, but the train's going over an abyss, so I'm sure going to try to stop it, and I'm certainly not going to pay for it!

Questions about the Passage

1. Why do you think Kathy Kelly speaks of being "converted" to civil disobedience (paragraph 5)? What does her word choice suggest about her understanding of civil disobedience?
2. What was the lesson that Kelly learned from the soldier in Missouri (paragraph 21)? Why do you think this lesson was important for someone involved in civil disobedience to know?
3. Why does Voices in the Wilderness inform the Justice Department before each of their actions? How is being public about breaking the sanctions important to civil disobedience?

Questions about the Argument

1. In the final paragraph, Kelly constructs a simile. In what way is her simile an argument to support the practice of civil disobedience? Restate the claim she is making.
2. Now look back at the entire interview and see if you can summarize Kelly's position as an argument. What claims does she make? What evidence does she provide to support her claims?
3. Do you find her argument persuasive? Be prepared to defend your answer with specific examples from the text.

Writing Assignments
Conversations

1. Imagine that you have organized a panel discussion about protesting an ongoing war. You may choose a real war or a possible one. You have invited three of the writers from this chapter to share their views. First, allow each person to present the reasons for opposition and the methods with which to oppose war. Then allow the respectful but skeptical audience to ask two or three questions. Try to differentiate the voices of the speakers as they answer each question from the audience. This conversation may also be done in class with students taking the roles of the speakers and the questioners in the audience.

2. Choose one Vietnam protest photograph. Interview the photographer and the people pictured. Ask the photographer to explain reasons for taking the photo and what he or she hoped to convey. Then ask the subjects to tell what was happening when the photo was taken. Do the photographer and the subjects agree about the meaning of the photo?

Writing Sequence One: Putting Your Money Where Your Mouth Is!

1. Choose three personal narratives from this chapter that explore the point at which the writer has had to make the decision to act upon a belief. What has led the writer to this point? What actions follow from that decision? What in the narrative convinces you that this decision is a conscientious response? Is it a response that you can see yourself making?

2. Make some connections between the three narratives. What ideas or motives do they have in common? How do they differ? On the basis of this small sample, what conclusions can you draw about why activists engage in civil disobedience?

3. Take the conclusion you developed for the previous question and turn it into a claim in your own argument. Your claim can be specifically about these peace activists or it can be a general one about the nature of either activists' motivations or civil disobedience itself. In support of your claim, you should use additional personal narratives either from this or other chapters, from interviews you may conduct, or from your own civil disobedience experience.

Writing Sequence Two: Capstone Argument

1. Looking back at the entire casebook, what is your position on civil disobedience? Have you changed your views after reading some of these writers? Whether your stance has altered or not, which readings have most affected the position you now take? Lay out the ways in which these readings have influenced you.

2. Write an argument in brief (see Chapter 3) that includes a claim you develop from your position in the last question. Use at least one reading from Chapter 4 or 5 plus at least two other readings from any chapter as support for your claim.
3. Make the best case you can against your argument in brief. Raise objections that writers from this book might bring up. Think of this as another argument in brief.
4. Now construct your full argument in defense of your claim. Be sure to counter the objections that you raised in Question 3. Provide plentiful evidence from the casebook to support your position.

A

Research Topics and Selected Civil Disobedience Bibliography

1. Define civil disobedience carefully, using the texts we have studied. Apply your definition to actions that have loosely been called civil disobedience. You may consider historical events, such as, for example, the Boston Tea Party; the work of helping slaves escape on the Underground Railroad; or, more recently, protests preventing women from entering clinics to obtain abortions or violent actions against abortion providers. Other possibilities include freeing laboratory animals to protest animal abuse or the destruction of labs where experiments on animals are performed. You might also examine actions of the antiglobalization movement or the gay rights movement.

2. Research John Brown's raid on Harpers Ferry in 1859. Trace the responses to the raid. What were contemporary views of his actions? For example, both Thoreau and Douglass wrote about Brown, sometimes admiringly. To what extent do you think the joining of nonviolence to civil disobedience, as it has been practiced in the twentieth century, might make our views of Brown differ from those of his nineteenth-century contemporaries?

3. Research the direction that the Student Nonviolent Coordinating Committee (SNCC) took after 1965 toward the use of violence. Examine the writings of Stokely Carmichael and others that made the case to abandon nonviolent resistance and civil disobedience. Compare the early SNCC actions and guiding principles to those of the later SNCC activists. Account for the change in the philosophy. How much has to do with the pace of progress toward civil rights?

How much might it have to do with the particular personalities involved? In other words, make a historical judgment on the issue.

4. Research the environmentalism movements and their activists. Do they draw on civil disobedience theories? You will find sources on this topic listed in the bibliography below.

5. Research peace and human rights groups that protest at the U.S. Army's Western Hemisphere Institute for Security Cooperation, known until 2001 as the School of the Americas, located in Fort Benning, Georgia. How do they use civil disobedience theory and practice? How effective have the protests been? Be sure to define what you mean by *effective*.

6. Examine the refusal (sometimes called the *refusenik*) movement in Israel in which military officers refuse to serve in the Israeli-occupied territories in Palestine. A section of the bibliography below has readings to get you started on this topic. Decide whether you consider the selective refusal of these officers to be true civil disobedience. You will need to state your definition of civil disobedience.

7. Research a civil disobedience activist, either one in this casebook or another person such as Philip Berrigan, Daniel Berrigan, Ammon Hennacy, Karl Meyer, David Dellinger, Roy Wilkins, James Farmer, or Sister Dorothy Marie Hennessey. What beliefs or experiences led him or her to civil disobedience?

8. There are many narratives of civil disobedience activists in this casebook. Many more can be found in oral histories of the major movements (see bibliography below). Choose a movement and locate several sources of narratives. Examine the narratives to see what factors lead people to the level of engagement we see in a Kathy Kelly, a Frederick Douglass, a John Lewis, or a Dorothy Day. Make a case for the necessary qualities of a civil disobedience activist.

9. Research whether your own religion has a tradition of civil disobedience. Does it differ from those represented in the casebook? Develop a claim that indicates how and why and in what respects it differs or resembles other religious traditions.

10. Take a careful look at the critiques of civil disobedience that were written in the 1960s. This era of the civil rights movement and the anti–Vietnam War protests brought the idea of civil disobedience into prominence. Responding to the actions and ideas of Dr. King and other activists, Supreme Court Justice Abe Fortas wrote *Concerning Dissent and Civil Disobedience* (1968). Others in turn replied, creating a conversation. In addition to Fortas, you might examine Alan Gewirth,

Herbert Storing, Harris Wofford, and Howard Zinn (complete listings in the bibliography below). Study the arguments. Choose the one or two that are most persuasive to you. Make a case for your choice.

11. Formulate a position statement on civil disobedience. Defend and attack that position in a debate, using any writers in this casebook and some of those listed in question 7, thus forming teams on either side.

12. Examine several newspaper editorial cartoons about the civil rights movement, anti–Vietnam War protests, the war in Iraq, or another issue of your choice. Be sure to acquaint yourself with the issues and history of the period you have chosen. What arguments do the cartoons make? How do they make these arguments? What common elements can you see? Are the cartoons effective in persuading viewers?

13. Research news photographs of particular important civil disobedience actions, such as Gandhi's mass demonstrations in India, the Birmingham demonstration of 1963, or protests against wars such as the Vietnam War, the Gulf War, or the war in Iraq. Choose photographs that seem to have had an impact on public opinion. In order to assess their impact, you will need to understand what public opinion was and how it changed. Analyze how they use visual argument to change public perceptions.

Selected Bibliography

These are good places to start your research. The footnotes and bibliographies in these sources will lead you to other pertinent material.

Civil Disobedience Theories and Activists

Bedau, Hugo, comp. Civil Disobedience: Theory and Practice. New York: Pegasus, 1969.

Carson, Clayborne, and Kris Shepard, eds. A Call to Conscience: The Landmark Speeches of Dr. Martin Luther King, Jr. New York: IPM/Warner, 2001.

Carton, Evan. "The Price of Privilege: 'Civil Disobedience' at 150." The American Scholar 67.4 (1998): 105.

Coffin, William S., and Morris I. Leibman. Civil Disobedience: Aid or Hindrance to Justice? Washington: American Enterprise Institute for Public Policy Research, 1972.

Dellinger, David. From Yale to Jail: The Life Story of a Moral Dissenter. New York: Pantheon, 1993.

Dudley, William. The Civil Rights Movement: Opposing Viewpoints. San Diego: Greenhaven, 1996.

Fortas, Abe. Concerning Dissent and Civil Disobedience. New York: World, 1968.

Garvey, T. G. "Frederick Douglass's Change of Opinion on the U.S. Constitution: Abolitionism and the 'Elements of Moral Power.' " ATQ: The American Transcendental Quarterly 9.3 (1995): 229–244.

Gewirth, Alan. "Civil Disobedience, Law, and Morality: An Examination of Justice Fortas' Doctrine." The Monist 54 (1970): 536–555.

Goldwin, Robert A., ed. On Civil Disobedience: American Essays, Old and New. Chicago: Rand, 1969.

Hare, A. Paul, and Herbert H. Blumberg, eds. Nonviolent Direct Action: American Cases: Social-Psychological Analyses. Washington: Corpus, 1968.

Harris, Paul. Civil Disobedience. Lanham: UP of America, 1989.

Iyer, Raghavan N., ed. The Essential Writings of Mahatma Gandhi. Delhi: Oxford UP, 1991.

Jack, Homer A. Gandhi Reader: A Sourcebook of His Life and Writings. Bloomington: Indiana UP, 1956.

Lynd, Staughton, and Alice Lynd, eds. Nonviolence in America: A Documentary History. Rev. ed. Maryknoll: Orbis, 1995.

Lyons, David. "Moral Judgment, Historical Reality, and Civil Disobedience." Philosophy and Public Affairs 27 (1998): 31–49.

Nanda, B. R. Gandhi and His Critics. Delhi: Oxford UP, 1985.

———. Mahatma Gandhi: A Biography. Delhi: Oxford UP, 1989.

Polner, Murray, and Naomi Goodman, eds. The Challenge of Shalom: The Jewish Tradition of Peace and Justice. Philadelphia: New Society, 1994.

Polner, Murray, and Jim O'Grady. Disarmed and Dangerous: The Radical Lives and Times of Daniel and Philip Berrigan. New York: Basic, 1997.

Sibley, Mulford Q. The Obligation to Disobey: Conscience and the Law. New York: Council on Religion and International Affairs, 1970.

Singer, Peter. Democracy and Disobedience. Oxford: Clarendon, 1973.

Storing, Herbert G. "The Case against Civil Disobedience." On Civil Disobedience: Essays Old and New. Ed. Robert A. Goldwin. Chicago: Rand McNally, 1968. 95–120.

Tolstoy, Leo. Writings on Civil Disobedience and Nonviolence. Philadelphia: New Society, 1987.

Walzer, Michael. Obligations: Essays on Disobedience, War, and Citizenship. Cambridge: Harvard UP, 1970.

Waskow, Arthur. "The Sword and the Plowshare as Tools of Tikkun Olam." Tikkun 17.3 (2002): 42–49.

Weinberg, Arthur C., and Lia Weinberg, eds. Instead of Violence: Writings by the Great Advocates of Peace and Nonviolence throughout History. New York: Grossman, 1963.

Zinn, Howard. "Law and Justice." Writings on Disobedience and Democracy. New York: Seven Stories, 1997. 368–401.

Civil Rights Movement

Allen, Barbara. "Martin Luther King's Civil Disobedience and the American Covenant Tradition." Publius 30.4 (2000): 71.

Beardslee, William R. The Way out Must Lead In: Life Histories in the Civil Rights Movement. Westport: Hill, 1983.

D'Emilio, John. Lost Prophet: The Life and Times of Bayard Rustin. New York: Free, 2003.

Dudley, William. The Civil Rights Movement: Opposing Viewpoints. San Diego: Greenhaven, 1996.

Greenberg, Cheryl L. A Circle of Trust: Remembering SNCC. New Brunswick: Rutgers UP, 1998.

Proudfoot, Merrill. Diary of a Sit-In. 2nd ed. Urbana: U of Illinois P, 1990.

Rustin, Bayard. Down the Line: The Collected Writings of Bayard Rustin. Chicago: Quadrangle, 1971.

Peace Movements

Chatfield, Charles. The American Peace Movement: Ideals and Activism. New York: Twayne, 1992.

Foley, Michael S. Confronting the War Machine: Draft Resistance during the Vietnam War. Chapel Hill: U of North Carolina P, 2003.

Gaylin, Willard. In the Service of Their Country: War Resisters in Prison. New York: Grosset & Dunlap, 1970.

Gioglio, Gerald. Days of Decision: An Oral History of Conscientious Objectors in the Military during the Vietnam War. Trenton: Broken Rifle, 1989.

Lynd, Alice. We Won't Go: Personal Accounts of War Objectors. Boston: Beacon, 1968.

Marullo, Sam, and John Lofland. Peace Action in the Eighties: Social
    Science Perspectives. New Brunswick: Rutgers UP, 1990.
O'Brien, Tim. If I Die in a Combat Zone: Box Me up and Ship Me
    Home. New York: Delacorte, 1973.
Small, Melvin, et al. Give Peace a Chance: Exploring the Vietnam Anti-
    war Movement: Essays from the Charles DeBenedetti Memorial
    Conference. Syracuse: Syracuse UP, 1992.
Tollefson, James W. The Strength Not to Fight: An Oral History of Con-
    scientious Objectors of the Vietnam War. Boston: Little, Brown,
    1993.
Zinn, Howard. The Power of Nonviolence: Writings by Advocates of
    Peace. Boston: Beacon, 2002.

Environmentalism

Berry, Wendell. "The Reactor and the Garden." The Gift of Good Land:
    Further Essays Cultural and Agricultural. New York: North Point,
    1981. 161–170.
Gomberg, Tooker. "A Friction to the Machine." Alternatives Journal
    27.2 (2001): 7.
Krawczyk, Betty. "A Prisoner of Conscience in the War of the Woods."
    Earth Island Journal 16.1 (2001): 40.
Kumar, Satish, and Jake Bowers. "Can the Use of Violence Be Justified
    as We Campaign for a Better World?" The Ecologist 30.8
    (2000): 20.
Little, Jane Braxton. "Crimes for Nature." American Forests 105.1
    (1999): 7–9.
Martin, Michael. "Ecosabotage and Civil Disobedience." Environmen-
    tal Ethics 12.4 (1990): 291.
Welchman, Jennifer. "Is Ecosabotage Civil Disobedience?" Philosophy
    and Geography 4.1 (2001): 97–107.

Israeli Refusers

Gazit, Shlomo. "Refusers: Renege!" Jerusalem Post 5 February 2002,
    Opinion: 8.
Gorenberg, Gershom. "The Thin Green Line." Mother Jones 27.5
    (2002): 48–55, 90.
Halkin, Hillel. "Of Soldiers, 'Outposts,' and 'Occupation.'" Jerusalem
    Post 13 June 2003, Opinion: 9B.

Harel, Amos, and Lily Galili. "Air Force to Oust Refusenik Pilots."
    haaretzdaily.com. 25 Sept. 2003 <http://www.haaretz.com>.
Menuhin, Ishai. "Saying No to Israel's Occupation." New York Times
    9 March 2002, A15.
Myre, Greg. "27 Israeli Pilots Say They Refuse to Bomb Civilians."
    New York Times 25 Sept. 2003, A12.
Sontag, Susan. "On Courage and Resistance." The Nation 276.17 (2003): 11.

Other Movements

Alcorn, Randy C. Is Rescuing Right? Breaking the Law to Save the
    Unborn. Downers Grove: InterVarsity, 1990.
Dixon, Nicholas. "The Morality of Anti-Abortion Civil Disobedience."
    Public Affairs Quarterly 11.1 (1997): 21.
Freeman, Jo, and Victoria L. Johnson. Waves of Protest: Social Move-
    ments since the Sixties. Lanham: Rowman, 1999.
Shepard, Benjamin H., and Ronald Hayduk. From ACT UP to the
    WTO: Urban Protest and Community Building in the Era of Glob-
    alization. London: Verso, 2002.
Washington and Lee University School of Law. "Protest and Resistance:
    Civil Disobedience in the 1990s." Washington and Lee Law
    Review 48.1 (1991): 15–252.

B

Using Sources in an Argumentative Research Essay

I. Research Resources

Writing an argumentative research essay demands that you learn to do many things—read arguments critically, synthesize other writers' work, and organize and support your own argument. But before you can do any of these things, you must locate relevant, reliable, and thoughtful sources for your essay. The types of critical skills you exercise in reading the texts in this book are also necessary for doing good research. Finding sources may be easy, but finding good sources is often hard because we must be able to distinguish the good from the bad, the thoughtful from the superficial, the reliable from the fly-by-night, and the open-minded from the biased.

Research often begins when you have chosen your research topic but not yet narrowed it or developed a working thesis or claim (see Chapter 3). What you discover about your research topic will help you to narrow your focus and then to take your own position. Students just beginning research in the modern college library have great resources to draw upon. But where should you begin?

There are four types of resources for the research you will likely do for a college argumentative research essay:

1. Field research, such as observations, interviews, surveys, and questionnaires
2. Your library (and connected libraries) catalog

3. InfoTrac College Edition, other databases, and other electronic sources such as CD-ROMs
4. The Internet

Field Research

The information and ideas necessary to understand some current topics can be obtained through research "in the field," direct observation and collection of material in the world. You might, for example, conduct an oral history interview with a veteran to learn how people experienced a particular war. You might e-mail civil disobedience activists and ask them their opinions of current world events; they will often respond to thoughtful questions from serious students. It is important to prepare well for field research, so be sure that you have carefully constructed your questions or interview procedure before you begin.

Library Catalogs

Every library maintains a catalog of its holdings of books, periodicals, and electronic publications, normally cataloged according to the Library of Congress or Dewey Decimal System. College and university libraries, as well as many public libraries, are often part of larger library networks that enable you to search the holdings of thousands of other libraries. You should become very familiar with the method to search your own library's catalog and with using the reference materials available in the library. Learn to use the search functions in your online library catalog. Consult the reference librarians; they are extremely knowledgeable and will assist you to do better searches in the library. Remember that most scholarship in the world is still found in the books and journals you can locate through the library catalog.

InfoTrac College Edition, Databases, and Other Electronic Sources

Libraries subscribe to databases that contain bibliographic information—indexes to publications, citations, and abstracts—and to databases that include full-text services that allow the user to read and download complete sources. Investigate what your library has available and how to access it. Many databases are now available to library patrons from off-campus via the library's Web site.

As part of your purchase of this book, you have access to InfoTrac College Edition. This full-text database, available to you at all times from your computer, includes over 5,000 journals going back in some cases nearly twenty years. You may search InfoTrac College Edition for articles in scholarly publications, journals of opinion, and news magazines. Often you will be able to download a portable document format (PDF) file, which is a true copy of the article as it appeared in print. This type of retrieval enables you to cite page numbers to the original place of publication.

The Internet

The Internet can be a wonderful source for information and ideas for the careful researcher. Government bodies, universities, publishers, individual scholars, and scholarly and professional organizations have published millions of valuable pages on the World Wide Web. Many newspapers and magazines now publish online versions of their current issues, although earlier material may not be accessible or free. Other material available is much more dubious, ranging from personal obsessions to deceptive Web sites that are selling a product or an ideology. It is vital to depend upon the guidance of your librarian or instructor as well as on your own critical analysis in evaluating Web sites. See your library Web site or your librarian for recommended sites when you begin your research.

You will also wish to search directly for your topic on the Internet. You can use keywords and subjects to locate material using search engines such as Google and Yahoo! Evaluate the sites you find this way using the steps below. Remember to record all publication information and the date you accessed the site because you will need these to use and cite the source in your essay.

Example of Doing Research

Suppose you were interested in exploring whether the Vietnam War could be considered a just war. How would you go about finding adequate and reliable sources?

Look at the four types of research resources above. You would probably not begin with *field research* because you would need to educate yourself before you interviewed or questioned anyone. You should begin with your library catalog.

Internet Site Evaluation Checklist

1. Is the site peer reviewed?
2. Does it give information about how to cite it? Such information is a good indication that the authors see themselves as part of the scholarly conversation.
3. Is there a named author? Who is it? What are his or her credentials? You may have to do research on the author.
4. Check the home page or welcome page. Is there a sponsoring organization? Have you heard of it? Is it reliable? What do the authors say about themselves? Do you have any way to check on them? Are they a recognized authority such as a university or well-known organization? Do not use Web sites where no author or no sponsoring organization is named.
5. Is there any kind of editorial policy or statement of purpose given? Read it carefully so you can judge the intention of the authors.
6. If the sites include text from other sources, can you be sure it is reliably reproduced? If material is scanned in, there is no way to tell if it was correctly and completely added. Look for PDF texts because you can see the original pages and locate the original in the library. You must be able, at the least, to verify the material, so there must be accurate citation of original publication data and/or hyperlinks to original material locations.
7. When was the site last updated? If some years ago, it may no longer be accurate or have been a fly-by-night project to begin with.
8. If it is a commercial site, what sorts of ads appear? Look carefully to see if the site is in fact only an advertisement disguised as information. Ads can also lead you to make critical judgments about the intended audience of the Web site, helping you to evaluate its contents.
9. Finally, there is no substitute for reading critically. You are the judge of the ethos of the Web site. Are you confident that the site is reliable, authoritative, and honest?

Library Catalog

Our library catalog at Loyola University Chicago found two books when we entered the keywords *Vietnam* and *just war* in the keyword catalog search:

Boyd Andrew J. *The Theory of Just War and Its Application to the American War in Vietnam.* Chicago: Loyola UP, 1991.

McNeal, Patricia F. *Harder than War: Catholic Peacemaking in Twentieth-Century America.* New Brunswick: Rutgers UP, 1992.

We can print all the publication information and library call number or save it to a file on our computer. We can even e-mail the information to ourselves or to someone else.

Once the books are located in the library, we can see if they lead in an interesting direction. Almost as important, we can use their bibliographies to find the names of other books and articles and can search the catalog for them.

InfoTrac College Edition and Other Databases

A search of InfoTrac College Edition for the keywords *Vietnam* and *just war* together finds three sources. One that looks especially promising is reprinted below as it appears:

> **KERREY'S CULPABILITY: Vietnam & the just-war tradition.** (participation of former Senator Bob Kerrey in Vietnam War and moral culpability implied by just-war theory) Gordon Marino.
>
> ***Commonweal*** June 1, 2001 v128 i11 p9 Mag.Coll.: 107M0094

Using InfoTrac College Edition assures us that the source has been selected as appropriate for college research. If we need to know more, we can pursue information about both Senator Bob Kerrey and the author, Gordon Marino, in other databases available in the library. Sen. Kerrey is easy to find through many standard biographical reference sources. However, Marino is harder. He is not for example, in *Who's Who* or *Contemporary Authors*. We can try to see if there is a note about the author in the publication itself, where we learn he is an associate professor of philosophy and director of the Hong/Kirkegaard Library at Saint Olaf College. If further research about him were necessary, we would look for other of his publications and for information about him on Saint Olaf's Web site.

We can also click on the Link button next to his article to find many other sources related to Vietnam. These need to be followed up. *Just war* by itself and *Vietnam* by itself as keywords will locate more sources as well.

The Internet

Using *Vietnam "just war"* to search Google finds 12,700 Web documents. One is a page on a Web site for the 15th Field Artillery Regiment http://www.landscaper.net/peace.htm. There is quite a bit of material on this Web site, but how much can you use? For example, this page includes a definition of just war that is not credited to an author or source. This is not a particularly reliable source for just war theory. The writers of the Web site are not authorities and do not claim to be authorities on just war. What could you use? The regimental history by the regimental historian, who is named, would be authoritative. You can check to see the statement of purpose and the history of the Web site. You can contact the Webmaster and ask questions. You can follow the links and evaluate them as well. Excerpts from other sources and quotations should not be used unless you can verify them.

Some research topics make evaluation especially difficult. For example, if you were researching World War II, you might use the words *German, WW II, British,* and *Jews* to search in Google. You would then come across the Web site http://www.heretical.com/mkilliam/wwii .html, which seems to have a large number of quotations from primary sources and newspapers. Initially, you might think the site was one you could use in your research.

However, the author's name is given, but not information about the author. And, as you begin to read, if you know anything about the subject, you will see the author is a Hitler supporter and twists facts terribly. If you then turn to the main page and click on some links, you will see it is a neo-Nazi site selling anti-Semitic books; there is even a swastika on one page. But if you knew nothing about the subject, you might believe this to be objective or at least truthful. Thus the Internet may not be a good place to begin research on a topic you know very little about.

II. Integrating Sources into Your Writing

In general, you will demonstrate your knowledge and credibility as a writer by controlling your use of source material. Remember that you are in charge, not the sources. Certainly utilize the ideas and facts another writer offers, but employ those to support your argument. Do not allow the sources to overshadow your claims.

Avoiding Plagiarism

Plagiarism is a form of fraud or theft in which a writer takes others' words or ideas and presents them as his or her own. Some plagiarism is the result of ignorance or carelessness. More seriously, some is deliberate, such as buying papers to hand in as your own or copying sources and passing them off as your own writing. All kinds of plagiarism violate the basic rules of the conversations we participate in. Inadvertent plagiarism prevents researchers from following up on sources and learning from them directly because sources are not named. Of course, deliberate plagiarism is equivalent to lying to people—never a good basis for a conversation. In addition, plagiarism often leads to severe penalties in both the academic and publishing worlds.

To avoid plagiarism, you must cite your source wherever you paraphrase, summarize, or quote. Both the sources of information—facts, dates, and events—and of ideas must be cited. You must give complete bibliographic data about all sources you use. You must use either the exact words of the source as a quotation or paraphrase or summarize the source's information or ideas in your own words.

Introducing Source Material

There are three ways to use material you have found in your research in your own argument: summary, paraphrase, and quotation. Each has its place. Whether you summarize, paraphrase, or quote, you need to introduce the material in some way. The easiest way is to begin with an attribution:

- According to Richard Falk, . . .
- As John Yoder points out, . . .

Be sure to give the full name of an author you are mentioning for the first time; thereafter you may use the last name only. It can add to your own authority as a writer to identify the authority of your source:

- The Islamic legal scholar Majid Khadduri notes . . .
- University of Chicago Divinity School professor Jean Bethke Elshtain believes that . . .

Give a context or other opening to make sense of a quotation, and be sure that your quotation is part of a grammatical sentence.

Summary

When you wish to state briefly information or an idea from a source, use summary. Use your own words to sum up the main facts or notions; leave out the details. Summary is especially appropriate for information.

Paraphrase

When you want to use information or ideas at greater length from a source, paraphrase it. To paraphrase means to put the passage into your own words, changing the structure as well as the words.

Quotation

Judicious quotation adds authority and credibility to your argumentative research writing. Choose passages that are important to your argument, that are well stated, or that you wish to examine in detail. Avoid using too many quotations. No reader wants to read a patchwork quilt of quotations stitched together by a writer with no words of his or her own. Introduce quotations carefully: Do not just plop them in. Quotations longer than four lines should be set off by indenting them ten spaces. If you remove anything from a quoted passage, you must indicate you have done so with ellipses. If you add anything to a quotation, perhaps to clarify a word, place square brackets around the addition.

III. Documenting Sources: MLA and APA Styles

All sources of information and ideas must be cited; you must state what the source is and which part of it you used. The exception is items that are common knowledge, such as, for instance, that the United States fought in World War II or that Christianity is the dominant religion of the West. Both the Modern Language Association (MLA) and the American Psychological Association (APA) have extensive guidelines for preparing papers and publications that include distinct styles of source citation. The styles both require that you keep careful records of your research so that you can accurately cite your sources. Instructors in the humanities generally require students to follow MLA guidelines. In the social sciences, instructors usually require APA format. Use the format your instructor assigns.

Both the MLA and APA formats work by giving a short reference to the source at the end of the passage quoted, paraphrased, or summarized. The reference is keyed to a complete bibliographic entry at the end of the paper, the Works Cited page for MLA, the References or Bibliography for APA.

For more extensive discussions of documentation forms, see the *MLA Handbook for Writers of Research Papers*, 6th edition, and the *APA Publication Manual*, 5th edition. In addition, both the MLA and the APA have advice about documenting sources, particularly electronic ones, on their respective Web sites, www.mla.org and www.apastyle.org.

Parenthetical Citation

The MLA format requires that you give the author's name and the page number in parentheses following the quotation, summary, or paraphrase. For APA, the author's name, the date or year of publication, and the page numbers are given. In either style, you do not need to repeat the author's name if you give it in the text.

MLA Style

1. Direct Quotation

      One major concern is "that America's pre-emptive war will lead directly to the use of the weapons whose mere possession the war is supposed to prevent" (Schell 15).

2. Author Named with Direct Quotation

      As Kelsay points out, "with respect to the example of Muhammad, then, it was possible to speak of use of lethal force which was right, in the sense of divinely sanctioned—even, divinely commanded" (45).

3. Summary or Paraphrase

      After the September 11, 2001, terrorist attacks, there were condemnations from almost all governments around the world, although in the Middle East there was public rejoicing in the streets at Americans' suffering (Longworth 19).

4. Two or Three Authors

      The main difference between the assassination of John F. Kennedy and that of Abraham Lincoln was that Kennedy was "a remembered physical presence" while Lincoln was "an image of the plastic arts" (Kempton and Ridgeway 63).

5. Two Books by the Same Author

To distinguish between two books by the same author that appear in your Works Cited, either include the title in the introduction to the passage or use a short version of the title in the parenthetical citation.

> Khadduri explains: "The world surrounding the Islamic state, composed of all other nations and territories that had not been brought under its rule, was collectively known as the 'territory of war'" (<u>Islamic Law of Nations</u> 12).

6. Corporate Author
Some publications are published under the name of an organization or other group. You can use the name of the organization just as you would an author. It is preferable to give the name in the introduction to the cited passage.

> The Chicago Public Schools Office of School and Community Relations notes that Local School Councils may set dress-code policy (vi).

7. Article in an Anthology
If you use an article in a book such as this casebook or any anthology, use the name of the author of the article, not the author or editor of the book.

8. No Author
Use the title in the parenthetical citation if there is no author. You should use a shortened title if possible, starting with the word by which it is alphabetized in the Works Cited.

> "We are menaced less by fleets and armies than by catastrophic technologies in the hands of the embittered few" (<u>National Security Strategy</u> 1).

9. Indirect Source
When you wish to use a passage quoted in another source and cannot locate the original, you may cite the source by naming the author of the quoted passage and placing the source you found it in the parenthetical citation.

> Burton Leiser describes terrorism as "seemingly senseless" (qtd. in Khatchadourian 35).

10. Scriptures
References to the names and parts of sacred writings, such as the Bible, the Qur'an, and the Upanishads, are not underlined. Biblical

citations give the book, chapter, and verse, and the standard abbreviations are preferred.

```
"They have healed the wound of my people
lightly, saying, 'Peace, peace,' when there is no
peace" (Jer.6:14).
```

11. Electronic Sources

When citing sources from databases and the Internet, follow the
rules for in-text parenthetical citation as much as possible. If there
are no page numbers given, you must cite the entire work. If the
source numbers its paragraphs, then include those as (par. 2) or
(pars. 8–9). It is a good idea to name the source in the text.

```
Alexander warns that it is easier to list
Just War principles than to apply them to a spe-
cific instance.
```

The Works Cited list gives Alexander's article retrieved through a
full-text database from <u>The Providence Journal-Bulletin.</u>

```
According to Prados, "There were no signifi-
cant changes in the CIA's intelligence sources on
Iraq, and in fact there was no real change in
what the agency was reporting" (29).
```

This article, from <u>The Bulletin of the Atomic Scientists,</u> was retrieved
as a PDF from InfoTrac College Edition. Therefore, a page number
can be given. If you retrieve it directly from the <u>Bulletin's</u> Web site,
you will not be able to cite a page number.

```
The White House Web site's History & Tours
section attributes Jefferson's election to the
vice presidency under John Adams to "a flaw in
the Constitution."
```

12. A Television or Radio Program, a Sound Recording, a Film or Video Recording, a Lecture, an Interview, or a Cartoon

These are all cited in the text as entire works. Thus the preferred
method is to include the title or the name of the person (such as the
director, performer, interviewee, or speaker) in the text. The title or
name should be the element that begins the entry in your Works Cited.

```
The Ramirez cartoon expresses a strong prowar
position. (The entry in the Works Cited list
```

gives the specific cartoon under the cartoonist's name, Mike Ramirez.)

Kathy Kelly inspired the students with her lecture on working for peace. (The lecture is listed under Kelly.)

Mrs. Wayani was married twice and has four children. (The interview with Mrs. Wayani appears under her name in the Works Cited list.)

Phillis Wheatley went to England with her master's son, Nathaniel Wheatley, as <u>Africans in America</u> explains. (The video recording is listed in the Works Cited list by its title.)

APA Style

1. Author with Direct Quotation

One major concern is "that America's pre-emptive war will lead directly to the use of the weapons whose mere possession the war is supposed to prevent" (Schell, 2003, p.15).

2. Author Named with Direct Quotation

As Kelsay (1993) points out, "with respect to the example of Muhammad, then, it was possible to speak of use of lethal force which was right, in the sense of divinely sanctioned—even, divinely commanded" (p.45).

3. Summary or Paraphrase

After the September 11, 2001, terrorist attacks, there were condemnations from almost all governments around the world, although in the Middle East there was public rejoicing in the streets at Americans' suffering (Longworth, 2001, p.19).

4. Two or Three Authors

APA uses an ampersand (&) between names in the parenthetical citation but not in the text itself.

The main difference between the assassination of John F. Kennedy and that of Abraham Lincoln was that Kennedy was "a remembered physical presence" while Lincoln was "an image of the plastic arts" (Kempton & Ridgeway, 1968, p.63).

5. Two Books by the Same Author
In the APA style, the different dates distinguish the different books. Khadduri's other book was published in 1955.

Khadduri (1966) explains: "The world surrounding the Islamic state, composed of all other nations and territories that had not been brought under its rule, was collectively known as the 'territory of war'" (p.12).

6. Corporate Author
The Chicago Public Schools Office of School and Community Relations (2000) notes that local school councils may set dress code policy (p.vi).

7. Article in an Anthology
As with MLA format, use the author of the article in the collection, not the author or editor of the book.

8. No Author
"We are menaced less by fleets and armies than by catastrophic technologies in the hands of the embittered few" (<u>National Security Strategy</u>, 2003, 1).

9. Indirect Source
Burton Leiser (1979) describes terrorism as "seemingly senseless" (as cited in Khatchadourian, 2003, p.35).

10. Scriptures
Identical to MLA format, references to the names and parts of sacred writings, such as the Bible, the Qur'an, and the Upanishads, are not underlined. Biblical citations give the book, chapter, and verse, and the standard abbreviations are preferred.

11. Electronic Sources
Give the author's name, the date of publication, and page or paragraph numbers, if they are available, just as you would with a print

source. If no author is given, use a shortened version of the title. If no date is given, use n.d. to indicate no date.

> Alexander (2003) warns that it is easier to list Just War principles than to apply them to a specific instance.

The References list gives Alexander's article retrieved through a full-text database from *The Providence Journal-Bulletin.*

> According to Prados (2003), "There were no significant changes in the CIA's intelligence sources on Iraq, and in fact there was no real change in what the agency was reporting" (p.29).

This article, from *The Bulletin the Atomic Scientists,* was retrieved as a PDF from InfoTrac College Edition. Therefore, a page number can be given. If you retrieve it directly from the *Bulletin*'s Web site, you will not be able to cite a page number.

> The White House Web site's History & Tours section attributes Jefferson's election to the vice presidency under John Adams to "a flaw in the Constitution."

12. **A Television or Radio Program, a Sound Recording, a Film or Video Recording, a Lecture, an Interview, or a Cartoon**
As in the MLA format, these sources are all cited in the text as entire works. Thus, the preferred method is to include the title or the name of the person (such as the director, performer, interviewee, or speaker) in the text. Unlike in MLA format, APA format considers an interview or unpublished lecture unrecoverable data and therefore does not include it in the References list, but it may be cited in the text as a personal communication.

> Mrs. Wayani was married twice and has four children (personal communication, October 17, 2003).

> Phillis Wheatley went to England with her master's son, Nathaniel Wheatley, as *Africans in America* explains.

The video recording is listed in the References list by its title.

The Works Cited and References Lists

All parenthetical citations refer to a work listed on the Works Cited page (MLA) or References list (APA). The reader must be able to find every source named in the body of your essay in the bibliographic listing, which appears at the end of the essay. Therefore the list is alphabetized by the authors' last names or, if no author is given, by the title of the source (excluding *a, an,* and *the* at the beginning of the title).

If you have kept a computer file of all your sources, you can easily arrange them alphabetically. Similarly, if you have kept bibliography note-cards, you can alphabetize these. If you have already prepared an annotated bibliography, remove the annotations and attach it to the paper.

MLA Style

The Works Cited page is double-spaced. The entries are typed in the "drop-and-hang" style: the first line of the entry is flush against the left margin, and each subsequent line of the entry is indented five spaces. A student paper using MLA style is printed at the end of this Appendix.

MLA Form for Books

Author. <u>Title of Book</u>. City: Publisher's Name in Shortened Form, date of publication.

Note that all the important words in the title are capitalized. MLA prefers that titles be underlined rather than italicized, but your instructor might prefer italics for titles. Publishers' names should be abbreviated; use UP for *University Press.*

1. Book by One Author

> Kelsay, John. <u>Islam and War: A Study in Compara-</u>
> <u>tive Ethics</u>. Louisville: Westminster, 1993.

2. Book by Two or More Authors
If a book has two or three authors, list them in the order they appear on the title page. Reverse only the name of the first author listed and separate the names by commas. If there are more than three authors, use the abbreviation et al. (Latin for *and others*) after the first author, or you may choose to list all the authors.

> Hammer, Michael, and James Champy. <u>Reengineering</u>
> <u>the Corporation: A Manifesto for Business</u>
> <u>Revolution</u>. New York: HarperBusiness, 1993.

Perls, Frederick, Ralph E. Hefferline, and Paul
    Goodman. <u>Gestalt Therapy: Excitement and
    Growth in the Human Personality</u>. New York:
    Dell, 1951.

3. Book with an Editor or Translator

Jack, Homer A., ed. <u>The Gandhi Reader: A
    Sourcebook of His Life and Writings</u>. New
    York: Grove, 1956.

Zohn, Harry, and Karl F. Ross, trans. <u>What If—?
    Satirical Writings of Kurt Tucholsky</u>. New
    York: Funk, 1967.

4. Corporate Author
List the book by the corporate author, such as an association or commission, even if there is an editor listed as well.

Central Conference of American Rabbis. <u>A Passover
    Haggadah: The New Union Haggadah</u>. Ed. Herbert
    Bronstein. New York: Central Conference of
    American Rabbis, 1974.

5. Article or Other Piece in an Anthology
Use the author of the article as the author. Put the title of the article in quotation marks. Give the editor's name after the title of the anthology, which is underlined. Follow the period after the date of the publication with the inclusive pages where the article is found.

Chang, Edward T. "America's First Multiethnic
    'Riots.'" <u>The State of Asian America:
    Activism and Resistance in the 1990s</u>. Ed.
    Karin Aguilar-San Juan. Boston: South End,
    1994. 101-17.

Kempton, Murray, and James Ridgeway. "Romans."
    <u>The Sense of the Sixties</u>. Ed. Edward Quinn
    and Paul J. Dolan. New York: Free, 1968.
    63-67.

6. Article in a Reference Book
Cite an article in an encyclopedia or dictionary the way you would one in an anthology (see above) except do not list the editor of the reference work. If the author of the article is given, use the name;

otherwise, cite by the title of the article. Common reference books that are published often in new editions do not need full publication data. You need only give the edition (if you can) and the date of publication. You may omit volume and page numbers if the entries are arranged alphabetically.

"Justice." The American Heritage College Dictionary. 3rd ed. 1997.

Kelly, P. M. "Gaia Hypothesis." The Harper Dictionary of Modern Thought. Ed. Alan Bullock and Stephen Trombley. Rev. ed. New York: Harper, 1988.

MLA Form for Articles

Author. "Title of the Article." Journal volume number (year): page numbers.
Author. "Title of the Article." Newspaper date of publication, edition: page numbers.
Author. "Title of the Article." Magazine date of publication: page numbers.

1. Article in a Scholarly Journal

Do not use the issue number unless the journal does not number pages continuously throughout the volume.

Windholz, Anne M. "An Emigrant and a Gentleman: Imperial Masculinity, British Magazines, and the Colony That Got Away." Victorian Studies 42 (1999–2000): 631–58.

Flanzbaum, Hilene. "Unprecedented Liberties: Re-Reading Phillis Wheatley." MELUS: The Journal of the Society for the Study of the Multi-Ethnic Literature of the United States 18.3 (1993): 71–81.

2. Article in a Newspaper

Schmetzer, Uli, "Spanish, Italian Backers of Iraq War Survive Vote." Chicago Tribune 27 May 2003, late ed., sec 1: 6.

3. Article in a Magazine

> Schell, Jonathan. "The Case against the War." <u>The Nation</u> 3 March 2003: 11–23.

> Meyerson, Harold. "The Most Dangerous President Ever." <u>American Prospect</u> May 2003: 25–28.

MLA Form for Electronic Sources

For electronic sources, you need to collect more information than you do for print sources because there is no uniform publication format as yet for Internet, World Wide Web, and other electronic publications. Be sure to record as much publication data as you can find about electronic sources, including especially the date you accessed the source. Electronic sources can disappear in a way print ones do not, so record your information right away. It is also a good idea to download and save or print a copy of the source.

Publication data you should collect and use to cite electronic sources:

1. Author's name (if given)
2. Title of the document
3. Information about print publication (if published previously or simultaneously in print)
4. Information about electronic publication (title of publication or Internet site)
5. Access information (date of access and URL of the document—but see exceptions below)

The basic Works Cited form is:

Author's name. "Title of the Document." Information about print publication. Information about electronic publication. Access information.

1. Article in a Periodical on the Web

> Prados, John. "A Necessary War? Not According to U. N. Monitors—or to U.S. Intelligence, Which Has Watched the Situation Even More Carefully." <u>Bulletin of the Atomic Scientists</u> 59.3 (2003): 8 pp. 27 May 2003 <http://www.thebulletin.org/issues/2003/mj03/mu03prados.html>.

Sometimes the URL becomes so long and complicated that it is difficult to transcribe. In such cases, give the URL of the site's search page instead.

> Gonzalez, David. "A Town of Tents and Civil
>   Disobedience." New York Times on the Web.
>   1 Aug. 2001. The New York Times Company.
>   9 Feb. 2002 <http://www.nytimes.com>.

2. Article through a Library Subscription Service

Often the URLs from these services are unique to the institution, are extremely long, or require access through your institution. In this case, access information should include the name of the database (underlined), the name of the service, the name of the library, and the date of access.

> Robnett, Belinda. "African-American Women in the
>   Civil Rights Movement, 1954–1965: Gender,
>   Leadership, and Micromobilization." American
>   Journal of Sociology 101 (1996): 1661–1693
>   JSTOR. Loyola U Chicago Lib. 2 March 2003
>   <http://www.jstor.org>.

3. Article from an Organization's Web Site

> "Not In Our Name: A Statement of Conscience
>   against War and Repression." Not In Our Name.
>   2002. Not In Our Name. 9 Jan. 2003
>   <http://www.nion.us/NION.HTM>.

4. Entire Internet Sites, Such as Online Scholarly Projects or Professional Sites

> Digital Schomburg African American Women Writers
>   of the 19th Century. 1999. The New York Public
>   Library. 10 June 2002 <http://149.123.1.8/
>   schomburg/writers_aa19/toc.html>.

MLA Form for Nonprint Sources

1. A Film or Video Recording

> Africans in America. Prod. Orlando Bagwell. WGBH
>   Educational Foundation. Videocasette. PBS
>   Video, 1998.

2. A Television or Radio Program

```
"White House Pressed to Stir Revolt in Iran."
    Narr. Steve Inskeep. All Things Considered.
    Natl Public Radio. WBEZ, Chicago. 31 May 2003.
```

3. An Interview

```
Wayani, Shashi. Personal Interview. 17 October
    2002.
```

4. A Lecture or Speech

```
Kelly, Kathy. Keynote Address. English Dept.
    Shared-Text Project. Loyola University,
    Chicago. 18 Sept. 2002.
```

5. A Cartoon or Comic Strip

Follow the cartoonist's name with the title if there is one. Use the label of either *Cartoon* or *Comic Strip* and then give the regular publication information.

```
Donnelly, Liza. Cartoon. New Yorker 21 and
    28 April 2003: 66.
```

APA Style

The References page is double-spaced. The entries are typed in the "drop-and-hang" style: the first line of the entry is flush against the left margin; each subsequent line of the entry is indented five spaces.

APA format differs from MLA in a number of important ways: Use only the initial or initials of an author's first and middle names with his or her last name: *Adams, J. Q.* Follow the name of the author with the date of publication in parentheses.

Capitalize only the first word of titles of books and articles and the first word after a colon. Do capitalize the main words of journals and newspapers. Do not put quotation marks around the titles of articles.

Italicize the titles of books and names of journals, newspapers, and magazines. Do not shorten publishers' names, although you may omit unimportant words such as *Publishers, Inc.,* or *Co.*

APA Form for Books

Author. (date of publication). *Title.* City of publication: Publisher.

1. Book by One Author

Kelsay, J. (1993). *Islam and war: A study in comparative ethics.* Louisville: Westminster/John Knox Press.

2. Book by Two or More Authors

APA only uses et al. if there are more than six authors. Use an ampersand to connect the last two authors.

Hammer, M., & Champy, J. (1993). *Reengineering the corporation: A manifesto for business revolution.* New York: HarperBusiness/Harper Collins.

Perls, F., Hefferline, R. E., & Goodman, P. (1951). *Gestalt therapy: Excitement and growth in the human personality.* New York: Dell.

3. Book with an Editor or Translator

Jack, H. A. (Ed.). (1956). *The Gandhi reader: A sourcebook of his life and writings.* New York: Grove Press.

Zohn, H., & Ross, K. F. (Trans.). (1967). *What if—? Satirical writings of Kurt Tucholsky.* New York: Funk & Wagnalls.

4. Corporate Author

Central Conference of American Rabbis. (1974). *A Passover haggadah: The new union hagaddah.* H. Bronstein (Ed.). New York: Author.

5. Article or Other Piece in an Anthology

Use the author or title of the article as the beginning of the entry. Put the inclusive page numbers after the title of the book in parentheses.

Chang, E. T. (1994). America's first multiethnic "riots." In K. Aguilar-San Juan (Ed.), *The state of Asian America: Activism and resistance in the 1990s* (pp.101–117). Boston: South End Press.

Kempton, M., & Ridgeway, J. (1968). Romans. In E. Quinn & P. J. Dolan (Eds.), *The sense of the sixties* (pp.63–67), New York: Free Press.

6. Article in a Reference Book

Justice. (1997). *The American heritage college dictionary* (3rd ed., p.738). Boston: Houghton Mifflin.

Kelly, P. M. (1988). Gaia hypothesis. In A. Bullock & S. Trombley (Eds.), *The Harper dictionary of modern thought* (p.341). New York: Harper & Row.

APA Form for Articles

Author. (date of publication). Title of article. *Title of publication, volume number,* page numbers.

1. Article in a Scholarly Journal

Windholz, A. M. (1999–2000). An emigrant and a gentleman: Imperial masculinity, British magazines, and the colony that got away. *Victorian Studies, 42,* 631–58.

Flanzbaum, H. (1993). Unprecedented liberties: Rereading Phillis Wheatley. *MELUS: The Journal of the Society for the Study of Multi-Ethnic Literature of the United States, 18*(3), 71–81.

2. Article in a Newspaper

Schmetzer, U. (2003, May 27). Spanish, Italian backers of Iraq war survive vote. *Chicago Tribune,* Sec. 1, p.6.

3. Article in a Magazine

Schell, J. (2003, March 3). The case against the war. *The Nation,* 11–23.

Meyerson, H. (2003, May) The most dangerous president ever. *American Prospect,* 25–28.

APA Form for Electronic Sources

Author. (Date of publication). Title of article. *Journal title, volume number,* issue number, page numbers [if given]. Retrieved date of access, from where: source URL.

1. **Article in a Periodical on the Web**
Give the retrieval date and URL only if you believe the electronic version differs from the print version.

> Prados, J. (2003). A necessary war? Not according
>   to U.N. monitors—or to U.S. intelligence,
>   which has watched the situation even more
>   carefully. *Bulletin of the Atomic Scientists,*
>   *59*(3). Retrieved May 27, 2003, from
>   http://www.thebulletin.org/issues/2003/mj03/
>   mj03prados.html.

2. **Article through a Library Subscription Service**
Give the date of retrieval and the name of the database service. Follow it with the article number if the database provides one.

> Robnett, B. (1996) African-American women in the
>   civil rights movement, 1954–1965: Gender,
>   leadership, and micromobilization. *American*
>   *Journal of Sociology, 101,* 1661–1693.
>   Retrieved March 2, 2003, from JSTOR database.

3. **Article from an Organization's Web Site**

> Not in Our Name (2002). *Not in our name: A state-*
>   *ment of conscience against war and repres-*
>   *sion.* Retrieved January 9, 2003, from
>   http://www.nion.us/NION.HTM.

4. **Entire Internet Sites, Such as Online Scholarly Projects or Professional Sites**

> The New York Public Library. (1999) *Digital*
>   *Schomburg African American women writers of*
>   *the 19th century.* Retrieved June 10, 2002,
>   from http://149.123.1.8/schomburg/
>   writers_aa19/toc.html.

APA Form for Nonprint Sources

1. **A Film or Video Recording**

> Bagwell, O. (Producer). (1998). *Africans in Amer-*
>   *ica.* [Videotape]. Boston: WGBH Educational
>   Foundation/PBS Video.

2. A Television or Radio Program

```
Inskeep, S. (Reporter). (2003, May 31). White
    House pressed to stir revolt in Iran. All
    things considered [Radio Program]. Chicago:
    WBEZ.
```

3. An Interview

Because interviews cannot be retrieved as a source, APA does not list them in the References list.

4. A Lecture or Speech

Unless the lecture was recorded, it is also considered a source that cannot be retrieved and is not listed in the References list.

5. A Cartoon or Comic Strip

```
Donnelly, L. (2003, April 21 & 28). [Cartoon].
    New Yorker, 66.
```

IV. Sample Student Paper in MLA Style

Format

Print or type your paper in an easily readable font type and size, such as Times New Roman 12 point. Justify the lines of the paper at the left margin only. Print only on one side, and use white, good-quality, 8 1/2 × 11-inch paper. Be sure to keep a backup copy on disk. Use one-inch margins on the sides and the top and bottom of the paper (except for page numbers). Double-space your paper, including quotations and the Works Cited list. Leave only one space after the period unless your instructor prefers two.

Put your name and the title of the paper on the first page as follows:

Name
Instructor's Name
Course Number
Date

Double-space and then center the title of your paper on the next line. Do not underline the title, put it in quotation marks, or type it in all capital letters. Capitalize the main words and underline only the words (such as a book title) you would underline in the text of the paper. Use the header function of your word-processing program to place your name and consecutive page numbers in the upper right corner of your pages.

You can see what a properly formatted research paper looks like in Saudur Rahman's paper that follows.

Saudur Rahman

Dr. Sharon Walsh

English 106

November 17, 2003

Gandhi and the Effectiveness of His Civil
Disobedience Movement

Who does not know of Mahatma Gandhi? It seems that many Americans know about Gandhi, but only as little as the fact that he was a leader in the Indian independence movement. There are even fewer people who know that Mahatma Gandhi practiced civil disobedience and noncooperation as a part of his movement of satyagraha. In "Satyagraha, Civil Disobedience, Passive Resistance, Non-co-operation," Gandhi defined satyagraha as "soul-force," which "excludes the use of violence" (222). Two mass demonstrations characterized by civil disobedience and nonviolence were directed against the Rowlatt Bills and the Salt Acts. These laws gave the British government stronger control of the Indian people's civil and economic lives. These movements of Gandhi have long been topics for debate. Many doubt that Gandhi's policy of noncooperation actually avoids violence. Some say that Gandhi's policy did not even help

India in achieving its independence because of its ineffectiveness. By analyzing the Rowlatt and Salt Acts satyagrahas, however, one can understand that it is not the policy of noncooperation, but the inadequacy of communication that causes violence. One can also understand that nonviolence, through its effect on public opinion, did indeed help India in its independence movement because although the outbreak of violence in the Rowlatt satyagraha only caused further repression by the British government, the truly nonviolent Salt Acts satyagraha helped the Indians gain democratic and congressional rights.

A close look at the Rowlatt satyagraha shows that the failure of the satyagraha was due to the inadequacy of communication. From Joan V. Bondurant's historical account of the Rowlatt satyagraha in "Gandhi's Satyagraha against the Rowlatt Bills," one learns that this satyagraha was the first implementation of Gandhi's policy of noncooperation in India (32). Regarding noncooperation, in his letter entitled, "An Appeal to His Followers," Gandhi writes:

If a government does a grave injustice, the subject must withdraw cooperation wholly or partially,

sufficiently to wean the ruler from his wickedness
. . . It would be a sin for me to serve General Dyer
and cooperate with him to shoot innocent men. (134)

In order to help the wicked ruler realize his
wickedness, it is important to boycott his
rule. He implies that he cannot participate in
a government whose moral standards are very
low. In order to withdraw his participation in
the British government, Gandhi launched the
Rowlatt satyagraha. The Rowlatt Bills were supposed to "strengthen the hand of the government
in the control of crime, including sedition"
(Bondurant 32). The Indians, however, found the
bills undemocratic, infringing their rights of
liberty and justice and jeopardizing the safety
of India (33). The campaign of 1919 was mainly
characterized by civil disobedience because
besides the Rowlatt Act, many other laws were
selected to be violated, such as laws regulat-
ing publication of literature (42). Although
the campaign was intended to be of a nonviolent
nature,

In response to violent retaliation by police,
and later to the arrest of leaders, violence broke
out in many places after the first day of mass
demonstration. Stone-throwing was reported in Delhi,
and elsewhere buildings were burned, telegraph

lines cut, and both English and Indian officers
killed. (37)

The campaign failed because Gandhi's expecta-
tion of keeping it nonviolent proved to be
unfulfilled.

   The failure of the Rowlatt satyagraha is
often cited as evidence for showing the
ineffectiveness of Gandhi's philosophy of
nonviolence. In order to study the cause of the
failure, however, it is important to look at
the lessons that Gandhi learned from the failure
of his first satyagraha in India. As a result
of the outbreak of violence, Gandhi changed his
methods of propagating his philosophy. He
"raised a corps of volunteers and commenced the
work of educating the public with regard to the
meaning and practice of Satyagraha" (Bondurant
39). Before the Rowlatt campaign, Gandhi had
only propagandized against the Rowlatt Bills and
had asked the people to pledge to nonviolence.
After the campaign's failure, however, Gandhi
realized that the masses needed practice and
thus he devised the Satyagraha Corps. This
effort to propagate his philosophy was the only
change that Gandhi made in his movement. If the
cause of the outbreak of violence had been due
to flaws in Gandhi's philosophy itself, then his

changes in policy should have proved insufficient and future <u>satyagrahas</u> should have resulted in outbreaks of violence too.

However, as time progressed, the <u>satyagrahas</u> proved to be more and more successful. An example of a <u>satyagraha</u> that took place about ten years after the Rowlatt <u>satyagraha</u> and proved to be successful is the Salt Acts <u>satyagraha</u>. H. J. N. Horsburgh and Thomas Weber give a historical account and an analysis of this <u>satyagraha</u> in "The Practice of Satyagraha," and "The Marchers Simply Walked Forward until Struck Down," respectively. The immediate objective of this <u>satyagraha</u> was the "repeal of the Salt Acts which created a government monopoly of salt and imposed a tax that caused hardship to the poor" (Horsburgh 92). In order to gain independence, the Indians needed to get rid of the British interference in their economic lives. The Indian masses marched on the Salt Works in order to seize control of their own resource. After the demonstrators disregarded a few warnings, the police methodically beat them down. As the <u>satyagrahis</u> remained nonviolent, the police became infuriated and used more violence toward the <u>satyagrahis</u>, but they did not raise even an arm to fend off the blows (Weber 276). In the more than ten years since the

Rowlatt <u>satyagraha</u>, the public had become fully aware of the requirements of <u>satyagraha</u>. Gandhi believed that any movement requires training and that "there was no *prima facie* reason why the masses, if trained, should be incapable of showing the discipline which in organized warfare a fighting force normally does" (qtd. in Iyer 299). Indeed, until the end of the campaign, not a single <u>satyagrahi</u> perpetrated violence, showing their soldier-like discipline. This change was solely the result of mass propagation of Gandhi's philosophy. Thus, as time passed, it became clear that it was not the philosophy of nonviolence but the inadequacy of communication that had caused the outbreak of violence in the Rowlatt <u>satyagraha</u>.

The success of the Salt Acts <u>satyagraha</u> also addresses a criticism of Gandhi's philosophy. In his collection of criticisms of Gandhi's philosophy of ahimsa, or nonviolence, Raghavan N. Iyer, in "<u>Ahimsa</u>," mentions a criticism that "to preach ahimsa to the masses is merely a means of perpetrating violence and chaos" (209). If one studies the Rowlatt <u>satyagraha</u> alone, one will indeed draw the conclusion that mass demonstration inevitably results in outbreaks of violence and chaos. However, the analysis of the Salt Acts <u>satyagraha</u> has shown

that preaching nonviolence does not have to
result in violence if the masses are trained
extensively enough. In the Rowlatt satyagraha,
the masses had not been trained extensively
because of Gandhi's "failure to anticipate the
overwhelming response among the masses which
his appeal invoked" (Bondurant 43). In his
essay entitled, "The Practice of Satyagraha or
Civil Disobedience: The Passive Resister's Discipline and Method," Gandhi admitted that
because satyagraha on a large scale was being
introduced in India for the first time in the
Rowlatt campaign, it was still in the "experimental stage" (75). He was therefore making new
discoveries, and one of these discoveries was
that the masses needed an extensive amount of
training. As soon as he had this realization,
he was able progressively to avoid violence
perpetrated by satyagrahis, and, eventually,
the Salt Acts satyagraha showed that to preach
nonviolence does not mean to precipitate violence and chaos.

Even those who agree that Gandhi's policies
did succeed in curtailing violence perpetrated
by the civil disobedients argue that his methods were ineffective. Iyer continues his collection of criticisms by adding that nonviolence is "merely a guide to individual conduct

and cannot be taken as a practicable technique
of universal application in the social and
political spheres" (209). However, an analysis
of the results of the successful <u>satyagrahas</u>
and those in which violence broke out shows
that the nonviolence movement did prove to be
effective. The successful nonviolent Salt Acts
<u>satyagraha</u> helped the Indian independence move-
ment. Through self-suffering, the Indian masses
swayed the public opinion against the British
government. Professor J. C. Kumarappa, a supporter of Gandhi, said, "Our primary object was
to show the world at large the fangs and claws
of the Government in all its ugliness and
ferocity" (qtd. in Weber 281). Through self-
suffering, the masses of India did indeed show
to the world how low Britain's moral standards
were. The atrocities that the police inflicted
on the unarmed men were horrifying. An American
journalist recorded, "In 18 years of reporting
in twenty-two countries I have never witnessed
such harrowing scenes as at Dharasana" (qtd. in
Horsburgh 93), the site of the demonstration.
Police behavior used to disperse nonviolent
gatherings included the following:

Lathi blows on head, chest, stomach, and joints;
lathi thrusts to private parts and abdominal regions;
stripping of men before beating; forceful removal of

loin cloths and thrusting of sticks into the anus;
squeezing of testicles until the victim lost con-
sciousness; dragging of wounded men by legs and
arms, often while they were being beaten; throwing
wounded men into thorn hedges or salt water; riding
horses over sitting and lying demonstrators; stick-
ing pins and thorns into bodies, even when the victims were unconscious; beating men to unconscious-
ness; and the use of 'foul language and blasphemy.'
(Weber 278-279)

These accounts of severe British oppression
through the use of lathi, or a metal-capped
staff, opened the eyes of millions of people.
The people lost their sympathy for and faith in
the British government (281). Through self-
suffering, the satyagrahis helped India realize
the true nature of the British rule, and with
that realization, Britain's rule over India was
sure to end soon.

    By appealing to public opinion, the satya-
grahis made the oppressors "examine their
behavior when it became increasingly out of
step with the moral standards of other international actors [such as the Americans] whose
opinions mattered to them" (284). The American
people saw a connection between the Boston Tea
Party and the Salt Acts satyagraha, and thus
the American press did an extensive coverage of

Gandhi. For example, <u>Time</u> magazine referred to Gandhi as a saint, and made him its Man of the Year for 1930 (283). This made the British feel embarrassed because their morality was out of step with the morality of their ally. The attention that the self-suffering drew was such that the British risked losing an important political ally (284). Gandhi understood that "the method of reaching the heart is to awaken public opinion. Public opinion, for which one cares, is a mightier force than that of gunpowder" (282). Gandhi's philosophy was right because eventually "Britain did give up India, not only because its power base had been eroded by the Second World War but also because of increasing opposition from the Indian masses who witnessed the ugliness of imperialism at places like Dharasana" (281).

For those who argue that Britain gave up its hold on India mainly because its power base was eroded by the Second World War, it is important to realize that Britain did not grant independence to the rest of its colonies until some decades later. Even the immediate results of the Salt Acts <u>satyagraha</u> show that it was nonviolence that helped India achieve its independence. The <u>satyagraha</u> resulted in a less burdensome interpretation of the Salt Laws and an

agreement that Congress should be represented
at future constitutional talks (Horsburgh 94).
A chance for representation allowed the Indians
some control over their own fate, which eventually resulted in complete independence from
British rule.

The effects of the outbreaks of violence, on
the other hand, show that violence was not an
effective means of achieving political goals.
In his article, "Terrorism in India during the
Freedom Struggle," Peter Heehs argues that
"violent resistance was preached and practiced
throughout the Independence movement and had
significant effect on its course and outcome"
(469). Evidence indicates, however, that violence affected the course of independence only
in a negative way. When violence broke out in
the Rowlatt <u>satyagraha</u>, the British government
"imposed severe repressive measures resulting
in further violence" (Bondurant 41). The
British imposed martial law in Amritsar due to
the outbreak of violence. And it was as a
result of this "martial law rule under General
Dyer that the infamous Jallianwala Bagh massacre emerged in Amritsar," in which "British
officers fired on a crowd gathered in a confined area, killing hundreds of helpless per

sons" (Bondurant 38). The British also forced
the Rowlatt Bill into law (38), subjecting the
Indians to forceful rule because the Rowlatt
Bill gave an increased authority to the British
in India's internal affairs. Thus, the imposi-
tion of martial law and the passage of the
Rowlatt Bills show that violence only resulted
in a setback for the Independence movement.

In conclusion, Gandhi's methods were indeed
more effective than the other available means
of the time. Because Britain had established an
empire in India and had treated the Indians as
subjects, instead of citizens, the Indian people had only two methods of fighting for their
independence. Initially, terrorism and violence
were the only means. Later, when Gandhi's movement became strong, the means of civil disobedience became available to the masses. Through
Gandhi's movement, everybody was able to participate in the Independence movement, whereas
in the terrorism movement, only a few people
were involved. The involvement of the masses
showed the British that they were not wanted in
India. Gandhi's philosophy proved to be so
effective that Martin Luther King, Jr., later
adopted his methods to fight for civil rights
in America. Even if Gandhi's method did sometimes provoke violence, it was only because it

was still in the experimental stage. Besides,
in a country where such laws as the Rowlatt
Bills prohibited people from making use of legislation, speeches, and writings, it was better
to adopt a method that sometimes led to violence than a method that was violence itself.
Because both methods involved breaking laws, it
was better to break laws in a nonviolent manner
so that the public sympathized with the nonviolent sufferer. These choices led to results
that helped the Independence movement.

Works Cited

Bondurant, Joan V. "Gandhi's Satyagraha against

   the Rowlatt Bills." Nonviolent Direct Action.

   American Cases: Social-Psychological

   Analyses. Ed. A. Paul Hare and Herbert H.

   Blumberg. Cleveland: Corpus, 1968.31-46.

Gandhi, Mohandas. "An Appeal to His Followers."

   Gandhi: Selected Writings. Ed. Ronald Duncan.

   New York: Harper & Row, 1971. 131-135.

Rahman 14

——. "The Practice of Satyagraha or Civil Disobe-
    dience: The Passive Resister's Discipline and
    Method." Gandhi: Selected Writings. Ed. Ronald
    Duncan. New York: Harper & Row, 1971. 65-76.

——. "Satyagraha, Civil Disobedience, Passive
    Resistance, Non-co-operation." [March 21,1921]
    Young India 1919-1922. New York: Huebsch,
    1923. 220-223.

Heehs, Peter. "Terrorism in India during the
    Freedom Struggle." Historian 55 (Spring
    1993): 469-482.

Horsburgh H. J. N. "The Practice of Satyagraha."
    Non-Violence and Aggression: A Study of
    Gandhi's Moral Equivalent of War. London:
    Oxford UP, 1968. 60-94.

Iyer, Raghavan N. "Ahimsa: Nonviolence as a Creed
    and a Policy." The Moral and Political

Rahman 15

Thought of Mahatma Gandhi. New York: Oxford

UP, 1973. 177–222.

——. "The Scope and Significance of Satyagraha."

The Moral and Political Thought of Mahatma

Gandhi. New York: Oxford UP, 1973. 293–344.

Weber, Thomas. "The Marchers Simply Walked For-

ward until Struck Down." Peace and Change 18

(July 1993): 267–289.

Index

Abolitionist movement, 177–209
  Declaration of Independence (Jefferson),
    178–183
  "Declaration of the National Anti-Slavery
    Convention"(Garrison), 183–189
  "Evolution of an Abolitionist, The"
    (Douglass), 189–199
  "True to my Word" (Parker), 202–207
  "Underground Railroad, The" (Still),
    199–202
Ad hominem attack (attack on the
  person), 30
Ad populum (pandering), 34
Affirm, 21
After this, because of this (post hoc ergo
  propter hoc), 32
"Against the System" (Rowland), 264–271
American Psychological Association (APA)
  format, 50
  APA style, 301, 305–307
  parenthetical citation, 302
  see also Works Cited and References Lists
Analogy
  argument by, 15–16
  faulty, 31–32
  see also Logos
Annotating a bibliography, 42–44
Antecedent, 21
Antigone (Sophocles), 61–92
APA format. *See* American Psychological
  Association (APA) format
APA Publication Manual, 301
Apology (Plato), 93–99
Argumentative research essay, 37–51
  annotating a bibliography, 42–44
  checklist for, 51
  conferring with instructor, 47
  creating a conservation among writer,
    readers, and authorities, 37–38
  essay drafts, 47–48
  essay revision, 49

focusing a thesis, 44
Modern Language Association (MLA)
  style student paper sample, 317–332
narrowing a topic and developing a
  working thesis or claim, 39
note-taking, 40–42
outline or argument in brief, 45–47
proofreading, 50
source selection and evaluation, 40
topic selection, 38–39
see also Research resources
Arguments, 5–7
  in the academic classroom and
    symposium, 7
  by analogy, 15–16
  Aristotelian, 7
  in private sphere, 6
  in professional and business domain, 6
  in the public forum, 6–7
  recognizing, 5
  Rogerian, 13
  Toulmin, 7, 24–25
Aristotelian argument, 7
Assumptions, 8–9
Attack on the person (ad hominem
  attack), 30
Audience, 7, 11–14, 45
Authority, use of, 10–11

Backing, 24
Bandwagon, 35
Begging the question, 32
Bibliographies, 41–44
  annotating, 42–44
  civil disobedience theories and
    activists, 289–291
  civil rights movement, 291
  environmentalism, 292
  Israeli Refusers, 292–293
  other movements, 293
  peace movements, 291–292

333

Credits

This page constitutes an extension of the copyright page. We have made every effort to trace the ownership of all copyrighted material and to secure permission from copyright holders. In the event of any question arising as to the use of any material, we will be pleased to make the necessary corrections in future printings. Thanks are due to the following authors, publishers, and agents for permission to use the material indicated.

Chapter 3.
41: Courtesy of Andrew Packman 43: Courtesy of Caitlin Cunningham 46: Courtesy of John Anneken

Chapter 4.
57: Hebrew Bible 58: Hebrew Bible 61: Christian Bible 61: Christian Bible 62: Solphocles, Antigone: Three Theban Plays, translated by C. A. Trypanis. (Aris and Phillips, 1986). 95: http://www.gutenberg.net/etext/1656 101: http://www.infomotions.com/etxts/philosophy/400BC–301BC/plato-crito-340.txt OR http://www.gutenberg.net/etext/1657

Chapter 5.
111: http://www.gutenberg.net/etext93/civil11.txt OR http ://www.infomotions.com/etexts/philosophy/1800–1899/thoreau-civil-182.txt 138: "A Letter from Tolstoy to Gandhi," 7 Sept. 1910, in Tolstoy's Letters. Vol. II, 1880-1910. Selected, edited, and translated by R. F. Christian. London: The Athelone Press, University of London, 1978, 706–708 143: From THE ESSENTIAL WRITINGS OF MAHATMA GANDHI by Raghavan Iyre. Reproduced by permission of Oxford University Press India, New Delhi. 145: "Definition of Terms: Satyagraha, Civil Disobedience, Passive Resistance, Non-Cooperation," 21 March 1921, in Youg India 1919–1922, ed. Mahatma Gandhi. New York: B. W. Buebsch, 1928 147: From THE ESSENTIAL WRITINGS OF MAHATMA GANDHI by Raghaven Iyer. Reproduced by permission of Oxford University Press India, New Delhi. 150: From THE ESSENTIAL WRITINGS OF MAHATMA GANDHI by Raghavan Iyer. Reproduced by permission of Oxford University Press India, New Delhi. 151: From THE ESSENTIAL WRITINGS OF MAHATMA GANDHI by Raghavan Iyer. Reproduced by permission of Oxford University Press India, New Delhi. 154: Mohandas K. Gandhi, "Zionism and Anti-Semitism," Harijan, 26 November 1938, in The Gandhi Reader, ed. Homer A. Jack. New York: Grove, 1956, pp. 317–321 157: Judah L. Magnes, "A Letter to Gandhi," (February 26,) 1939, in The Challenge of Shalom: The Jewish Tradition of Peace and Justice, ed. Murray Polner and Naomi Goodman. Philadelphia: New Society Publishers, 1994, pp. 55–58. 163: Reprinted by arrangement with the Estate of Martin Luther King Jr., c/o Writers House as agent for the proprietor, New York, NY. Copyright 1963 Martin Luther King Jr., copyright renewed 1991 Coretta Scott King.

Chapter 6.
135: Leo Tolstoy, "Letter to Dr. Eugen Heinrich Schmitt" (c. 1895, trans. Aylmer Maude) in Leo Tolstoy: Writings on Civl Disobedience and Nonviolence. Philadlephia: New Society Publishers, 1987. 169–172. 185: 190: William Lloyd Garrison, "Declaration of the National Anti-Slavery Convention," December 14, 1833, in William Lloyd Garrison and the Fight Against Slavery: Selection from The Liberator, ed. William E. Cain. Boston: Bedford Books, 1995, pp. 90–94. 197: Douglass (Blassingame ed.) FREDERICK DOUGLASS PAPERS. Series I, Volume 1. pp. 20–23. Copyright 1979 Yale University Press. 200: Douglass (Blassingame ed.) FREDERICK DOUGLASS PAPERS. Series I, Volume 3. pp. 204–26. Copyright 1979 Yale University Press. 204: "Stationmaster and Conductor on the Underground Railroad," from Life and Times of Frederick Douglass, boston: Dewitt, Fiske, 1892, 328–331. 206: Selection from William Still, "Mary Epps,